INTERNETWORKING LANs AND WANs
Concepts, Techniques and Methods

Internetworking is one of the fastest growing markets in the field of computer communications. However, the interconnection of LANs and WANs tends to cause significant technological and administrative difficulties. This book provides valuable guidance, enabling the reader to avoid the pitfalls and achieve successful connection.

1993 0 471 93568 9

THE MULTIPLEXER REFERENCE MANUAL

Designed to provide the reader with a detailed insight into the operation, utilization and networking of six distinct types of multiplexers, this book will appeal to practising electrical, electronic and communications engineers, students in electronics, network analysts and designers.

1993 0 471 93484 4

PRACTICAL NETWORK DESIGN TECHNIQUES

Many network design problems are addressed and solved in this informative volume. Gil Held confronts a range of issues including through-put problems, line facilities, economic trade-offs and multiplexers. Readers are also shown how to determine the numbers of ports, dial-in lines and channels to install on communications equipment in order to provide a defined level of service

1991 0 471 93007 5 (Book)
0 471 92942 5 (Disk)
0 471 92938 7 (Set)

NETWORK MANAGEMENT
Techniques, Tools and Systems

Techniques, tools and systems form the basis of network management. Exploring and evaluating these three key areas, this book shows the reader how to operate an effective network.

1992 0 471 92781 3

Please refer to the inside-back cover for further details

LAN TESTING AND TROUBLESHOOTING

LAN TESTING AND TROUBLESHOOTING

Reliability
Tuning
Techniques

Gilbert Held
4-Degree Consulting
Macon, Georgia,
USA

JOHN WILEY & SONS
Chichester ● New York ● Brisbane ● Toronto ● Singapore

Other Wiley Editorial Offices

John Wiley & Sons, Inc., 605 Third Avenue,
New York, NY 10158-0012, USA

Jacaranda Wiley Ltd, 33 Park Road, Milton,
Queensland 4064, Australia

John Wiley & Sons (Canada) Ltd, 22 Worcester Road,
Rexdale, Ontario M9W 1L1, Canada

John Wiley & Sons (Asia) Pte Ltd, 2 Clementi Loop #02-01,
Jin Xing Distripark, Singaporc 0512

Library of Congress Cataloging-in-Publication Data

Held, Gilbert, 1943–
    LAN testing and troubleshooting
reliability, tuning, techniques/
Gilbert Held.
        p.   cm.
    Includes bibliographical references and index.
    ISBN 0 471 95880 8 (alk. paper)
    1. Local area networks (Computer networks) — Management.
I. Title.
TK5105.7.H447   1996
004.6'8 — dc20   95–53982
                                                              CIP

British Library Cataloguing in Publication Data

A catalogue record for this book is available from the British Library

ISBN 0 471 95880 8

Typeset in 10$\frac{1}{2}$/12pt Bookman by Aarontype, Bristol
Printed and bound in Great Britain by Bookcraft (Bath) Ltd
This book is printed on acid-free paper responsibly manufactured from sustainable forestation,
for which at least two trees are planted for each one used for paper production.

CONTENTS

PREFACE

Local Area Networks in many respects are similar to the weather, with changes in the operational state of a network often unpredictable. Like our friendly weather forecaster who relies upon satellite photographs, barometric readings and intuition based upon years of experience, the network manager, analyst or administrator depends upon certain tools and techniques to isolate LAN problems prior to initiating corrective action.

Recognizing that local area network problems can suddenly appear and may be difficult to resolve, this book was written as a modular guide to network testing, troubleshooting and tuning. By observing the flow of frames on a network you can often obtain the ability to adjust or tune your network to obtain a higher level of performance, alleviating problems prior to their appearance. Thus, tuning can be viewed as a mechanism for both increasing network performance as well as delaying the appearance of many network utilization related problems.

Although tuning is a powerful technique to alleviate or postpone many network utilization related problems, other LAN problems require the application of testing and troubleshooting. While testing and troubleshooting techniques and procedures are related to one another, there are distinct differences between the two. In addition, there are two types of testing you can perform proactive and reactive. Proactive testing occurs prior to a problem arising and encompasses a wide range of operations, from simply monitoring traffic to injecting a signal and observing the result of the signal injection. In comparison, reactive testing occurs in response to a problem and has its roots in wide area network testing. Reactive testing involves the use of hardware or software to inject a known value represented by a voltage, current or frame of information onto a network. By observing the result of the injection of information you may gain an insight to one or more network related problems and obtain the ability to initiate corrective action.

Although testing is usually performed in response to the appearance of a network related problem you can perform testing at any time. In comparison, troubleshooting occurs in response to the appearance of one or more network related problems. Thus, testing can be proactive or reactive, while troubleshooting is always reactive. However, both testing and troubleshooting in many instances rely upon the use of a common set of tools to isolate and correct problems. Due to this, it is often common to discuss testing and troubleshooting methods as an entity, while separating the two when discussing a methodology to perform a series of tests.

By providing detailed information on testing and troubleshooting tools and techniques you can use this book as a guide to performing both proactive and reactive local area network test related operations. In addition, a methodology section is included in the first chapter of this book to provide you with guidelines to facilitate your testing and troubleshooting operations. This section is based upon my experience over the past ten years in managing the interconnection of a large number of LANs through a nationwide wide area network. From knowledge gained during this time I have had the fortune to be able to write a book on the subject, and at the same time the misfortune of encountering at first hand a wide variety of operational problems that tested the patience of network users while those problems were isolated and resolved. Hopefully, this chapter will share with you the learning curve obtained from my experience which will facilitate your ability to isolate and resolve network related problems.

As a professional author I highly value readers' comments. Please feel free to write me through my publisher whose address is on the copyright page of this book. Let me know if there are topics I may have missed that should be included in a second edition, topics I should expand upon or areas that may not warrant the degree of attention provided for in this book. Through your comments and suggestions we can both go forward to provide future readers with the most relevant information required to support local area networking.

Gilbert Held
Macon, GA

ACKNOWLEDGEMENTS

In previously authored books I noted that the preparation and publication of a manuscript is a team effort. This book is no exception, requiring the efforts of many persons on both sides of the Atlantic.

I would like to take the opportunity to sincerely thank my Publishing Editor at John Wiley & Sons, Ann-Marie Halligan. I truly appreciate her effort in backing this writing project. I would also like to thank Robert Hambrook, the Senior Production Editor at John Wiley & Sons for guiding my manuscript through the production process into the book you are reading.

As an author who perhaps travels too frequently and decided some time ago that notebook computers are too difficult to recharge, especially at 30 000 feet, I write the old-fashioned way — by hand. Having spent the night in too many hotel rooms where my portable electrical adapters did not fit into electrical outlets I can personally state that this is an area that requires standardization. Until electrical outlets become standardized, the magic of turning my notes and diagrams into a professional manuscript lies in the talented hands of Ms Junnie Heath and Mrs Linda Hayes for whom I am most appreciative.

Last but not least, once again I wish to thank my family for their understanding. Writing a book is no simple task, requiring work during many evenings and weekends, and their cooperation and understanding is truly appreciated.

1

INTRODUCTION

A logical development based upon the increase in the use of personal computers in academia, business and government was a requirement to permit the sharing of information between computers. This requirement was satisfied through the development of different types of local area network technologies, such as Ethernet, Token-Ring and the emerging ATM network which should be readily available within the next few years.

Since LANs represent communications systems based upon a combination of hardware and software, they are no different than other hardware and software based technologies with respect to the fact that problems can be expected to occur. Where LANs differ from other hardware and software based technologies is in their complexity. Hardware in the form of connectors, cables, adapter boards, computer ROM code and server platforms must interact with personal computer and network operating systems as well as application and utility programs developed by independent vendors. Considering the fact that a typical LAN, assuming we could define typical, represents millions of lines of coding from numerous software developers as well as thousands of pieces of hardware manufactured by firms literally spanning the globe, it's actually a small miracle that you can obtain interoperability when a network is constructed. Contributing to this 'miracle' is the fact that there are various standards that govern the operation of hardware and software. Thus, the small miracle is no miracle but instead represents the application of a well thought out series of standards.

Although a working LAN can be considered to represent a testimony to the ingenuity of hardware and software developers and system integrators, when network problems occur their isolation and resolution can be extremely difficult. This difficulty results from the interaction of numerous hardware components and software modules, each of which can be the cause of one or more network problems. As a result, the ability to effectively test and troubleshoot LANs depends upon several factors. First, a general knowledge of the operation of LAN hardware and software is necessary. This knowledge permits you to understand how to test and troubleshoot different LAN components as well as compare the results of different tests to normal LAN operational characteristics. Next, detailed knowledge of such hardware and software operations as frame compositions, personal computer and network operating system interaction and packet decoding may be required to isolate the cause of certain types of network- and application program-related problems. Third and most important, knowledge of the cause and effect of common LAN problems can considerably assist you in your problem isolation and resolution effort. This knowledge is akin to having your own database of LAN problem information, enabling you to recognize problem symptoms, verify the apparent cause of certain problems and then initiate corrective action.

To provide readers with practical information required to test and troubleshoot LANs this book was written as a series of modular chapters, with each chapter focused upon a specific LAN related area. Each chapter, with the exception of Chapter 2, is linked to the succeeding chapter based upon a logical progression of hardware and software testing you should consider performing to isolate network problems. Chapter 2, which covers Ethernet and Token-Ring frame operations, serves as an in-depth examination of data flow on Ethernet and Token-Ring networks. The information in this chapter acquaints you with the normal operation of each type of network as well as different error conditions you can note by monitoring the flow of frames on each network. From Chapter 3 onward each chapter is linked in a logical progression with chapter modularity providing you with the ability to focus your attention upon a specific network-related topic if you require an immediate reference to a specific net-working problem which you feel is being caused by a certain hardware module or software component. Thus, this book can also be used as a reference to the operation of different LAN hardware components and software modules.

To facilitate the use of this book the following section of this chapter presents an overview of succeeding chapters. Once this is accomplished, a testing methodology section describes how you can use the contents of each chapter in an orderly manner to facilitate determining the cause of different types of network-related problems. After you are able to identify the cause of a problem you can initiate appropriate action to return the network to its desired operational state.

1.1 OVERVIEW OF SUCCEEDING CHAPTERS

As previously discussed, the focus of this section is to provide an overview of the content of succeeding chapters in this book. Since chapter titles are far more meaningful than their numeric identifiers, each of the following chapters is first identified by its title in the following subsection headings.

1.1.1 Ethernet and Token-Ring frame operations

Chapter 2 is focused upon explaining the operations of Ethernet and Token-Ring networks. This is accomplished by describing the access protocol, topology and frame composition for each network. From reading this chapter you will obtain an appreciation for the manner by which Ethernet and Token-Ring networks transport information, errors that effect the transmission of frames and how certain types of errors can be observed by monitoring network frames.

1.1.2 Workstation setup

In Chapter 3 we turn our attention to one of the most overlooked areas with respect to resolving LAN problems, the setup of hardware and software on a workstation. Due to the large number of options you may have to consider when installing a network adapter card, the section in Chapter 3 covering hardware can be used as a guide for verifying your adapter card settings. In focusing upon software, Chapter 3 examines the use of AUTO-EXEC.BAT and CONFIG.SYS files as well as the appropriate setup required to operate multiple protocol stacks. Concerning the latter, both ODI and NDIS are covered, to include the modules required for the operation of multiprotocol stacks as well as how different software modules should be loaded to support multiple stack operations.

When adding a workstation to a network or reconstructing files after a hard drive crash, it's often easy to improperly load files in a sequence other than their required sequence or to inappropriately set a number of software module parameters that can affect network performance. Thus, the software section of Chapter 3 can assist you both in the initial setup of a workstation as well as in a subsequent setup due to changing operational requirements.

1.1.3 Cable testing

Once a workstation is properly configured its ability to access a network requires a connection to the LAN cable infrastructure. Thus, in Chapter 4 we turn our attention to the topic of cable testing, focusing our attention upon the characteristics of different types of cable and the use of different cable tests to isolate cable-related problems.

After your workstation and cable connections are verified to be operative, communications problems typically fall into one of three broad areas: frame recognition problems that may not be observable from cable testing, network operating system-related problems or packet content problems. Each of these areas is covered in the remaining chapters in this book.

1.1.4 Working at the data link layer

In Chapter 5 we turn our attention to the use of hardware and software analyzers to observe the flow of information at the data link layer. In doing so I will note the relationship between data link layer errors and network utilization problems, since symptoms associated with the latter condition can result from data link layer errors and data link layer errors can build up to cause network utilization problems.

1.1.5 Checking the network operating system

Once the data link layer is checked a logical progression in attempting to isolate network problems is to turn your attention to the network operating system which is the focus of Chapter 6. In this chapter I will examine the use of several software tools to observe workstation and server network operating system statistics. This information will provide you with the ability to obtain network layer packet statistics. Those statistics can be extremely useful in determining the cause of many server related problems as well as for tuning your LAN.

1.1.6 Fault and performance management with SNMP and RMON

Although information in the previously mentioned chapters is usually sufficient to isolate the cause of most network problems, a key problem is obtaining access to different network performance information, especially when one network is geographically separated from another. Fortunately there are a set of standards which define the operation of network monitoring to include the monitoring of remote networks. Those standards, the Simple Network Management Protocol (SNMP) and the Remote Monitoring (RMON) Management Information Base (MIB), provide a standardized mechanism for a management console obtained from one vendor to monitor equipment obtained from another vendor.

In Chapter 7 I will focus my attention upon fault and performance management with SNMP and RMON. First I will explain the three components of SNMP and their relationship to one another. This will be followed by examining different types of Ethernet and Token-Ring RMON groups and the statistics you can obtain through the operation of standardized remote network monitoring.

1.1.7 Packet decoding

Although we would all like to believe that equipment operates correctly there are a variety of reasons that can inhibit or adversely affect LAN communications. If we focus our attention upon software, an improper configuration file or an error in a program occurring via a coding 'glitch' can result in information being misdirected or misinterpreted, or even a network crash. One method used to determine that software is the culprit is to examine the flow of data on the LAN. To do so requires packet decoding which is covered in Chapter 8.

In Chapter 8 I will first describe several methods you can use for packet decoding and then focus upon things to look for. In doing so space does not permit full coverage of the large number of LAN protocols in use. Due to this, I will largely focus Chapter 8 upon packet decoding techniques and methods, providing you with the tools necessary to better understand this testing and troubleshooting area.

1.1.8 Network tuning techniques

While alleviating networking problems boosts network performance, until Chapter 9 I will defer a discussion of a large number of specific techniques you can use to tune LANs to enhance their performance. In Chapter 9 I will directly focus my attention upon this topic. Since the WAN connection between geographically separated LANs represents a prime performance bottleneck due to the relatively low speed of WANs in comparison to LANs, I will primarily direct my attention in Chapter 9 upon internetwork tuning. Thus, I will focus my attention upon techniques you can consider to enhance the performance of such internetworking equipment as bridges and routers.

1.2 TESTING AND TROUBLESHOOTING METHODOLOGIES

It probably appears awkward to discuss testing and troubleshooting methodologies in an introductory chapter. Using conventional wisdom, I would probably defer discussing this topic until later, if not at the end of this book. However, due to the importance of developing appropriate testing and troubleshooting methodologies I felt it would be more appropriate to discuss this topic now. In doing so I will focus my attention on developing a sequence of actions you should consider rather than applying specific testing and troubleshooting tools and techniques. Thus, my primary goal is to acquaint you with a sequence of steps you should consider that can be used to facilitate isolating the cause of different types of network-related problems which then serve as a foundation for correcting those problems.

Figure 1.1 illustrates in flow chart form the major steps associated with troubleshooting to include testing associated

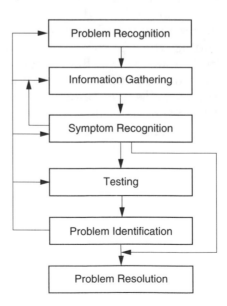

Figure 1.1   Major steps in the toubleshooting process

with the troubleshooting process. In examining Figure 1.1 note that depending upon your success in the problem isolation process you may be required to reinitiate one or more previously performed steps. This is indicated by the feedback loops illustrated in Figure 1.1.

1.2.1 Problem recognition

The first step in the troubleshooting process is to recognize you have a network-related problem. The problem recognition process may be initiated by a trouble report from a network user or through periodic testing. Regardless of the reporting source, once you become aware of the fact that a problem exists the next logical step in the troubleshooting process is to obtain as much information as possible concerning the problem. That step can be considered to represent the information gathering process.

1.2.2 Information gathering

As previously explained, the information gathering process step is a direct result of the problem recognition step. Although you would logically attempt to acquire as much information as possible during the problem recognition step you will more than likely have to obtain additional information. This resulted in the rationale for my separating the information gathering step from the problem recognition step.

During the information gathering step you would attempt to obtain as much information as possible concerning the problem. A good starting point is to attempt to obtain answers to the well-known reporters' questions – who, what, when, where, how and why. Obviously, if you can find the answer to 'why', you could probably skip the intermediate steps and directly resolve the problem.

In addition to obtaining answers to as many of the typical reporters' questions as possible you would attempt to determine, if appropriate, the type of equipment being used and equipment configuration information. This can be extremely important in attempting to resolve certain types of workstation related problems.

Another key area to focus upon during the information gathering process is to determine if any recent changes were made to a workstation's hardware or software, if new cabling occurred on a hub, the network operating system was reloaded or a new application program was loaded onto the network. Quite often a simple workstation or network change can undo hours or days of prior effort. For example, I remember spending several hours to set up someone's workstation to enable multiple stack operations by loading new software and changing the AUTO-EXEC.BAT and CONFIG.SYS files on that person's computer. About three months later his hard drive had to be reformatted and he used a four-month-old backup tape to restore his data. Unfortunately, he failed to mention this when he reported the inability to access the Internet, resulting in our help desk spending a considerable amount of time checking cabling, the status of a Domain Name Server (DNS) and other network equipment.

Once you complete your preliminary information gathering you would attempt to use that information to recognize the cause of the problem. This next step, which can be considered to represent a symptom recognition step, may require you to obtain additional information. Thus, a feedback loop is shown linking the symptom recognition step to the previously discussed information gathering step.

1.2.3 Symptom recognition

During the symptom recognition step you would attempt to use data from the problem recognition and information gathering steps to determine if the symptoms of the problem match information about the problem to include data obtained concerning the hardware and software environment. This step can be extremely important as many times it's relatively easy to perform a series of tests that will be unproductive if you do not correctly identify the symptoms of the problem.

The symptom recognition step sometimes can be compared to a cause and effect analysis. The effect represents the problem, while the cause, which at this point in the troubleshooting process may be unknown, is what you are attempting to identify. For many network-related problems you may use historical data in the form of trouble logs as well as network knowledge and even intuition to develop a list of potential causes of the problem. Once this step is completed, you would initiate one or more tests to isolate the correct cause of the problem. For certain problems, the symptom recognition process may result in your ability to bypass other steps in the troubleshooting process and directly initiate the problem resolution process. This is indicated by the forward branch from the symptom recognition step to the problem resolution step in Figure 1.1. For other problems for which you may recognize one or more symptoms that could be the result of different causes you would then initiate testing as a mechanism to isolate the cause of the problem.

1.2.4 Testing

Testing during the troubleshooting process can be considered to represent the step whereby you attempt to identify or verify the cause of the problem. In doing so you would use previously obtained information to select one or more tests or a logical progression of tests. For example, if the symptom recognition process appears to identify a problem at the physical layer you should initiate your testing process with one or more tests appropriate to physical layer testing and consider other tests if your first test or series of tests produce inconclusive results. Based upon your testing methodology you will hopefully obtain information that can be used to recognize the cause of the problem.

1.2.5 Problem identification

Problem identification represents the process of applying knowledge obtained from end-users, equipment configuration settings or test results to identify the cause of the problem. For those of us with prior experience working on wide area networks the problem identification step is similar to what persons in the WAN world refer to as fault recognition. Regardless of terminology, this step represents the process of determining the cause of the problem so that it can be resolved.

1.2.6 Problem resolution

Simply stated, the problem resolution step represents the process of fixing the problem. While this is the ultimate goal of the troubleshooting process it may not represent the actual last step in the troubleshooting process. If the network problem required the implementation of an alternative procedure, such as a router using the switched telephone network as a mechanism to compensate for the outage of a leased line, once the problem is resolved you should terminate any previously initiated alternative procedure. In addition, once a problem is resolved you should inform those persons affected of the resolution of the problem. Thus, the major steps in the troubleshooting process illustrated in Figure 1.1 are by no means all-inclusive, nor does the flowchart represent all possible steps you may wish to consider.

Troubleshooting is both an art and a science, requiring both knowledge and experience to be performed effectively. The major steps in the troubleshooting process represent a foundation you can tailor to your own needs, based upon your network environment and the types of problems you encounter.

2

ETHERNET AND TOKEN-RING FRAME OPERATIONS

The ability to effectively test and troubleshoot local area networks requires knowledge concerning how LANs operate to include their access methods, cabling infrastructure and the composition of frames used to transport information. In writing this book space constraints, as well as the availability of my previously published books covering Ethernet and Token-Ring networks, precluded a full review of Ethernet and Token-Ring LAN characteristics. Instead, I decided to concentrate primarily on providing a review of the composition of Ethernet and Token-Ring frame operations. I felt this would be more appropriate, as a majority of network-related problems can be detected by observing either the flow of frames or the display of network management information which relates to various frame fields. Thus, readers requiring detailed information covering Ethernet and Token-Ring access protocols and their cabling infrastructure are referred to this author's previously published books, *Ethernet Networks* (second edition) and *Token-Ring Networks*, both published by John Wiley & Sons.

In this chapter I will first focus my attention upon the composition of different types of Ethernet frames. In reality, there is only one Ethernet frame, while the CSMA/CD frame format standardized by the IEEE is technically referred to as an 802.3 frame. As I will note later in this chapter, the physical 802.3 frame can have several logical formats. For consistency and ease of reference, I will refer to Carrier Sense Multiple Access/Collision Detection (CSMA/CD) operations collectively as Ethernet, and

when appropriate, indicate differences between Ethernet and the
IEEE 802.3 Ethernet-based CSMA/CD standards. After describing
the general composition of Ethernet and IEEE 802.3 frames, I will
examine the function of the fields within each frame as well as the
manner by which the placement of frames on the media is
controlled – a process known as media access control. This will
be followed by a similar examination oriented towards the Token-
Ring frame format and the function of each frame field within a
Token-Ring frame. In doing so, I will cover the three types of
Token-Ring frames defined by the IEEE 802.5 standard.

2.1 ETHERNET FRAME COMPOSITION

Figure 2.1 illustrates the general frame composition of Ethernet
and IEEE 802.3 frames. You will note that they differ slightly. An
Ethernet frame contains an eight-byte preamble, while the IEEE
802.3 frame contains a seven-byte preamble followed by a one-
byte start of frame delimiter field. A second difference between
the composition of Ethernet and IEEE 802.3 frames concerns
the two-byte Ethernet type field. That field is used by Ethernet to
specify the protocol carried in the frame, enabling several
protocols to be carried independently of one another. Under
the IEEE 802.3 frame format, the type field was replaced by a
two-byte length field which specifies the number of bytes that
follow that field as data. In addition, to enable different types of
protocols to be carried in a frame and correctly identified, the
802.3 frame format subdivides the data field into subfields.

Ethernet

Preamble	Destination Address	Source Address	Type	Data	Frame Check Sequence
8 bytes	6 bytes	6 bytes	2 bytes	45–1500 bytes	4 bytes

IEEE 802.3

Preamble	Start of Frame Delimiter	Destination Address	Source Address	Length	Data	Frame Check Sequence
7 bytes	1 byte	2/6 bytes	2/6 bytes	2 bytes	45–1500 bytes	4 bytes

Figure 2.1 Ethernet and IEEE 802.3 frame formats

Those subfields include a Destination Service Access Point (DSAP), Source Service Access Point (SSAP) and Control field which prefixes a reduced data field. The use of those fields defines a Logical Link Control (LLC) layer residing within an 802.3 frame and will be discussed later in this chapter along with some common framing variations.

The differences between Ethernet and IEEE 802.3 frames, while minor, make the two incompatible with one another. This means that your network must contain all Ethernet compatible network interface cards (NICs) and all IEEE 802.3 compatible NICs, or adapter cards that can examine the frame and automatically determine its type, a process described later in this chapter. Fortunately, the fact that the IEEE 802.3 frame format represents a standard means that most vendors now market 802.3 compliant hardware and software. Although a few vendors continue to manufacture Ethernet or dual functioning Ethernet/ IEEE 802.3 hardware, such products are primarily used to provide organizations with the ability to expand previously developed networks without requiring the wholesale replacement of NICs. Although the IEEE 802.3 standard has essentially replaced Ethernet because of their similarities and the fact that 802.3 was based upon Ethernet, we will consider both to be Ethernet.

Now that we have an overview of the structure of Ethernet and 802.3 frames, let's probe deeper and examine the composition of each frame field. We will take advantage of the similarity between Ethernet and IEEE 802.3 frames to examine the fields of each frame on a composite basis, noting the differences between the two when appropriate.

2.1.1 Preamble field

The preamble field consists of eight (Ethernet) or seven (IEEE 802.3) bytes of alternating 1 and 0 bits. The Ethernet chip set contained on the network interface adapter places the preamble and following start of frame delimiter on the front of each frame transmitted on the network.

The purpose of the preamble field is to announce the frame and to enable all receivers on the network to synchronize themselves to the incoming frame. In addition, this field by itself (under Ethernet) or in conjunction with the start of frame delimiter field (under the IEEE 802.3 standard) ensures there is a minimum spacing period of 9.6 ms between frames for error detection and recovery operations.

2.1.2 Start of frame delimiter field

This field is applicable only to the IEEE 802.3 standard, and can be viewed as a continuation of the preamble. In fact, the composition of this field continues in the same manner as the format of the preamble, with alternating 1 and 0 bits used for the first six bit positions of this one-byte field. The last two bit positions of this field are 11 – this breaks the synchronization pattern and alerts the receiver that frame data follows.

Both the preamble field and the start of frame delimiter field are removed by the Ethernet chip set or controller when it places a received frame in its buffer. Similarly, when a controller transmits a frame, it prefixes the frame with those two fields (if it is transmitting an IEEE 802.3 frame) or a preamble field (if it is transmitting a true Ethernet frame).

2.1.3 Destination address field

The destination address identifies the recipient of the frame. Although this may appear to be a simple field, in reality its length can vary between IEEE 802.3 and Ethernet frames. In addition, each field can consist of two or more subfields, whose settings govern such network operations as the type of addressing used on the LAN, and whether or not the frame is addressed to a specific station or more than one station. To obtain an appreciation for

A. 2 byte field (IEEE 802.3)

I/G *	15 address bits

|←——— 16 bit address field ———→|

B. 6 byte field (Ethernet and IEEE 802.3)

I/G *	U/L	46 address bits

|←——————— 48 bit address field ———————→|

I/G bit subfield '0' = individual address '1' = group address
U/L bit subfield '0' = universally administered addressing
                    '1' = locally administered addressing

* Set to '0' in source address field

Figure 2.2   Source and destination address field formats

the use of this field, let's examine how this field is used under the IEEE 802.3 standard as one of the two field formats applicable to Ethernet.

Figure 2.2 illustrates the composition of the source and destination address fields. As indicated, the two-byte source and destination address fields are applicable only to IEEE 802.3 networks, while the six-byte source and destination address fields are applicable to both Ethernet and IEEE 802.3 networks. A user can select either a two- or a six-byte destination address field; however, with IEEE 802.3 equipment, all stations on the LAN must use the same addressing structure. Today, almost all 802.3 networks use six byte addressing, since the inclusion of a two-byte field option was designed primarily to accommodate early LANs that use 16-bit address fields.

I/G subfield

The one-bit I/G subfield is set to a 0 to indicate that the frame is destined to an individual station, or 1 to indicate that the frame is addressed to more than one station—a group address. One special example of a group address is the assignment of all 1's to the address field. Hex FF-FF-FF-FF-FF-FF is recognized as a broadcast address, and each station on the network will receive and accept frames with that destination address.

When a destination address specifies a single station, the address is referred to as a unicast address. A group address that defines multiple stations is known as a multicast address, while a group address that specifies all stations on the network is, as previously mentioned, referred to as a broadcast address.

U/L subfield

The U/L subfield is applicable only to the six-byte destination address field. The setting of this field's bit position indicates whether the destination address is an address that was assigned by the IEEE (universally administered) or assigned by the organization via software (locally administered).

Universal vs locally administered addressing

Each Ethernet Network Interface Card (NIC) contains a unique address burned into its read-only memory (ROM) at the time of manufacture. To ensure this universally administered address is not duplicated, the IEEE assigns blocks of addresses to each manufacturer. These addresses normally include a three-byte prefix, which identifies the manufacturer and is assigned by the IEEE, and a three-byte suffix, which is assigned by the adapter manufacturer to its NIC. For example, the prefix hex 02-60-8C identifies an NIC manufactured by 3Com.

Table 2.1 lists the three-byte identifiers associated with ten manufacturers of Ethernet network interface cards. Through the use of a table of three-byte identifiers and associated manufacturer names, diagnostic hardware or software can be programmed to read the source and destination address fields within frames and identify the manufacturer of the originating and destination adapter cards.

Although the use of universally administered addressing eliminates the potential for duplicate network addresses, it does not provide the flexibility obtainable from locally administered addressing. For example, under locally administered addressing, you can configure mainframe software to work with a predefined group of addresses via a gateway PC. Then, as you add new stations to your LAN, you simply use your installation program to assign a locally administered address to the NIC instead of using its universally administered address. As long as your mainframe computer has a pool of locally administered addresses that includes your recent assignment, you do not have to modify your mainframe communications software configuration. Since the modification of mainframe communications software typically requires recompiling and reloading, the attached network must become inoperative for a short period of time. Because a large mainframe may service hundreds to thousands of users, such changes are normally performed late in the evening or at a

Table 2.1   Representative Ethernet manufacturer IDs

Manufacturer	Three-byte identifier
3Com	02-60-8C
Cabletron	00-00-1D
Excelan	08-00-14
NEC	00-00-4C
NeXT	00-00-0F
Novell	00-00-1B
Synoptics (Bay Networks)	00-00-81
Western Digital	00-00-C0
Xerox	00-00-AA
Xircom	00-80-C7

weekend. Thus, the changes required for locally administered addressing are more responsive to users than those required for universally administered addressing.

2.1.4 Source address field

The source address field identifies the station that transmitted the frame. Like the destination address field, the source address can be either two or six bytes in length.

The two-byte source address is supported only under the IEEE 802.3 standard and requires the use of a two-byte destination address; all stations on the network must use two-byte addressing fields. The six-byte source address field is supported by both Ethernet and the IEEE 802.3 standard. When a six-byte address is used, the first three bytes represent the address assigned by the IEEE to the manufacturer for incorporation into each NIC's ROM. The vendor then normally assigns the last three bytes for each of its NICs.

2.1.5 Type field

The two-byte type field is applicable only to the Ethernet frame. This field identifies the higher-level protocol contained in the data field. Thus, this field tells the receiving device how to interpret the data field.

Under Ethernet, multiple protocols can exist on the LAN at the same time. Xerox served as the custodian of Ethernet address ranges licensed to NIC manufacturers and defined the protocols supported by the assignment of type field values. Table 2.2 lists four common Ethernet type field identifiers to include their hex values. Note that the value of the type field always exceeds decimal 1500 (hex 05-DC) and provides a mechanism for a receiving station to determine the type of frame on the network since a length field (described next) cannot exceed decimal 1500.

Table 2.2 Ethernet type field identifiers

Protocol specified	Hex value
Address Resolution Protocol (ARP)	08-06
AppleTalk	80-9B
AppleTalk ARM	80-F3
Netware IPX/SPX	81-37

Under the IEEE 802.3 standard, the type field was replaced by a length field, which precludes compatibility between pure Ethernet and 802.3 frames.

2.1.6 Length field

The two-byte length field, applicable to the IEEE 802.3 standard, defines the number of bytes contained in the data field. Under both Ethernet and IEEE 802.3 standards, the minimum size frame must be 64 bytes in length from preamble through FCS fields. This minimum size frame ensures that there is sufficient transmission time to enable Ethernet NICs to detect collisions accurately, based on the maximum Ethernet cable length specified for a network and the time required for a frame to propagate the length of the cable. Based on the minimum frame length of 64 bytes and the possibility of using two-byte addressing fields, this means that each data field must be a minimum of 46 bytes in length.

Because the data field cannot exceed 1500 bytes, the length field's maximum value cannot exceed 1500 decimal. Concerning its minimum value, when the data field contains less than 46 bytes, the data field is padded to reach 46 bytes in length. However, the length field does not include padding and reflects the actual number of characters in the data field.

2.1.7 Data field

As previously discussed, the data field must be a minimum of 46 bytes in length to ensure that the frame is at least 64 bytes in length. This means that the transmission of one byte of information must be carried within a 46-byte data field; if the information to be placed in the field is less than 46 bytes long, the remainder of the field must be padded. Although some publications subdivide the data field to include a PAD subfield, the latter actually represents optional fill characters that are added to the information in the data field to ensure a length of 46 bytes. The maximum length of the data field is 1500 bytes.

2.1.8 Frame check sequence field

The frame check sequence field, applicable to both Ethernet and the IEEE 802.3 standard, provides a mechanism for error detection. Each chip set transmitter computes a cyclic redundancy check (CRC) that covers both address fields, the type/length field, and the data field. The transmitter then places the computed CRC in the four-byte FCS field.

The CRC treats the previously mentioned fields as one long binary number. The n bits to be covered by the CRC are considered to represent the coefficients of a polynomial $M(X)$ of degree $n - 1$. Here, the first bit in the destination address field corresponds to the X^{n-1} term, while the last bit in the data field corresponds to the X^0 term. Next, $M(X)$ is multiplied by X^{32} and the result of that multiplication process is divided by the following polynomial:

$$G(X) = X^{32} + X^{26} + X^{23} + X^{22} + X^{16} + X^{12} + X^{11} + X^{10} + X^8$$

$$+X^7 + X^5 + X^4 + X^2 + X + 1$$

Note that the term X^n represents the setting of a bit to a 1 in position n. Thus, part of the generating polynomial $X^5 + X^4 + X^2 + X^1$ represents the binary value 11011.

This division produces a quotient and a remainder. The quotient is discarded, and the remainder becomes the CRC value placed in the four-byte FCS field. This 32-bit CRC reduces the probability of an undetected error to one bit in every 4.3 billion, or approximately one bit in 2^{32-1} bits.

Once a frame reaches its destination, the chip set's receiver uses the same polynomial to perform the same operation upon the received data. If the CRC computed by the receiver matches the CRC in the FCS field, the frame is accepted. Otherwise, the receiver discards the received frame, as it is considered to have one or more bits in error. The receiver will also consider a received frame to be invalid and discard it under two additional conditions. Those conditions occur when the frame does not contain an integral number of bytes, or when the length of the data field does not match the value contained in the length field. The latter condition, obviously, is only applicable to the 802.3 standard, since an Ethernet frame uses a type field instead of a length field.

2.2 ETHERNET MEDIA ACCESS CONTROL: FUNCTIONS

Under the IEEE 802 series of standards, the data link layer of the OSI Reference Model was subdivided into two sublayers – logical link control (LLC) and medium access control (MAC). The frame formats previously examined represent the manner in which LLC information is transported. Directly under the LLC sublayer is the MAC sublayer.

The MAC sublayer, which is the focus of this section, is responsible for checking the channel and transmitting data if the channel is idle, checking for the occurrence of a collision, and taking a series of predefined steps if a collision is detected. Thus, this layer provides the required logic to control the network.

Figure 2.3 illustrates the relationship between the physical and LLC layers with respect to the MAC layer. The MAC layer is an interface between user data and the physical placement and retrieval of data on the network. To better understand the functions performed by the MAC layer, let us examine the four major functions performed by that layer – transmitting data operations, transmitting medium access management, receiving data operations, and receiving medium access management. Each of those four functions can be viewed as a functional area, since a group of activities is associated with each area.

Table 2.3 lists the four MAC functional areas and the activities associated with each area. Although the transmission and reception of data operations activities are self-explanatory, the

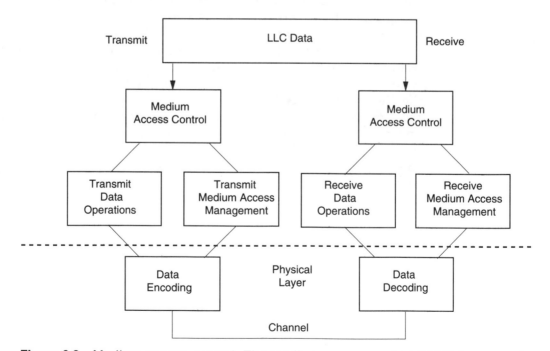

Figure 2.3 Medium access control. The medium access control (MAC) layer can be considered an interface between user data and the physical placement and retrieval of data on the network

Table 2.3 MAC functional areas

Transmit Data Operations	• Accept data from the LLC sublayer and construct a frame by appending preamble and start of frame delimiter; insert destination and source address, length count; if frame is less than 64 bytes, insert sufficient PAD characters in the data field. • Calculate the CRC and place in the FCS field.
Transmit Medium Access Management	• Defer transmission if the medium is busy. • Delay transmission for a specified interframe gap period. • Present a serial bit stream to the physical layer for transmission. • Halt transmission when a collision is detected. • Transmit a jam signal to ensure that news of a collison propagates throughout the network. • Reschedule retransmissions after a collision until successful, or a specified retry limit is reached.
Receive Data Operations	• Discard all frames not addressed to the receiving station. • Recognize all broadcast frames and frames specifically addressed to station. • Perform a CRC check. • Remove preamble, start of frame delimiter, destination and source addresses, length count, FCS; if necessary, remove PAD fill characters. • Pass data to LLC sublayer.
Receive Medium Access Management	• Receive a serial bit stream from the physical layer. • Verify byte boundary and length of frame. • Discard frames not an even eight bits in length or less than the minimum frame length.

transmission and reception of media access management require some elaboration. Therefore, let's focus our attention on the activities associated with each of those functional areas.

2.2.1 Transmit media access management

CSMA/CD can be described as a *listen-before-acting* access method. Thus, the first function associated with transmit media access management is to find out whether any data is already being transmitted on the network and, if so, to defer transmission. During the listening process, each station attempts to sense the carrier signal of another station, hence the prefix *carrier sense* (CS) for this access method. Although broadband networks use RF modems that generate a carrier signal, a baseband network has no carrier signal in the conventional sense of a carrier as a periodic waveform altered to convey information. Thus, a logical question you may have is how the MAC sublayer on a baseband network can sense a carrier signal if there is no carrier. The answer to this question lies in the use of a digital signaling method known as *Manchester encoding*, that a station can monitor to note whether another station is transmitting.

To understand the Manchester encoding signaling method used by baseband Ethernet LANs, let us first review the method of digital signaling used by computers and terminal devices. In that signaling method, a positive voltage is used to represent a binary 1, while the absence of voltage (0 volts) is used to represent a binary 0. If two successive 1 bits occur, two successive bit positions then have a similar positive voltage level or a similar zero voltage level. Since the signal goes from 0 to some positive voltage and does not return to 0 between successive binary 1's, it is referred to as a *unipolar non-return to zero signal* (NRZ). This signaling technique is illustrated at the top of Figure 2.4.

Although unipolar non-return to zero signaling is easy to implement, its use for transmission has several disadvantages. One of the major disadvantages associated with this signaling method involves determining where one bit ends and another

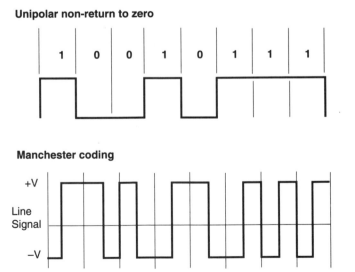

Figure 2.4 Unipolar non-return to zero (NRZ) signaling and Manchester coding. In Manchester coding, a timing transition occurs in the middle of each bit and the line code maintains an equal amount of positive and negative voltage

begins. Overcoming this problem requires synchronization between a transmitter and receiver by the use of clocking circuitry, which can be relatively expensive.

To overcome the need for clocking, baseband LANs use *Manchester* or *Differential Manchester* encoding. In Manchester encoding, a timing transition always occurs in the middle of each bit, while an equal amount of positive and negative voltage is used to represent each bit. This coding technique provides a good timing signal for clock recovery from received data, due to its timing transitions. In addition, since the Manchester code always maintains an equal amount of positive and negative voltage, it prevents direct current (DC) voltage buildup, enabling repeaters to be spaced farther apart from one another.

The lower part of Figure 2.4 illustrates an example of Manchester encoding. Note that a low to high voltage transition represents a binary 1, while a high to low voltage transition represents a binary 0. Although NRZ encoding is used on broadband networks, the actual data is modulated after it is encoded. Thus, the presence or absence of a carrier is directly indicated by the presence or absence of a carrier signal on a broadband network.

Collision detection

As previously discussed, under Manchester coding a binary 1 is represented by a high-to-low voltage transition, while a binary 0 is represented by a low-to-high voltage transition. Thus, an examination of the voltage on the medium of a baseband network enables a station to determine whether a carrier signal is present.

If a carrier signal is found, the station with data to transmit will continue to monitor the channel. When the current transmission ends, the station will then transmit its data, while checking the channel for collisions. Since Ethernet and IEEE 802.3 Manchester encoded signals have a 1-volt average DC voltage level, a collision results in an average DC level of 2 volts. Thus, a transceiver or network interface card can detect collisions by monitoring the voltage level of the Manchester line signal.

Jam pattern

If a collision is detected during transmission, the transmitting station will cease transmission of data and initiate transmission of a jam pattern. The jam pattern consists of 32 to 48 bits. These bits can have any value other than the CRC value that corresponds to the partial frame transmitted before the jam. The transmission of the jam pattern ensures that the collision lasts long enough to be detected by all stations on the network.

Wait time

Once a collision is detected, the transmitting station waits a random number of slot times before attempting to retransmit. Here the term *slot* represents 512 bits on a 10-Mbps network, or a minimum frame length of 64 bytes. The actual number of slot times the station waits is selected by a randomization process, formerly known as a *truncated binary exponential backoff*. Under this randomization process, a random integer r defines the number of slot times the station waits before listening to determine whether the channel is clear. If it is, the station begins to retransmit the frame, while listening for another collision.

If the station transmits the complete frame successfully and has additional data to transmit, it will again listen to the channel as it prepares another frame for transmission. If a collision occurs on a retransmission attempt, a slightly different procedure is followed. After a jam signal is transmitted, the station simply doubles the previously generated random number and then waits the prescribed number of slot intervals prior to attempting a retransmission. Up to 16 retransmission attempts can occur before the station aborts the transmission and declares the occurrence of a multiple collision error condition.

Figure 2.5 illustrates the collision detection process by which a station can determine that a frame was not successfully transmitted. At time t_0 both stations A and B are listening and fail to detect the occurrence of a collision, and at time t_1 station A commences the transmission of a frame. As station A's frame begins to propagate down the bus in both directions, station B begins the transmission of a frame, since at time t_2 it appears to station B that there is no activity on the network.

Shortly after time t_2 the frames transmitted by stations A and B collide, resulting in a doubling of the Manchester encoded signal level for a very short period of time. This doubling of the Manchester encoded signal's voltage level is detected by station B at time t_3, since station B is closer to the collision than station A. Station B then generates a jam pattern that is detected by station A.

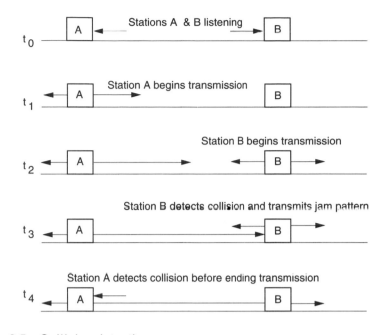

Figure 2.5 Collision detection

2.2.2 Service primitives

As previously mentioned, the MAC sublayer isolates the physical layer from the LLC sublayer. Thus, one of the functions of the MAC sublayer is to provide services to the LLC. To accomplish this task, a series of service primitives was defined to govern the exchange of LLC data between a local MAC sublayer and its peer LLC sublayer.

The basic MAC service primitives used in all IEEE MAC standards include the medium access data request (MA_DATA. request), medium access data confirm (MA_DATA.confirm), medium access data indicate (MA_DATA.indicate), and medium access data response (MA_DATA.response).

MADATA.request

The medium access data request is generated whenever the LLC sublayer has data to be transmitted. This primitive is passed from layer n to layer $n - 1$ to request the initiation of service, and results in the MAC sublayer formatting the request in a MAC frame and passing it to the physical layer for transmission.

MADATA.confirm

The medium access data confirm primitive is generated by the MAC sublayer in response to a MA_DATA.request generated by the local LLC sublayer. The confirm primitive is passed from layer $n-1$ to layer n, and includes a status parameter that indicates the outcome of the request primitive.

MADATA.indicate

The medium access data indicate primitive is passed from layer $n-1$ to layer n to indicate that a valid frame has arrived at the local MAC sublayer. Thus, this service primitive denotes that the frame was received without CRC, length, or frame alignment error.

MADATA.response

The medium access data response primitive is passed from layer n to layer $n-1$. This primitive acknowledges the MA_DATA.indicate service primitive.

2.2.3 Primitive operations

To illustrate the use of MAC service primitives, let us assume that station A on a network wants to communicate with station B. As illustrated in Figure 2.6, the LLC sublayer of station A requests transmission of a frame to the MAC sublayer service interface via the issue of an MA_DATA.request service primitive. In response to

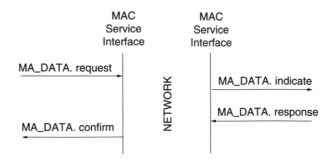

Figure 2.6 Relationship of medium access control service primitives

the MA_DATA.request, a frame is transmitted to station B. Upon receipt of that frame, the MAC sublayer at that station generates an MA_DATA.indicate to inform the LLC sublayer of the arrival of the frame. The LLC sublayer accepts the frame and generates an MA_DATA.response to inform the MAC sublayer that it has the frame. That response flows across the network to station A, where the MAC sublayer generates an MA_DATA.confirm to inform the LLC sublayer that the frame was received without error.

2.3 ETHERNET LOGICAL LINK CONTROL

The logical link control (LLC) sublayer was defined under the IEEE 802.2 standard to make the method of link control independent of a specific access method. Thus, the 802.2 method of link control spans Ethernet (IEEE 802.3), Token Bus (IEEE 802.4), and Token-Ring (IEEE 802.5) local area networks. Functions performed by the LLC include generating and interpreting commands to control the flow of data, including recovery operations when a transmission error is detected.

Link control information is carried within the data field of an IEEE 802.3 frame as an LLC Protocol Data Unit. Figure 2.7 illustrates the relationship between the IEEE 802.3 frame and the LLC Protocol Data Unit.

2.3.1 The LLC Protocol Data Unit

Service Access Points (SAPs) function much like a mailbox. Since the LLC layer is bounded below by the MAC sublayer and bounded above by the network layer, SAPs provide a mechanism for exchanging information between the LLC layer and the MAC and

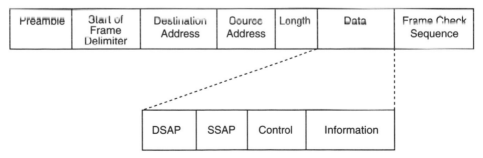

Figure 2.7 Formation of LLC Protocol Data Unit. Control information is carried within a MAC frame

network layers. For example, from the network layer perspective, a SAP represents the place to leave messages about the services requested by an application.

The Destination Service Access Point (DSAP) is one byte in length, and is used to specify the receiving network layer process which is an IEEE term to denote the destination upper-layer protocol. The Source Service Access Point (SSAP) is also one byte in length. The SSAP specifies the sending network layer process which is in effect the source upper-layer protocol. Both DSAP and SSAP addresses are assigned by the IEEE and are always the same since destination and source protocols must always be the same. For example, hex address FF represents a DSAP broadcast address.

The Control field provides information that can indicate the type of service and protocol format. For example, if the frame is transporting NetWare data, the control field will contain the hex value 03, which indicates that the frame uses the unnumbered format for connectionless services. Prior to discussing the types and classes of service defined by the 802.2 standard, let us examine two additional IEEE 802.3 logical frame formats.

2.3.2 Ethernet_SNAP frame

The Ethernet_SNAP (Subnetwork Access Protocol) frame provides a mechanism for obtaining a type field identifier associated with a pure Ethernet frame in an IEEE 802.3 frame. To accomplish this, the data field is subdivided similarly to the previously illustrated LLC Protocol Data Unit shown in Figure 2.7; however, two additional subfields are added after the Control field. Those fields are an organization code of three bytes and an Ethernet type field of two bytes. Figure 2.8 illustrates the format of an Ethernet_SNAP frame.

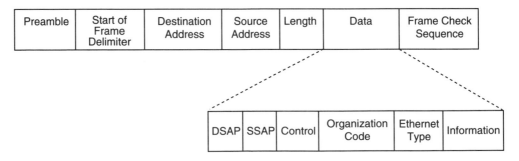

Figure 2.8   Ethernet_SNAP frame format

A value of hex AA is placed in the DSAP and SSAP fields to indicate that the frame is an Ethernet_SNAP frame. The Control field functions similarly to the previously described LLC Protocol Data Unit, indicating the type and class of service where hex 03 would indicate a connectionless service unnumbered format.

The Organization Code field references the assigner of the value in the following Ethernet type field. For most situations, a hex value of 00-00-00 is used to indicate that the Ethernet type field value was assigned by Xerox. When the organization code is hex 00-00-00, the Ethernet type field will contain one of the entries previously listed in Table 2.2.

2.3.3 NetWare Ethernet_802.3 frame

One additional logical variation of the IEEE 802.3 frame format that warrants an elaboration is known as the NetWare Ethernet_802.3 frame. Instead of using the IEEE 802.2 subfields to form a LLC protocol data unit, Novell places the IPX header immediately after the length field, reducing the maximum data field length by 30 bytes. The NetWare Ethernet_802.3 frame can only be used to transport NetWare IPX traffic and represents a common level of frustration when an administrator attempts to use this frame format to transport a different protocol.

2.3.4 Receiver frame determination

A receiving station can distinguish between different types of Ethernet frames and correctly interpret data transported in those frames. To do so, it must examine the value of the field following the source address field, which is either a type or a length field. If the field value exceeds 1500 decimal, the field must be a type subfield. Thus, the frame is a 'raw' Ethernet frame. If the value is less than 1500, the field is a length field and the two bytes following that field, which represent the first two bytes of an IEEE 802.3 frame's data field, must be examined. If those two bytes have the value hex FF-FF, the frame is a NetWare Ethernet_802.3 frame used to transport IPX. If the value of the two bytes is hex AA-AA, the frame is an Ethernet_SNAP frame. Any other value in those bytes means the frame is an IEEE_802.3 frame.

It is important during the LAN installation process to bind the appropriate protocol to the frame type capable of transporting the protocol. Table 2.4 lists several examples of protocols that can be bound to different types of Ethernet frames.

Table 2.4 Protocols vs frame type

Frame type	Protocols that can be bound
Ethernet	NetWare, AppleTalk, Phase I, TCP/IP
IEEE 802.3	NetWare, FTAM
NetWare Ethernet_802.3	NetWare only
Ethernet_SNAP	NetWare, AppleTalk, Phase II, TCP/IP

2.3.5 Types and classes of service

Under the 802.2 standard, there are three types of service available for sending and receiving LLC data. These types are discussed in the next three paragraphs. Figure 2.9 provides a visual summary of the operation of each LLC service type.

Type 1

Type 1 is an unacknowledged connectionless service. The term *connectionless* refers to the fact that transmission does not occur between two devices as if a logical connection were established. Instead, transmission flows on the channel to all stations; however, only the destination address acts upon the data. As the name of this service implies, there is no provision for the acknowledgement of frames. Neither are there provisions for flow control or for error recovery. Therefore, this is an unreliable service.

Despite those shortcomings, Type 1 is the most commonly used service, since most protocol suites use a reliable transport mechanism at the transport layer, thus eliminating the need for reliability at the link layer. In addition, by eliminating the time needed to establish a virtual link and the overhead of acknowledgements, a Type 1 service can provide a greater throughput than other LLC types of services.

Type 2

The Type 2 connection-oriented service requires that a logical link be established between the sender and the receiver prior to information transfer. Once the logical connection is established, data will flow between the sender and receiver until either party

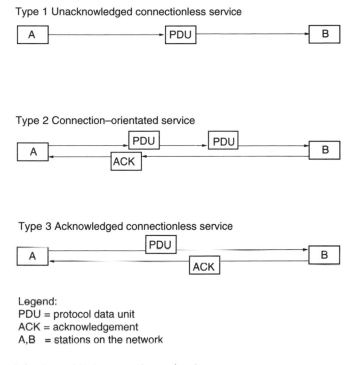

Figure 2.9   Local link control service types

terminates the connection. During data transfer, a Type 2 LLC service provides all of the functions lacking in a Type 1 service, using a sliding window for flow control.

Type 3

The Type 3 acknowledged connectionless service contains provision for the setup and disconnection of transmission; it acknowledges individual frames using the stop-and-wait flow control method. Type 3 service is primarily used in an automated factory process-control environment, where one central computer communicates with many remote devices that typically have a limited storage capacity.

Classes of service

All logical link control stations support Type 1 operations. This level of support is known as Class I service. The classes of service supported by LLC indicate the combinations of the three LLC service types supported by a station. Class I supports Type 1 service, Class II supports both Type 1 and Type 2, Class III supports Type 1 and Type 3 service, while Class IV supports all three service types. Since service Type 1 is supported by all classes, it can be considered a least common denominator, which enables all stations to communicate using a common form of service.

Service primitives

The LLC sublayer uses service primitives similar to those that govern the exchange of data between the MAC sublayer and its peer LLC sublayer. In doing so, the LLC sublayer supports the Request, Confirm, Indicate, and Response primitives described in Section 2.2 of this chapter. The major difference between the LLC and MAC service primitives is that the LLC sublayer supports three types of services. As previously discussed, the available LLC services are unacknowledged connectionless, connection-oriented, and acknowledged connectionless. Thus, the use of LLC service primitives varies in conjunction with the type of LLC service initiated. For example, a connection-oriented service uses service primitives in the same manner as that illustrated in Figure 2.6. If the service is unacknowledged connectionless, the only service primitives used are the Request and Indicate, since there is no Response nor Confirmation.

2.4 TOKEN-RING FRAME OPERATIONS

In this section we will examine Token-Ring frame operations, enabling us to understand the manner in which different frame fields are used for such functions as access control, error checking, routing of data between interconnected networks, and other Token-Ring network functions. In addition, by obtaining an understanding of the composition of Token-Ring frames, we will obtain the ability to recognize the cause of different types of problems, their potential effect upon a network, and actions we can consider to correct such problems.

A Token-Ring network consists of ring stations representing devices that attach to a ring and an attaching medium. Concerning the latter, the attaching medium can be shielded, twisted-pair, or fiber optic cable, each having constraints concerning transmission distance and number of stations allowed on the network.

A ring station, also referred to as a station or workstation, transfers data to the ring in a transmission unit referred to as a frame. Frames are transmitted sequentially from one station to another physically active station in a clockwise direction. The next active station is referred to as downstream neighbor, which regenerates the frame as well as performing MAC address checking and other functions. In performing a Medium Access Control (MAC) address check, the station compares its address to the destination address contained in the frame. If the two match or if the station has a functional address that matches the frame destination's address, the station copies the data contained in the frame. While performing the previously described operations, the station performs a number of error checks based upon the composition of data in the frame and reports errors via the generation of different types of error reporting frames. Thus, it is important to understand the composition of the fields within the Token-Ring frames as they govern the operation of a Token-Ring network.

2.4.1 Transmission formats

Three types of transmission formats are supported on a Token-Ring network – token, abort, and frame. The token format as illustrated in Figure 2.10(a) is the mechanism by which access to the ring is passed from one computer attached to the network to another device connected to the network. Here the token format consists of three bytes, of which the starting and ending delimiters are used to indicate the beginning and end of a token frame. The middle byte of a token frame is an access control byte. Three bits are used as a priority indicator, three bits are used as a reservation indicator, while one bit is used for the token bit, and another bit position functions as the monitor bit.

When the token bit is set to a binary 0 it indicates that the transmission is a token. When it is set to a binary 1 it indicates that data in the form of a frame is being transmitted.

The second Token-Ring frame format, Figure 2.10(b), signifies an abort token. In actuality there is no token, since this format is indicated by a starting delimiter followed by an ending delimiter. The transmission of an abort token is used to abort a previous transmission.

The third type of Token-Ring frame format, Figure 2.10(c), occurs when a station seizes a free token. At that time the token format is converted into a frame which includes the addition of

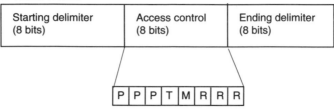

a. Token format

Starting delimiter (8 bits)	Access control (8 bits)	Ending delimiter (8 bits)

P	P	P	T	M	R	R	R

b. Abort token format

Starting delimiter	Access control

c. Frame format

Starting delimiter (8 bits)	Access control (8 bits)	Frame control (8 bits)	Destination address (48 bits)	Source address (48 bits)	Routing information (optional)

Information variable	Frame check sequence (32 bits)	Ending delimiter (8 bits)	Frame status (8 bits)

Figure 2.10 Token, abort, and frame formats (P: priority bits, T: token bit, M: monitor bit, R: reservation bits)

frame control, addressing data, an error detection field and a frame status field. At any given point in time, only one token can reside on a ring, represented as either a token format, an abort token format, or a frame. By examining each of the fields in the frame we will also examine the token and token abort frames due to the commonality of fields between each frame.

2.4.2 Starting/ending delimiters

The starting and ending delimiters mark the beginning and ending of a token or frame. Each delimiter consists of a unique code pattern which identifies it to the network. To understand the composition of the starting and ending delimiter fields requires us to review the method by which data is represented on a Token-Ring network using Differential Manchester encoding.

Differential Manchester encoding

Figure 2.11 illustrates the use of Differential Manchester encoding, comparing its operation to non-return to zero (NRZ) and conventional Manchester encoding.

In Figure 2.11(a), NRZ coding illustrates the representation of data by holding a voltage low (−V) to represent a binary 0 and high (+V) to represent a binary 1. This method of signaling is called non-return to zero since there is no return to a 0 V position after each data bit is coded.

One problem associated with NRZ encoding is the fact that a long string of 0 or 1 bits does not result in a voltage change. Thus, to determine that bit m in a string of n bits of 0's or 1's is set to a 0 or 1 requires sampling at predefined bit times. This in turn requires each device on a network using NRZ encoding to have its own clocking circuitry.

To avoid the necessity of building clocking circuitry into devices, a mechanism is required for encoded data to carry clocking information. One method by which encoded data carries clocking information is obtained from the use of Manchester encoding which is illustrated in Figure 2.11(b) and which represents the signaling method used by Ethernet. In Manchester encoding, each data bit consists of a half-bit time signal at a low voltage (−V) and another half-bit time signal at the opposite positive voltage (+V). Every binary 0 is represented by a half-bit time at a low voltage and the remaining bit time at a high voltage.

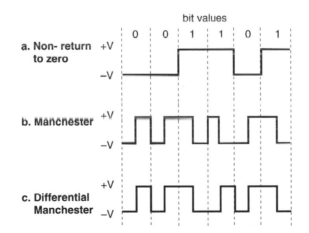

Figure 2.11 Differential Manchester encoding. In Differential Manchester encoding, the direction of the signal's voltage transition changes whenever a binary 1 is transmitted but remains the same for a binary 0

Every binary 1 is represented by a half-bit time at a high voltage followed by a half-bit time at a low voltage. By changing the voltage for every binary digit, Manchester encoding ensures that the signal carries self-clocking information.

In Figure 2.11(c), Differential Manchester encoding is illustrated. The difference between Manchester encoding and Differential Manchester encoding occurs in the method by which binary 1's are encoded. In Differential Manchester encoding, the direction of the signal's voltage transition changes whenever a binary 1 is transmitted, but remains the same for a binary 0. The IEEE 802.5 standard specifies the use of Differential Manchester encoding and this encoding technique is used on Token-Ring networks at the physical layer to transmit and detect four distinct symbols – a binary 0, a binary 1, and two non-data symbols.

Non-data symbols

Under Manchester and Differential Manchester encoding there are two possible code violations that can occur. Each code violation produces what is known as a non-data symbol and is used in the Token-Ring frame to denote starting and ending delimiters similar to the use of the flag in an HDLC frame. However, unlike the flag whose bit composition 01111110 is uniquely maintained by inserting a 0 bit after every sequence of five set bits and removing a 0 following every sequence of five set bits, Differential Manchester encoding maintains the uniqueness of frames by the use of non-data J and non-data K symbols. This eliminates the bit stuffing operations required by HDLC.

The two non-data symbols each consist of two half-bit times without a voltage change. The J symbol occurs when the voltage is the same as that of the last signal, while the K symbol occurs when the voltage becomes opposite to that of the last signal. Figure 2.12 illustrates the occurrence of the J and K non-data symbols based upon different last bit voltages. Readers will note in comparing Figure 2.12 to Figure 2.11(c)c that the J and K non-data symbols are distinct code violations that cannot be mistaken for either a binary 0 or a binary 1.

Now that we have an understanding of the operation of Differential Manchester encoding and the composition of the J and K non-data symbols, we can focus our attention upon the actual format of each frame delimiter.

The start delimiter field marks the beginning of a frame. The composition of this field is the bits and non-data symbols

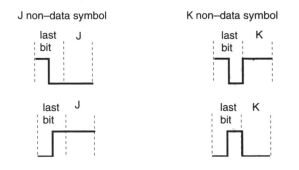

Figure 2.12 J and K non-data symbol composition. J and K non-data symbols are distinct code violations that cannot be mistaken for data

JK0JK000. The end delimiter field marks the end of a frame as well as denoting whether or not the frame is the last frame of a multiple frame sequence using a single token or if there are additional frames following this frame.

The format of the end delimiter field is JK1JK1IE, where I is the intermediate frame bit. If I is set to 0, this indicates it is the last frame transmitted by a station. If I is set to 1, this indicates that additional frames follow this frame.

E is an Error-Detected bit. The E bit is initially set to 0 by the station transmitting a frame, token, or abort sequence. As the frame circulates the ring, each station checks the transmission for errors. Upon detection of a Frame Check Sequence (FCS) error, inappropriate non-data symbol, illegal framing, or another type of error, the first station detecting the error will set the E bit to a value of 1. Since stations keep track of the number of times they set the E bit to a value of 1, it becomes possible to use this information as a guide to locating possible cable errors. For example, if one workstation accounted for a very large percentage of E bit settings in a 72-station network, there is a high degree of probability that there is a problem with the lobe cable to that workstation. The problem could be a crimped cable or a loose connector and represents a logical place to commence an investigation in an attempt to reduce E bit errors.

2.4.3 Access control field

The second field in both token and frame formats is the access control byte. As illustrated in Figure 2.10(a), this byte consists of four subfields and serves as the controlling mechanism for gaining access to the network. When a free token circulates the

Table 2.5 Priority bit settings

Priority bits	Priority
000	Normal user priority, MAC frames that do not require a token and response type MAC frames
001	Normal user priority
010	Normal user priority
011	Normal user priority and MAC frames that require tokens
100	Bridge
101	Reserved
110	Reserved
111	Specialized Station Management

network the access control field represents one-third of the length of the frame since it is prefixed by the start delimiter and suffixed by the end delimiter.

The lowest priority that can be specified by the priority bits in the access control byte is 0 (binary 000), while the highest is 7 (binary 111), providing eight levels of priority. Table 2.5 lists the normal use of the priority bits in the access control field. Workstations have a default priority of 3 (001), while bridges have a default priority of 4 (100).

To reserve a token, a workstation will attempt to insert its priority level in the priority reservation subfield. Unless another station with a higher priority bumps the requesting station, the reservation will be honored and the requesting station will obtain the token. If the token bit is set to 1, this serves as an indication that a frame follows instead of the ending delimiter.

A station that needs to transmit a frame at a given priority can use any available token that has a priority level equal to or less than the priority level of the frame to be transmitted. When a token of equal or lower priority is not available, the ring station can reserve a token of the required priority through the use of the reservation bits. In doing so the station must follow two rules. First, if a passing token has a higher priority reservation than the reservation level desired by the workstation, the station will not alter the reservation field contents. Secondly, if the reservation bits have not been set or indicate a lower priority than that desired by the station, the station can now set the reservation bits to the required priority level.

Once a frame is removed by its originating station, the reservation bits in the header will be checked. If those bits have a non-zero value, the station must release a non-zero priority token, with the actual priority assigned based upon the priority used by the station for the recently transmitted frame, the reservation bit settings received upon the return of the frame, and any stored priority.

On occasion, the Token-Ring protocol will result in the transmission of a new token by a station prior to that station having the ability to verify the settings of the access control field in a returned frame. When this situation arises, the token will be issued according to the priority and reservation bit settings in the access control field of the transmitted frame.

Figure 2.13 illustrates the operation of the priority (P) and reservation (R) bit fields in the access control field. In this example, the prevention of a high-priority station from monopolizing the network is illustrated by station A entering a priority-hold state (Figure 2.13(b)). This occurs when a station originates a token at a higher priority than the last token it generated. Once in a priority-hold state, the station will issue tokens that will bring the priority level eventually down to zero as a mechanism to prevent a high-priority station from monopolizing the network.

The monitor bit

The monitor bit is used to prevent a token with a priority exceeding zero or a frame from continuously circulating on the Token-Ring. This bit is transmitted as a 0 in all tokens and frames, except for a device on the network which functions as an active monitor and thus obtains the capability to inspect and modify that bit.

When a token or frame is examined by the active monitor it will set the monitor bit to a 1 if it was previously found to be set to 0. If a token or frame is found to have the monitor bit already set to 1 this indicates that the token or frame has already made at least one revolution around the ring and an error condition has occurred, usually caused by the failure of a station to remove its transmission from the ring or the failure of a high-priority station to seize a token. When the active monitor finds a monitor bit set to 1 it assumes an error condition has occurred. The active monitor then purges the token or frame and releases a new token onto the ring. Now that we have an understanding of the role of the monitor bit in the access control field and the operation of the active monitor on that bit, let's focus our attention upon the active monitor.

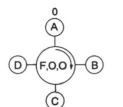

a. Station A generates a frame using a non–priority token P, R = 0,0.

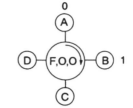

b. Station B reserves a priority 1 in the reservation bits in the frame P, R = 0,1; Station A enters a priority–hold state.

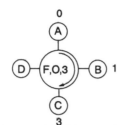

c. Station C reserves a priority of 3, overriding B's reservation of 1; P, R = 0,3.

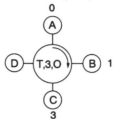

d. Station A removes its frame and generates a token at reserved priority level 3; P, R = 3,0

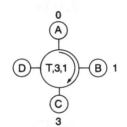

e. Station B repeats priority token and makes a new reservation of priority level 1; P, R = 3,1.

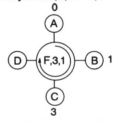

f. Station C grabs token and transmits a frame with a priority of 3; P, R = 3,1.

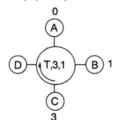

g. Upon return of frame to Station C it's removed. Station C generates a token at the priority just used; P, R = 3,1.

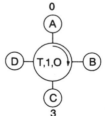

h. Station A in a priority-hold state grabs token and changes its priority to 1; P, R = 1,0. Station A stays in priority-hold state until priority reduced to 0.

Legend;

, = stations

Number outside station identifier indicates priority level.

Figure 2.13   Priority and reservation field utilization

The active monitor

The active monitor is the device that has the highest address on the network. All other stations on the network are considered as standby monitors and watch the active monitor.

As previously explained, the function of the active monitor is to determine if a token or frame is continuously circulating the ring in error. To accomplish this the active monitor sets the monitor count bit as a token or frame goes by. If a destination workstation fails or has its power turned off the frame will circulate back to the active monitor, where it is then removed from the network. In case the active monitor should fail or be turned off, the standby monitors watch the active monitor by looking for an active monitor frame. If one does not appear within 7 seconds, the standby monitor that has the highest network address then takes over as the active monitor.

In addition to detecting and removing frames that might otherwise continue to circulate the ring, the active monitor performs several other ring management functions. Those functions include the detection and recovery of multiple tokens and the loss of a token or frame on the ring, as well as initiation of a token when a ring is started. The loss of a token or frame is detected by the expiration of a timer whose time-out value exceeds the time required for the longest possible frame to circulate the ring. The active monitor restarts this timer and each time it transmits a starting delimiter which precedes every frame and token. Thus, if the timer expires without the appearance of a frame or token, the active monitor will assume the frame or token was lost and initiate a purge operation, which is described later in this section.

2.4.4 Frame control field

The frame control field informs a receiving device on the network of the type of frame that was transmitted and how it should be interpreted. Frames can be either logical link control (LLC) or reference physical link functions according to the IEEE 802.5 medium access control (MAC) standard. A medium access control frame carries network control information and responses, while a logical link control frame carries data.

The eight-bit frame control field has the format FFZZZZZZ, where FF are frame definition bits. The upper part of Table 2.6 indicates the possible settings of the frame bits and the

Table 2.6 Frame control field subfields

Frame type field F bit settings	Assignment
00	MAC frame
01	LLC frame
10	Undefined (reserved for future use)
11	Undefined (reserved for future use)

Frame type field Z bit settings	Assignment[a]
000	Normal buffering
001	Remove ring station
010	Beacon
011	Claim token
100	Ring purge
101	Active monitor present
110	Standby monitor present

[a] When F bits are set to 00, Z bits are used to notify an adapter that the frame is to be expressed buffered.

assignment of those settings. The ZZZZZZ bits convey medium access control (MAC) buffering information when the FF bits are set to 00. When the FF bits are set to 01 to indicate an LLC frame, the ZZZZZZ bits are split into two fields, designated rrrYYY. Currently, the rrr bits are reserved for future use and are set to 000. The YYY bits indicate the priority of the logical link control (LLC) data. The lower part of Table 2.6 indicates the value of the Z bits when used in MAC frames to notify a Token-Ring adapter that the frame is to be expressed buffered.

2.4.5 Destination address field

Although the IEEE 802.5 standard supports both 16-bit and 48-bit address fields, IBM's implementation requires the use of 48-bit address fields. IBM's destination address field is made up of five subfields as illustrated in Figure 2.14. The first bit in the destination address identifies the destination as an individual station (bit set to 0) or as a group (bit set to 1) of one or more stations. The latter provides the capability for a message to be broadcast to a group of stations.

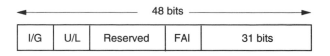

Figure 2.14 Destination address subfields (I/G: individual or group bit address identifier; U/L: universally or locally administered bit identifier; FAI: functional address indicator). The reserved field contains the manufacturer's identification in 22 bits represented by six hex digits

Universally administered address

Similar to an Ethernet universally administered address, a Token-Ring universally administered address is a unique address permanently encoded into an adapter's ROM. Because it is placed into ROM, it is also known as a burned-in address. The IEEE assigns blocks of addresses to each vendor manufacturing Token-Ring equipment, which ensures that Token-Ring adapter cards manufactured by different vendors are uniquely defined. Token-Ring adapter manufacturers are assigned universal addresses that contain an organizationally unique identifier. This identifier consists of the first six hex digits of the adapter card address and is also referred to as the manufacturer identification. For example, cards manufactured by IBM will begin with the hex address 08-00-5A or 10-00-5A, whereas adapter cards manufactured by Texas Instruments will begin with the address 40-00-14. Table 2.7 lists vendor universal address prefixes assigned by the IEEE.

Locally administered address

A key problem with the use of universally administered addresses is the requirement to change software coding in a mainframe computer whenever a workstation connected to the mainframe via a gateway is added or removed from the network. To avoid constant software changes, locally administered addressing can be used. This type of addressing functions similarly to its operation on an Ethernet LAN, temporarily overriding universally administered addressing; however, the user is now responsible for ensuring the uniqueness of each address. To accomplish locally administered addressing, a statement is inserted into a configuration file which sets the adapter's address at adapter-open time, normally when a station is powered on or a system reset operation is performed.

Table 2.7 Vendors assigned universal address prefix

6-digit address Prefix	Vendor	6-digit address Prefix	Vendor
00-00-0D	RND	48-00-09	HP
00-00-A6	NwkGnl	48-00-0A	Nestar
00-00-C9	Prteon	48-00-10	AT&T
00-01-3A	Agilis	48-00-14	Exceln
00-01-C8	TmsCrd	48-00-17	NSC
00-DD-00	UB	48-00-1E	Apollo
00-DD-01	UB	48-00-20	Sun
08-00-5A	IBM	48-00-25	CDC
10-00-58	DG	48-00-28	TI
10-00-5A	IBM	48-00-2B	DEC
10-00-D8	DG	48-00-36	Intrgr
48-00-0C	Cisco	48-00-39	Spider
40-00-14	TI	48-00-45	Xylogx
40-00-22	VisTec	48-00-47	Sequnt
40-00-2A	TRW	48-00-49	Univtn
40-00-65	NwkGnl	48-00-4C	Encore
40-00-9F	Amrstr	48-00-4E	BICC
40-00-A9	NSC	48-00-67	ComDes
40-00-AA	Xerox	48-00-68	Ridge
40-00-B3	Cimlin	48-00-69	SilGrf
40-00-C0	WstDig	48-00-6A	AT&T
40-00-C9	Prteon	48-00-6E	Exceln
40-00-DD	Gould	48-00-7C	Vtalnk
42-07-01	Intrln	48-00-89	Kinetx
42-60-8C	3Com	48-00-8B	Pyramd
42-CF-1F	CMC	48-00-8D	Xyvisn
48-00-02	Bridge	48-00-90	Retix
48-00-03	ACC	50-00-14	TI
48-00-05	Symblx	EA-00-03	DEC
48-00-08	BBN	EA-00-04	DECnet

Functional address indicator

The functional address indicator subfield in the destination address identifies the function associated with the destination address, such as a bridge, active monitor or configuration report server.

The functional address indicator indicates a functional address when set to 0 and the I/G bit position is set to a 1 – the latter indicating a group address. This condition can only occur when the U/L bit position is also set to a 1 and results in the ability to generate locally administered group addresses that are called functional addresses. Table 2.8 lists the functional addresses defined by the IEEE. Currently, 21 functional addresses have been defined out of a total of 31 that are available for use, with the remaining addresses available for user definitions or reserved for future use.

Address values

The range of addresses that can be used on a Token-Ring primarily depends upon the settings of the I/G, U/L, and FAI bit positions. When the I/G and U/L bit positions are set to 00 the manufacturer's universal address is used. When the I/G and U/L bits are set to 01, individual locally administered addresses are used in the defined range listed in Table 2.8. When all three bit positions are set, this situation indicates a group address within the range contained in Table 2.9. If the I/G and U/L bits are set to 11 but the FAI bit is set to 0, this indicates that the address is a functional address. In this situation the range of addresses is

Table 2.8   IEEE functional addresses

Active Monitor	C0-00-00-00-00-01
Ring Parameter Server	C0-00-00-00-00-02
Network Server Heartbeat	C0-00-00-00-00-04
Ring Error Monitor	C0-00-00-00-00-08
Configuration Report Server	C0-00-00-00-00-10
Synchronous Bandwidth Manager	C0-00-00-00-00-20
Locate–Directory Server	C0-00-00-00-00-40
NetBIOS	C0-00-00-00-00-80
Bridge	C0-00-00-00-01-00
IMPL Server	C0-00-00-00-02-00
Ring Authorization Server	C0-00-00-00-04-00
LAN Gateway	C0-00-00-00-08-00
Ring Wiring Concentrator	C0-00-00-00-10-00
LAN Manager	C0-00-00-00-20-00
User-defined	C0-00-00-00-80-00
	through
	C0-00-40-00-00-00
ISO OSI ALL ES	C0-00-00-00-40-00
ISO OSI ALL IS	C0-00-00-00-80-00
IBM discovery non-server	C0-00-00-01-00-00
IBM resource manager	C0-00-00-02-00-00
TCP/IP	C0-00-00-04-00-00
6611-DECnet	C0-00-20-00-00-00
LAN Network Manager	C0-00-40-00-00-00

Table 2.9 Token-Ring addresses

	Bit settings			
	I/G	U/L	FAI	Address or address range
Individual, universally administered	0	0	0/1	Manufacturer's serial no.
Individual, locally administered	0	1	0	40-00-00-00-00-00 to 40-00-7F-FF-FF-FF
Group address	1	1	1	40-00-80-00-00-00 to 40-00-FF-FF-FF-FF
Functional address	1	1	0	C0-00-00-00-00-01 to C0-00-FF-FF-FF-FF (bit-sensitive)
All stations broadcast	1	1	1	FF-FF-FF-FF-FF-FF
Null address	0	0	0	00-00-00-00-00-00

bit-sensitive, permitting only those functional addresses previously listed in Table 2.8.

A number of destination ring stations can be identified through the use of a group address. Table 2.10 lists a few of the standard group addresses that have been defined when the I/G, U/L and FAI bits are set to 1.

In addition to the previously mentioned addresses, there are two special destination address values that are defined. An address of all 1's (FF-FF-FF-FF-FF-FF) identifies all stations as destination stations. If a null address is used in which all bits are set to 0 (00-00-00-00-00), the frame is not addressed to any workstation. In this situation it can only be transmitted but not received, enabling you to test the ability of the active monitor to purge this type of frame from the network.

Table 2.10 Representative standardized group addresses

Bridge	80-02-43-00-00-00
Bridge management	80-01-43-00-00-08
Novell IPX	90-00-72-00-00-40
Hewlett-Packard probe	90-00-90-00-00-80
Vitalink gateway	90-00-3C-A0-00-80
Customer use	D5-00-20-00-XX-XX
DECnet phase IV station addresses	55-00-20-00-XX-XX

Figure 2.15 Source address field (RI: routing information bit identifier; U/L: universally or locally administered bit identifier). The 46 address bits consist of 22 manufacturer identification bits and 24 universally administered bits when the U/L bit is set to 0. If set to 1, a 31-bit locally administered address is used with the manufacturer's identification bit set to 0

2.4.6 Source address field

The source address field always represents an individual address which specifies the adapter card responsible for the transmission. The source address field consists of three major subfields as illustrated in Figure 2.15. When locally administered addressing occurs, only 24 bits in the address field are used since the 22 manufacturer identification bit positions are not used.

The routing information bit identifier identifies the fact that routing information is contained in an optional routing information field. This bit is set when a frame is routed across a bridge using IBM's source routing technique.

2.4.7 Routing information field

The routing information field is optional and is included in a frame when the RI bit of the source address field is set. Figure 2.16 illustrates the format of the optional routing information field. If this field is omitted, the frame cannot leave the ring it was originated on under IBM's source routing bridging method. Under transparent bridging, the frame can be transmitted onto another ring. The routing information field is of variable length and contains a control subfield and one or more two-byte route designator fields when included in a frame as the latter are required to control the flow of frames across one or more bridges.

The maximum length of the routing information field (RIF) is 18 bytes. Since each RIF field must contain a two-byte routing control field, this leaves a maximum of 16 bytes available for use by up to eight route designators. As illustrated in Figure 2.16, each two-byte route designator consists of a 12-bit ring number and a four-bit bridge number. Thus, a maximum total of 16 bridges can be used to join any two rings in an Enterprise Token-Ring network.

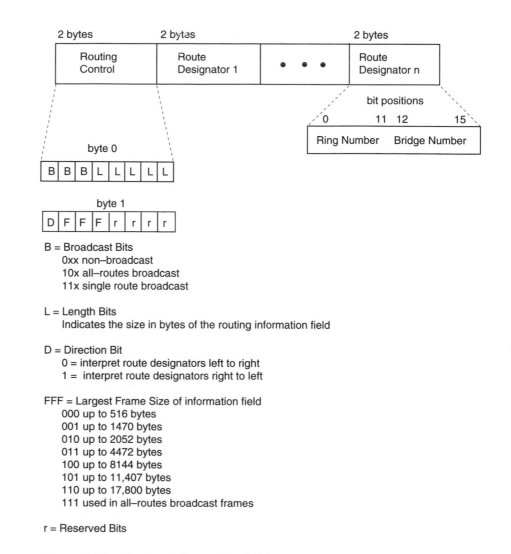

Figure 2.16 Routing information field

2.4.8 Information field

The information field is used to contain Token-Ring commands and responses as well as to carry user data. The type of data carried by the information field depends upon the F bit settings in the frame type field. If the F bits are set to 00 the information field carries medium access control (MAC) commands and responses that are used for network management operations. If the F bits are set to 01 the information field carries logical link control (LLC) or user data. Such data can be in the form of portions of a file being transferred on the network or an electronic mail message being routed to another workstation on the network. The information field is of variable length and can be considered to represent the higher level protocol enveloped in a Token-Ring frame.

In the IBM implementation of the IEEE 802.5 Token-Ring standard the maximum length of the information field depends upon the Token-Ring adapter used and the operating rate of the network. Token-Ring adapters with 64 kilobytes of memory can handle up to 4.5 kilobytes on a 4 Mbps network and up to 18 kilobytes on a 16 Mbps network.

2.4.9 Frame check sequence field

The frame check sequence field contains four bytes which provide the mechanism for checking the accuracy of frames flowing on the network. The cyclic redundancy check data included in the frame check sequence field covers the frame control, destination address, source address, routing information and information fields. If an adapter computes a cyclic redundancy check that does not match the data contained in the frame check sequence field of a frame, the destination adapter discards the frame information and sets an error bit (E bit) indicator. This error bit indicator, as previously discussed, actually represents a ninth bit position of the ending delimiter and serves to inform the transmitting station that the data was received in error.

2.4.10 Frame status field

The frame status field serves as a mechanism to indicate the results of a frame's circulation around a ring to the station that initiated the frame. Figure 2.17 indicates the format of the frame

A = Address – Recognized Bits
B = Frame – Copied Bits
r = Reserved Bits

Figure 2.17 Frame status field. The frame status field denotes whether the destination address was recognized and whether the frame was copied. Since this field is outside CRC checking, its subfields are duplicated for accuracy

status field. The frame status field contains three subfields that are duplicated for accuracy purposes since they reside outside CRC checking. One field (A) is used to denote whether an address was recognized, while a second field (C) indicates whether the frame was copied at its destination. Each of these fields is one bit in length. The third field, which is two bit positions in length (rr), is currently reserved for future use.

2.5 TOKEN-RING MEDIUM ACCESS CONTROL

As previously discussed, a MAC frame is used to transport network commands and responses. As such, the MAC layer controls the routing of information between the LLC and the physical network. Examples of MAC protocol functions include the recognition of adapter addresses, physical medium access management, and message verification and status generation. A MAC frame is indicated by the setting of the first two bits in the frame control field to 00. When this situation occurs, the content of the information field which carries MAC data is known as a vector.

2.5.1 Vectors and subvectors

Only one vector is permitted per MAC frame. That vector consists of a major vector length (VL), a major vector identifier (VI), and zero or more subvectors.

As indicated in Figure 2.18, there can be multiple subvectors within a vector. The vector length (VL) is a 16-bit number that gives the length of the vector, including the VL subfield in bytes. VL can vary between decimal 4 and 65 535 in value. The minimum value that can be assigned to VL results from the fact that the smallest information field must contain both VL and VI subfields. Since each subfield is two bytes in length, the minimum value of VL is 4.

When one or more subvectors is contained in a MAC information field, each subvector contains three fields. The subvector length (SVL) is an eight-bit number which indicates the length of the subvector. Since an eight-bit number has a maximum value of 255 and cannot indicate a length exceeding 256 bytes (0–255), a method was required to accommodate subvector values (SVV) longer than 254 bytes. The method used is the placement of hex FF in the SVL field to indicate

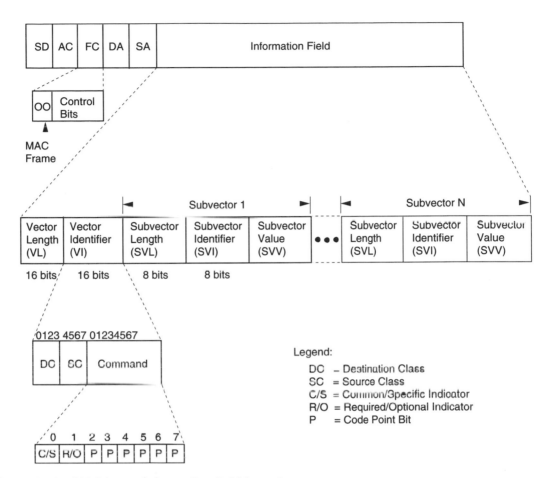

Figure 2.18 MAC frame information field format

that SVV exceeds 254 bytes. Then, the actual length is placed in the first two bytes following SVL. Finally, each SVV contains the data to be transmitted. The command field within the major vector identifier contains bit values referred to as code points which uniquely identify the type of MAC frame. Figure 2.18 illustrates the format of the MAC frame information field, while Table 2.11 lists currently defined vector identifier codes for six MAC control frames defined under the IEEE 802.5 standard.

2.5.2 MAC control

As previously discussed, each ring has a station known as the active monitor which is responsible for monitoring tokens and

Table 2.11   Vector identifier codes

Code value	MAC frame meaning
010	Beacon (BCN)
011	Claim token (CL_TK)
100	Purge MAC frame (PRG)
101	Active monitor present (AMP)
110	Standby monitor present (SMP)
111	Duplicate address test (DAT)

taking action to prevent the endless circulation of a token on a ring. Other stations function as standby monitors and one such station will assume the functions of the active monitor if that device should fail or be removed from the ring. For the standby monitor with the highest network address to take over the functions of the active monitor, the standby monitor needs to know there is a problem with the active monitor. If no frames are circulating on the ring but the active monitor is operating, the standby monitor might falsely presume the active monitor has failed. Thus, the active monitor will periodically issue an active monitor present (AMP) MAC frame. This frame must be issued every 7 seconds to inform the standby monitors that the active monitor is operational. Similarly, standby monitors periodically issue a standby monitor present (SMP) MAC frame to denote they are operational.

If an active monitor fails to send an AMP frame within the required time interval, the standby monitor with the highest network address will continuously transmit claim token (CL_TK) MAC frames in an attempt to become the active monitor. The standby monitor will continue to transmit CL_TK MAC frames until one of three conditions occurs:

- A MAC CL_TK frame is received and the sender's address exceeds the standby monitor's station address.
- A MAC beacon (BCN) frame is received.
- A MAC purge (PRG) frame is received.

If one of these conditions occurs, the standby monitor will cease its transmission of CL_TK frames and resume its standby function.

Purge frame

If a CL_TK frame issued by a standby monitor is received back without modification and neither a beacon nor purge frame is received in response to the CL_TK frame, the standby monitor becomes the active monitor and transmits a purge MAC frame. The purge frame is also transmitted by the active monitor each time a ring is initialized or if a token is lost. Once a purge frame is transmitted, the transmitting device will place a token back on the ring.

Beacon frame

In the event of a major ring failure, such as a cable break or the continuous transmission by one station (known as jabbering), a beacon frame will be transmitted. The transmission of BCN frames can be used to isolate ring faults. For an example of the use of a beacon frame, consider Figure 2.19 in which a cable fault results in a ring break. When a station detects a serious problem with the ring, such as the failure to receive a frame or token, it transmits a beacon frame. That frame defines a failure domain which consists of the station reporting the failure via the transmission of a beacon and its nearest active upstream neighbor (NAUN), as well as everything between the two.

If a beacon frame makes its way back to the issuing station, that station will remove itself from the ring and perform a series of diagnostic tests to determine if it should attempt to reinsert itself into the ring. This procedure ensures that a ring error

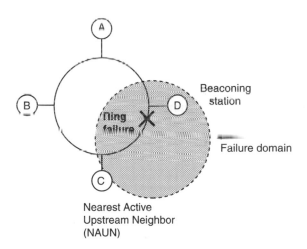

Figure 2.19 Beaconing. A beaconing frame indicates a failure occurring between the beaconing station and its nearest active upstream neighbor – an area referred to as a failure domain

caused by a beaconing station can be compensated for by having that station remove itself from the ring. Since beacon frames indicate a general area where a failure occurred, they also initiate a process known as auto-reconfiguration. The first step in the auto-reconfiguration process is the diagnostic testing of the beaconing station's adapter. Other steps in the auto-reconfiguration process include diagnostic tests performed by other nodes located in the failure domain in an attempt to reconfigure a ring around a failed area.

Duplicate address test frame

The last type of MAC command frame is the duplicate address test (DAT) frame. This frame is transmitted during a station initialization process when a station joins a ring. The station joining the ring transmits a MAC DAT frame with its own address in the frame's destination address field. If the frame returns to the originating station with its address-recognized (A) bit in the frame control field set to 1, this means that another station on the ring is assigned that address. The station attempting to join the ring will send a message to the ring network manager concerning this situation and will not join the network.

Station insertion

Depending upon the type of LAN adapter installed in your workstation, you may observe a series of messages of the format 'Phase X' followed by the message 'Completed' or 'Passed' when you power on your computer. Those messages refer to a five-phase ring insertion process during which your workstation's Token-Ring adapter attempts to become a participant on the ring. Table 2.12 lists the steps in the ring insertion process.

Table 2.12 Ring station insertion process

Phase 0: Lobe testing
Phase 1: Monitor check
Phase 2: Duplicate address check
Phase 3: Participation in neighbor notification
Phase 4: Request initialization

During the lobe testing phase, the adapter transmits a series of Lobe Media Test MAC frames to the multistation access unit (MAU). Those frames should be wrapped at the MAU, resulting in their return to the adapter. Assuming the returned frames are received correctly, the adapter sends a 5-volt DC current, which opens a relay at the MAU port and results in an attachment to the ring.

After the station attaches to the ring, it sets a value in a timer known as the Insert-timer and watches for an AMP, SMP or Purge MAC frame prior to the timer expiring. If the timer expires, a token claiming process is initiated. If the station is the first station on the ring, it then becomes the active monitor.

Once the Monitor Check Phase is completed, the station transmits a Duplicate Address Test frame during which the destination and source address fields are set to the station's universal address. If a duplicate address is found when the A bit is set to 1, the station cannot become a participant on the ring and detaches itself from the ring.

Assuming the station has a unique address, it next begins the neighbor notification process. During this ring insertion phase, the station learns the address of its nearest active upstream neighbor (NAUN) and reports its address to its nearest active downstream neighbor.

The address learning process begins when the active monitor transmits an AMP frame. The first station that receives the frame and is able to copy it sets the address-recognized (A) and frame-copied (C) bits to '1.' The station then saves the source address from the copied frame as the NAUN address and initiates a Notification–Response timer. As the frame circulates the ring, other active stations only repeat it as its A and C bits were set.

When the Notification–Response timer of the first station downstream from the active monitor expires, it broadcasts an SMP frame. The next station downstream copies its NAUN address from the source address field of the SMP frame and sets the A and C bits in the frame to '1.' Then it starts its own Notification–Response time which, upon expiration, results in that station transmitting its SMP frame. As the SMP frames originate from different stations, the notification process proceeds around the ring until the active monitor copies its NAUN address from an SMP frame. At this point, the active monitor sets its Neighbor-Notification Complete flag to 1, which indicates that the neighbor notification process was successfully completed.

The final phase in the ring insertion process occurs after the neighbor notification process is completed. During this phase, the station's adapter transmits a Request Initialization frame to the ring parameter server. The server responds with an Initialize-Ring-Station frame which contains values that enable all stations on the ring to use the same ring number and soft error report time value, thereby completing the insertion process.

2.6 TOKEN-RING LOGICAL LINK CONTROL

In concluding this chapter, I will examine the flow of information within a Token-Ring network at the logical link control (LLC) sublayer. Similar to Ethernet, the Token-Ring LLC sublayer is responsible for performing routing, error control, and flow control. In addition, this sublayer is responsible for providing a consistent view of a LAN to upper OSI layers, regardless of the type of media and protocols used on the network.

Figure 2.20 illustrates the format of an LLC frame which is carried within the information field of the Token-Ring frame. As previously discussed in this chapter, the setting of the first two bits in the frame control field of a Token-Ring frame to 01 indicates that the information field should be interpreted as an LLC frame. The portion of the Token-Ring frame which carries LLC information is known as a protocol data unit and consists of either three or four fields, depending upon the inclusion or omission of an optional information field. The control field is similar to the control field used in the HDLC protocol and defines three types of frames – information (I-frames) are used for sequenced messages, supervisory (S-frames) are used for status and flow control, while unnumbered (U-frames) are used for unsequenced, unacknowledged messages.

2.6.1 Service access points

Service access points (SAPs) can be considered interfaces to the upper layers of the OSI Reference Model, such as the network layer protocols. A station can have one or more SAPs associated with it for a specific layer and can have one or more active sessions initiated through a single SAP. Thus, we can consider a SAP to function similarly in scope to a mailbox, containing an address which enables many types of mailings to reach the box. However, instead of mail, SAP addresses identify different network layer processes or protocols and function as locations where messages can be left concerning desired network services.

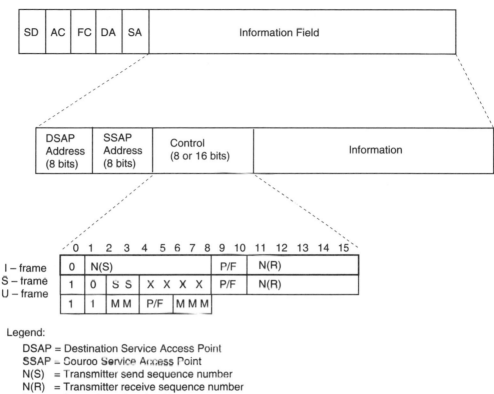

Legend:

DSAP = Destination Service Access Point
SSAP = Source Service Access Point
N(S) = Transmitter send sequence number
N(R) = Transmitter receive sequence number
S = Supervisory function bits
M = Modifier function bits
X = Reserved bits (set to zero)
P/F = Poll/final bit

Figure 2.20 Logical link control frame format

DSAP

The first field in the LLC protocol data unit is the destination services access point (DSAP). The DSAP address field identifies one or more service access points for which information is to be delivered.

SSAP

The second field in the LLC protocol data unit is the source services access point (SSAP). The SSAP address field identifies the service access point which transmitted the frame. Both DSAP and SSAP addresses are assigned to vendors by the IEEE to ensure that each is unique.

Both DSAPs and SSAPs are eight-bit fields; however, only seven bits are used for addressing, which results in a maximum of 128 distinct addresses available for each service access point. The eighth DSAP bit indicates whether the destination is an individual or a group address, while the eighth SSAP bit indicates whether the PDU contains a request or a response.

The control field contains information which defines how the LLC frame will be handled. U-frames are used for what is known as connectionless service in which frames are not acknowledged, while I-frames are used for connection-oriented services in which frames are acknowledged.

2.6.2 Types and classes of service

The types and classes of service supported by Token-Ring are the same as those supported by Ethernet, described in Section 2.3. Thus, readers are referred to Section 2.3 for information concerning the types and classes of service supported by a Token-Ring LAN.

3

WORKSTATION SETUP

Growing up, many people would have received a daily dose of vitamins from a caring mother, administered as preventative medicine. Although I haven't figured out how to feed a workstation, by verifying its setup I am normally able to either prevent or reduce potential problems from materializing. Thus, this author views a detailed understanding and review of the setup of a workstation's hardware and software as preventative medicine.

In this chapter I will focus my attention upon the relationship between network adapter cards that provide a physical connection to a local area network and the hardware and software of the workstation. First I will examine some of the hardware problems that can occur due to improper adapter card settings that result in conflicts between the network adapter card and the computer in which it is installed. Once this is accomplished I will turn my attention to software used to provide a local area network connection through the adapter card. In doing so I will examine the role of packet drivers, protocol stacks and the use of the AUTOEXEC.BAT, CONFIG.SYS and other important files on workstations. The term 'network adapter card' will be used interchangeably with 'network interface card' and the abbreviation NIC, as all three terms are synonymous references to an adapter card which provides a workstation with the ability to transmit information onto a LAN and receive information from the media.

3.1 HARDWARE

Although network adapter cards vary considerably between vendors as well as within a vendor's product line, there are several adapter card parameters that warrant checking to avoid

Table 3.1 Workstation hardware adapter settings to consider

- Base address of port used for CPU I/O
- Direct Memory Address (DMA) Channel
- Interrupt Request (IRQ) line
- Operating Rate
- Node Address

---

potential network problems. Some vendors include a program which can be used to display different hardware settings as well as reconfigure those settings via software. Other vendors provide dual-inline package (DIP) switches and jumpers on their network adapter cards which require physical intervention to change factory default settings, if required.

Table 3.1 lists hardware settings that many adapter cards permit users to change. In the remainder of this section I will examine each of the adapter card hardware settings listed in Table 3.1.

3.1.1 CPU port

Ports are used by computers for data transfer. Under DOS and other computer operating systems there are two types of ports commonly supported – CPU ports and operating system ports. Operating system ports, such as LPTx and COMx, where 'x' indicates a port number representing a particular parallel or serial port, are normally well known to users. Those ports are accessed by the operating system or Read Only Memory Basic Input Output System (ROM-BIOS) function calls.

CPU ports represent a low level data transfer capability which is directly accessed by the microprocessor in the workstation. The operating system uses some CPU ports to communicate with the keyboard as well as for disk drive data transfer operations. Other CPU ports may be used to send data to the speaker or to a network adapter card. Since each CPU port is identified by an address you will want to ensure that the port address setting on your network adapter card does not represent a conflict with another address used for a different device.

For the IBM PC and compatible computers common base port I/O hex addresses are listed in Table 3.2. Some adapter cards use I/O port addresses to control the memory addresses used by the

Table 3.2 Common I/O addresses
used by network adapter cards

- 0A20-0A2F
- 1A20-1A2F
- 2A20-2A2F
- 3A20-3A2F
- 4A20-4AEF

adapter card. Thus, you can use port I/O address settings not only to avoid adapter card conflicts but, in addition, to avoid memory conflicts. If you install two network adapter cards in a workstation you will have to configure both your software and network adapter cards to use different port addresses.

3.1.2 Direct Memory Access

Direct Memory Access (DMA) represents a method of data transfer used to move large quantities of data as well as specialized hardware used to perform the data transfer.

The rationale for DMA hardware is that its use permits data transfer to occur simultaneously with other tasks being performed by the microprocessor, similar to multitasking. An external device, such as a network adapter card, can initiate a DMA data transfer with computer memory. To do so it communicates with the DMA via a DMA channel. As in my discussion concerning ports, you do not want two adapter cards to use the same DMA channel. DMA channels typically supported by network adapter cards include channels 0, 1, 5, 6 and 7.

3.1.3 IRQ line

Each device that wants to obtain the attention of the microprocessor in a computer does so through the use of an interrupt request or IRQ. The device places a signal on its interrupt request (IRQ) line which causes the processor to suspend what it is doing in order to determine what action the device wants the processor to perform. On older PCs there are only eight IRQ lines, numbered from 0 to 7, while PC AT and compatible computers have 16 IRQ lines. However, to obtain eight additional IRQ lines PC AT-compatible systems use IRQ 2 for a second interrupt controller chip which makes it unavailable for use on AT-type computers.

From a performance perspective the interrupt controller associates higher priorities with lower IRQs. Thus, the system timer is assigned IRQ 0, while the keyboard is assigned IRQ 1. Three of the more common IRQ lines that can be used by network adapter cards are 10, 11 and 12 which are not pre-allocated to functions. However, since older PCs only support IRQs 0 through 7, those IRQ lines will not be acceptable for use with PC and PC XT compatible computers. Instead IRQ 2 or 3 can normally be used since IRQ 2 is not allocated in PCs and IRQ 3 is assigned to a second serial port.

When selecting an IRQ line you should consider your hardware configuration as well as the software you intend to use. Concerning hardware, if the computer has more than one physical parallel port which is using interrupts they may be set to use IRQ 5 and 7. Even if you do not have a second serial port IRQ 3 may not be available as certain network adapter cards, such as IBM's SDLC adapter, are set to use that interrupt line. Concerning software, some communications programs are designed to operate with a specific interrupt line or with a limited number of lines. Thus, you should carefully consider the operating requirements of both hardware and software when selecting an interrupt line for use by your network adapter card.

3.1.4 Operating rate

Although some network adapters, such as Ethernet 10Base-T, have a fixed operating rate, other adapter cards, such as Token-Ring, have dual operating rates. A few Token-Ring adapter cards require their operating rate to be set through the use of a jumper, DIP switch setting, or software. Although you do not have to actually set the operating rate of a dual speed adapter card, without examining what operating rate the default setting on cards that cannot automatically adjust to the network operating rate represents you may install a device set to the incorrect operating rate. Another common problem associated with Token-Ring network adapter cards is the fact that for several years IBM manufactured adapters limited to a 4 Mbps operating rate. Although those older network adapter cards cannot be used in a 16 Mbps Token-Ring network, the closure of a branch and the transportation of equipment to another location often result in a mixture of equipment at the new location that people will eventually attempt to use. By carefully examining equipment prior to its use you may be able to alleviate many hours of aggravation.

3.1.5 Node address

Each network adapter card is manufactured with a unique address burnt into read only memory (ROM) contained on the adapter. That address is referred to as the adapter's universally administered address and is six bytes or 48 bits in length. Under IEEE standards adapter cards can be set to recognize an address assigned by the network administrator. That address is referred to as the locally administered address and overrides the pre-assigned universally administered address.

Unlike the universally administered address that is unique from adapter to adapter, human error can result in duplicate locally administered addresses. Thus, care should be taken to ensure locally administered addresses are unique if this addressing scheme is used.

3.2 SOFTWARE

The major difference between the setup of hardware and software is the fact that the latter normally provides more options that you must consider. Software required to operate on a workstation to provide LAN access depends upon five main areas. Those areas are the operating system used on the workstation, the network operating system, how the computer will be used, the use of special applications, and the locations where communications software resides.

3.2.1 Workstation software

Common workstation operating systems include DOS, OS/2, UNIX, Windows NT, Windows 95 and System 7. Examples of network operating systems include NetWare, TCP/IP, IBM LAN Server, Microsoft LAN Manager, Banyan VINES and Windows NT. The way a computer is used, e.g. as a workstation, a server or a peer-to-peer workstation, may require different software setups. Similarly, the use of special application programs, such as terminal emulators that are used either through the LAN or via a hot key to a coaxial cable connection to a mainframe or minicomputer, can also require a special configuration so that hot keys do not conflict with LAN software operations. One common problem when using Windows 3.1 to access a network is the failure to use the Windows Setup facility to recognize the network operating system the workstation uses. When this occurs, the workstation may periodically freeze during certain network operations and may even reboot itself, resulting in a loss of work previously performed but not saved. Last but far from least, how you will use the workstation will govern the software you must operate on the workstation. Will the workstation use one LAN protocol or multiple protocols? The answer to this question as well as consideration of the previously mentioned areas will determine the communications software modules required to operate with the network adapter card.

Since this author could not attempt to cover but a small fraction of the large number of distinct combinations of the five major areas previously described, it was felt that this section would be more productive for readers by focusing upon an examination of the communications software modules required for a DOS workstation to support access to different networks and network applications. Doing so will permit an explanation of the operation of different software modules and the order in which they must be loaded, which can serve as a foundation for attempting to understand how to set up software on workstations to satisfy other networking scenarios.

3.2.2 The protocol stack

The ability of an application program on a workstation to communicate via a local area network is dependent upon a group of communications software modules referred to as a protocol stack. The protocol stack can be thought of as an interface between an application and the network adapter which supports the orderly flow of information onto and from the network. Figure 3.1 illustrates the relationship between an application program running on a workstation, the communications software used to form a protocol stack, and the network adapter card.

To access the network the application calls a procedure contained in the protocol stack. The protocol stack in turn sends a request to the network via the network adapter card. When the information flow is reversed, the adapter receives information from the network and generates an interrupt which informs the protocol stack to retrieve data from the card. The protocol stack then informs the application that information is available for its use and provides the information upon a request generated by the application.

A set of standards referred to as the application programming interface (API) governs the transfer of information between

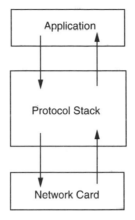

Figure 3.1 Relationship between an application program, protocol stack and network card

applications and protocol stacks. Another set of standards defines the composition of a protocol stack as well as how multiple stacks can be supported.

Standards

Standards that define the composition of a protocol stack are based upon the operating system used by the workstation and the network operating system. Concerning the latter, the protocol stack operating on a workstation must support the data transport mechanism of the network operating system. Examples of data transport mechanisms include NetBIOS, IPX, TCP/IP and Logical Link Control (LLC). Standards that define the interface between multiple stacks fall into two major camps – Open Data-Link (ODI) jointly developed by Apple Computer and Novell (see Section 3.3) and the Network Driver Interface Specification (NDIS) jointly developed by 3Com and Microsoft (see Section 3.4). Two additional standard protocol managers are the Packet Driver Specification (PDS) from FTP Software and the Adapter Support Interface (ASI) from IBM.

PDS evolved from a series of hardware drivers developed at Clarkson University and are often referred to as the Clarkson Packet Drivers. The setup when a packet driver is used is relatively simple, requiring only the identification of the software interrupt when the driver is loaded. Then the protocol stack is loaded and interfaces with the packet driver through the software interrupt.

ASI is implemented in IBM's Token-Ring LAN Support Program. It uses a protocol manager and a hardware interface to support different protocol interfaces. In doing so ASI requires drivers to be written to the ASI interface which enables ASI and ODI or NDIS to be implemented on the same workstation.

Table 3.3 summarizes the data transport mechanisms used by 20 popular types of network software as well as their ability to be used with either of the two major multiple protocol stack standards. Readers should note, however, that communications is among the most rapidly evolving technologically based fields. Thus, the support for protocol stacks listed in Table 3.3 will more than likely change after this book is published and should be carefully checked.

Rationale for multiprotocol stacks

To illustrate the rationale for the development of multiple protocol stack standards requires a review of single protocol

Table 3.3 Network software data transport and multiple protocol stack support

Network software	Data transport	Multiple protocol stack support
Artisoft Lantastic	NetBIOS	—
Attachmate Extra! over IPX	IPX	—
Attachmate Extra! over LLC	LLC	—
FTP PC/TCP	LLC	NDIS or ODI
Banyan VINES	LLC	NDIS
IBM Communications Manager	LLC	—
IBM LAN Server version 3.X	NetBIOS	NDIS
IBM LAN Server version 2.X	NetBIOS	—
IBM PC/3270 over LLC	LLC	—
IBM PC/3270 over NetBIOS	NetBIOS	—
IBM PC LAN	NetBIOS	—
IBM System/36 PC Support Program	LLC	—
IBM TCP/IP	LLC	NDIS
Microsoft LAN Manager version 2.X	NetBIOS	NDIS
Novell NetWare	IPX	ODI
Novell NetWare for SAA	IPX	ODI
Novell Personal NetWare	IPX	ODI
Novell LAN WorkPlace for DOS	TCP/IP	ODI
Wall Data Rumba	IPX	—
Wollongong Pathway Access TCP/IP	LLC	NDIS or ODI

stack arrangements as well as the limitations associated with this approach to networking. Most implementations of NetWare through version 3.11 required the network administrator to use the program WSGEN to generate IPX.COM which would include a network adapter card driver. Once this was accomplished the generated version of IPX.COM and another program known as NETx.COM, where x represents the version number, would be loaded onto a workstation. NETx.COM is a workstation shell which filters commands entered from the keyboard. This shell passes DOS commands to DOS and passes network commands to IPX for transmission onto the network. Since the shell sits atop IPX, the AUTOEXEC.BAT file of a DOS workstation connected to a NetWare LAN would contain the following statements:

```
C:\path\IPX
C:\path\NETX
F:
```

In the above statements the path normally represents a directory commonly named NETWORK or NETWARE, where the network files reside. The statement F: simply changes the user to drive F, which is normally the first network drive used by NetWare.

When used in this manner IPX, to include its built in network adapter card driver, retains exclusive control over the use of the adapter card. While this may not be an inconvenience for many persons, if you have a requirement to execute an application that requires the use of a different network protocol then problems would occur. You would have to create a different AUTO-EXEC.BAT file with a new set of commands to load a different protocol stack, rename your existing AUTOEXEC.BAT file for later reuse and reboot your computer. As an alternative, you could install a second network adapter in your workstation and use a second protocol stack dedicated to that adapter card. For example, assume your organization had a NetWare LAN which was connected to the Internet via an Internet access provider. The protocol used on the Internet is TCP/IP. Thus, you would have to either reconfigure your workstation's AUTOEXEC.BAT file and reboot your computer or obtain a second network adapter card and a separate protocol stack for TCP/IP operations, neither of which is a pleasing answer to the problem. The TCP/IP protocol stack differs slightly from the protocol stack illustrated in Figure 3.1 in two primary areas. First, the stack can contain the application. Secondly, instead of a built-in network adapter card driver like IPX.COM, a separate packet drive is normally used. However, the packet driver functions in a similar manner to the

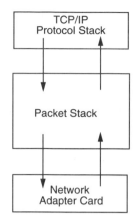

Figure 3.2   Typical layering of a TCP/IP protocol stack

built in network adapter driver in that it provides exclusive control over the operation of the adapter card as long as the TCP/IP protocol stack is memory-resident. Figure 3.2 illustrates the typical layering of a TCP/IP protocol stack which uses a separate packet driver to control the network adapter card.

Now that we have an appreciation for the role of single protocol stacks and the problems associated with operating multiple protocol stacks, let's focus our attention in Sections 3.3 and 3.4 upon ODI and NDIS and the software setup configurations required to properly operate multiple protocol stacks on a workstation.

3.3 SOFTWARE: ODI OPERATION

The Open Data-Link Interface (ODI) standard was released by Novell and Apple Computer in 1989. With the growth in the use of the Internet the use of ODI correspondingly increased as it provides a standard interface between a common network adapter card and multiple protocols. The ODI specification isolates the network adapter card from the protocol stacks, permitting multiple stacks to operate without specific knowledge of the hardware architecture of the network adapter card.

Figure 3.3 illustrates the ODI architecture for operating dual protocol stacks with a common network adapter card. In this illustration it was assumed that NetWare and TCP/IP protocol stacks are to use a common network adapter card.

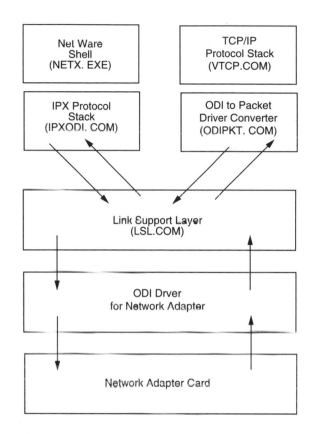

Figure 3.3   ODI architecture shown supporting NetWare and TCP/IP protocol stacks

3.3.1 Link Support Layer

In the ODI architecture illustrated in Figure 3.3 for running multiple stacks the Link Support Layer program (LSL.COM), which is the protocol manager, is supplied by Novell and is used to form a standard link for the simultaneous support of multiple protocols. Thus, LSL.COM must be loaded prior to loading the LAN driver normally provided by the vendor that manufactured the network adapter card, even though the driver sits below LSL in the stack.

3.3.2 LAN drivers

Examples of LAN drivers include TOKEN.COM for an IBM Token-Ring adapter, MADGEODI.COM for a Madge Token-Ring adapter and NE2000.COM for an NE2000 Ethernet adapter. ODI LAN drivers are also known as Multi-Link Interface Drivers (MLIDs) since they can control multiple adapters at the physical layer while regulating communications between those network adapter cards and the protocol stacks resident in workstation memory.

3.3.3 The NetWare stack

In the NetWare stack shown in the top left part of Figure 3.3 IPXODI.COM provides the Network (IPX) and Transport (SPX is built into IPX) layers of the OSI reference model and resembles the IPX.COM single protocol stack, enabling NETx.EXE, the NetWare shell, to be layered on top of IPXODI.COM. The initialization sequence of commands included in a workstation's AUTOEXEC.BAT file to use ODI with a single NetWare protocol stack would become:

```
C:\path\LSL.COM
C:\path\LANDRIVER
C:\path\IPXODI.COM
C:\path\NETX.EXE
F:
LOGIN GHELD
```

Here LANDRIVER represents the ODI network adapter card driver that supports a specific vendor's adapter card, such as the previously mentioned TOKEN.COM, MADGEODI, or NE2000.COM.

3.3.4 The TCP/IP protocol stack

To add the TCP/IP protocol stack you would add the appropriate statements to your AUTOEXEC.BAT file. Those statements must follow the execution of LSL.COM but can either precede or succeed the statements used to invoke the NetWare protocol stack. For example, assume the appropriate packet driver is contained in the file ODIPKT and the TCP/IP program is contained in the file TCPIP, while both files are located in the directory TCP. Then, the AUTOEXEC.BAT file would contain the following statements with the REM(ark) statements optionally added for clarity.

```
REM *Install NetWare*
C:\NETWARE\LSL.COM
C:\NETWARE\LANDRIVER
C:\NETWARE\IPXODI.COM
C:\NETWARE\NETx.EXE
F:
LOGIN GHELD
REM *Install TCP/IP*
C:\TCP\ODIPKT
C:\TCP\TCPIP
```

3.3.5 Using a shim

One of the problems associated with the use of packet drivers is the fact that they do not directly interface with LSL.COM nor with other protocol managers. Thus, if you wanted to support another protocol stack through the use of the Packet Drive Specification or a Clarkson Packet Driver you must obtain a software module referred to as a 'shim'. The shim provides the interface between the PDS protocol manager and LSL.COM or another protocol manager, such as the NDIS PROTMAN which is described later in this chapter. Figure 3.4 illustrates the location of a shim within a protocol stack.

3.3.6 Working with IPXODI

One common problem facing network users is a requirement for additional memory to execute memory intensive application programs. Although the DOS MEMMAKER program can provide you with considerable assistance in obtaining additional memory, it does not recognize the fact that certain programs, such as IPXODI.COM, are not all-inclusive and can be loaded as an entity or in parts.

IPXODI.COM consists of three parts IPX, SPX and Novell's Remote Diagnostics Responder. You can save memory by forgoing the loading of SPX or the Remote Diagnostics Responder. By entering the command IPXODI with the 'd' switch (IPXODI d) only IPX and SPX will be loaded, saving 4 kilobytes of memory. By entering the command IPXODI with the 'a' switch (IPXODI a) only IPX will be loaded, saving 8 kilobytes of memory. Prior to using either switch you should first determine the activities the workstation user intends to perform. For example, Novell's Remote Console (RCONSOLE) program requires SPX and the

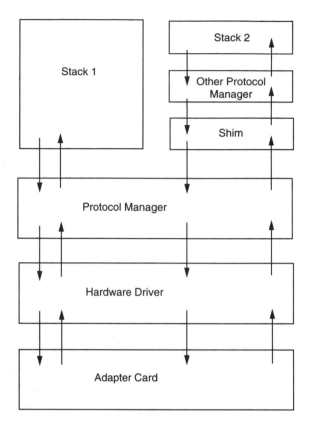

Figure 3.4 Using a shim to support multiple stacks developed for different protocol managers

Remote Diagnostics Responder. Thus, a workstation user who will use RCONSOLE could not use either IPXODI switch to save memory.

3.3.7 NET.CFG

One important file not shown in Figure 3.3 and until now not discussed is NET.CFG. This file describes the network adapter card configuration to the ODI driver and should be located in the same directory as the IPXODI and NETx files.

NET.CFG is an ASCII text file that can contain up to four main areas of information which describes the environment of a workstation. Those areas include a link support area, protocol area, link driver area, and parameter area.

Link support area

The link support area is used to define the number of communications buffers and memory set aside for those buffers. This
area is required to be defined when running TCP/IP; however,
since IPX does not use buffers or memory pools maintained by LSL
you can skip this section if you are only using a NetWare protocol
stack. The following illustration represents an example of the
coding of the link support area in the NET.CFG file to support TCP/
IP. The actual coding you would enter depends upon the network
adapter card to be used and you would obtain the appropriate
information from the manual accompanying the adapter card.

```
LINK SUPPORT
   BUFFERS 8 1144
   MemPool 4096
   MaxStacks 8
```

Protocol area

The protocol area is used to bind one or more protocols to specific
network adapter cards. By default, IPXODI binds to the network
adapter in the lowest system expansion slot as it scans slots in
their numerical order. If you have two or more network adapter
cards in a workstation you can use the protocol area to specify
which protocols you want to bind to each card. You can also
accomplish this at the link driver area by specifying 'Slot n' where
'n' is the slot number of the network adapter card you are
configuring. Assuming you wish to bind IPX to a 3Com adapter
card whose address is 3C5X9, you would add the following
statements to the NET.CFG file:

```
Protocol
   PROTOCOL IPX
   BIND 3C5X9
```

Since each computer using TCP/IP requires an IP address, the IP
address information must be included in the NET.CFG file if you
intend to use the TCP/IP protocol stack. For example, if the
network administrator assigned your computer the IP address
133.49.108.05, the IP address information would be entered as
follows:

```
PROTOCOL TCP/IP
ip_address 133.49.108.05
```

When using TCP/IP each workstation on the network is assigned the address of a default router by the network administrator. Thus, another statement commonly added to the NET.CFG file includes the address of the router that the workstation will use. For example, if the router's address is 133.49.108.17, then you would add the following statement to the NET.CFG file in its protocol area:

ip_router 133.49.108.17

The ip_address and ip_router statements can be avoided if the network administrator sets up a Reverse Address Resolution Protocol (RARP) server configured with IP and hardware addresses for workstations on the network. Then, when the workstation is powered on it will broadcast an RARP packet that will contain its hardware address. The RARP server will respond with the workstation's IP address associated with the hardware address. In the next section we will examine the Madge Smart Plus Token-Ring card's Link Driver statements which support this addressing method.

Link driver area

The link driver area is used to set the hardware configuration of the network adapter card so it is recognized by LAN drivers. If you are only using Novell's IPX, the first line of your NET.CFG file is a Link Driver statement which tells NETX the type of LAN card installed in the workstation, such as

Link Driver MADGEODI

The reason this statement becomes the first statement is that the Link Support area is omitted and, if you only have one adapter card, you do not require a protocol area.

If you're using a Madge Smart Plus Token-Ring card your link driver area would appear as follows:

```
Link Driver MADGEODI
     Frame TOKEN-RING
     Frame TOKEN-RING_SNAP
     Protocol   IPX    EO      TOKEN-RING
     Protocol   IP     800     TOKEN-RING_SNAP
     Protocol   ARP    806     TOKEN-RING_SNAP
     Protocol   RARP   8035    TOKEN-RING_SNAP
```

The Frame statement tells LSL the types of frames that can be used by the adapter, while the protocol statements inform LSL of the protocol number associated with each protocol to be supported. In this example TCP/IP requires the addition of frame and protocol statements (TOKEN-RING_SNAP) to be added to the link driver area. If you were using an Ethernet NE2000 card, your link driver area in the NET.CFG file would appear as follows:

```
Link Driver NE2000
    INT 5
    PORT 300
    Frame Ethernet_802.3
    Frame Ethernet_II
    Protocol IPX 0 Ethernet_802.3
    Protocol IP 8137 Ethernet_II
```

In this example the frame statements define the types of frames that will be supported by the adapter cards. Although most adapter cards include software that automatically construct or modify the NET.CFG file, upon occasion you may have to customize the contents of that file. To do so you can use the manual accompanying the network adapter card which will normally indicate the statements required to be placed in the file.

Virtual Load Modules

The introduction of NetWare 4.0 resulted in the replacement of NETX by Virtual Load Modules (VLMs) that sit behind DOS. In comparison, NETX sat in front of DOS and acted as a filter to identify and act upon network requests entered from the keyboard. VLMs are referred to as the NetWare DOS Requester as they use DOS redirection to satisfy file and print service requests. Since VLMs replace NETX.EXE, you would load VLM.EXE in the position previously used for NETX.EXE. That is, the sequence of commands placed in your AUTOEXEC.BAT file to initialize the NetWare protocol stack would appear as follows:

```
C:\NETWARE\LSL
C:\NETWARE\LANDRIVER
C:\NETWARE\IPXODI
C:\NETWARE\VLM.EXE
F:
LOGIN GHELD
```

To modify the AUTOEXEC.BAT file to support dual stack operations you could add the appropriate commands either after invoking LSL or after the 'Login' statement.

3.4 SOFTWARE: NDIS OPERATION

Although the Network Driver Interface Specification (NDIS) provides a dual stack capability similar to that provided by ODI its setup for operation varies considerably from the previously discussed dual stack mechanism. Figure 3.5 illustrates the relationship between NDIS software modules, upper layer protocol stacks and the network adapter card.

3.4.1 CONFIG.SYS use

Unlike ODI which represents a series of files loaded from an AUTOEXEC.BAT file, NDIS was designed as a series of device drivers which are loaded through the CONFIG.SYS file. In a DOS environment the first statement in the CONFIG.SYS file required for NDIS is:

DEVICE=drive:\path\PROTMAN.DOS

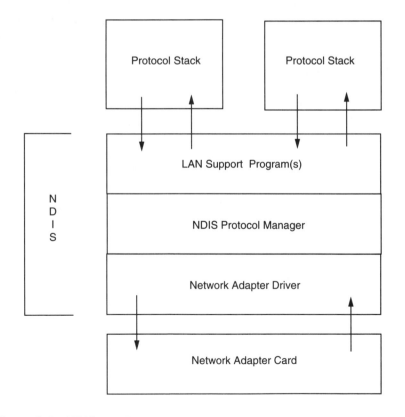

Figure 3.5   NDIS architecture

For OS/2, the file becomes PROTMAN.OS2. Both PROTMAN.DOS and PROTMAN.OS2 are the NDIS Protocol Manager for each workstation operating DOS or OS/2. The Protocol Manager reads the file PROTOCOL.INI which contains initialization parameters and stores the contents of that file in memory for use by other NDIS drivers. Thus, a short discussion of PROTOCOL.INI file is in order.

3.4.2 PROTOCOL.INI overview

The PROTOCOL.INI file can be considered to represent the NDIS equivalent of the NET.CFG file associated with ODI. Although most network products will automatically create or modify the PROTOCOL.INI file, some products require users to create or modify that file. In addition, you may be able to enhance network performance by modifying an existing parameter set by a network program which does not consider your total user environment.

Entries in PROTOCOL.INI occur in sections, with each section name surrounded in square brackets ([ ]). Under each section name are one or more named configuration entries which appear in the format 'name=value'. Although configuration entries can appear anywhere in a line under the section name, normal practice is to indent each entry three character positions to enhance readability.

The first section in the PROTOCOL.INI file has the heading [PROTMAN_MOD]. The first configuration entry for both DOS and OS/2 is the device name PROTMAN$. Thus, the first section entry becomes:

    [PROTMAN_MOD]
       DriverName=PROTMAN$

Other entries in the [PROTMAN_MOD] section are optional and can include keywords Dynamic, Priority and Bindstatus in assignment statements. The Dynamic statement can be set to 'YES' (Dynamic=YES) to support both static and dynamic binding, or 'NO' (Dynamic=NO) to set the Protocol Manager to operate only in static mode which is its default. In static mode protocol drivers are loaded once at system initialization and remain in memory. In dynamic mode drivers load at the point in time when they are bound by Protocol Manager. In addition, if the drivers support a dynamic unloading capability they can be unloaded if the software unbinds them when they are not needed, freeing memory.

The Priority keyword is used to specify the order of priority of protocol processing modules. Under NDIS an incoming LAN packet is first offered to the protocol with the highest priority. Other protocols will see the packet only if a higher protocol does not first recognize and process the packet. Protocols not specified in a priority list are the last to inspect incoming packets.

The Bindstatus keyword is used to specify whether Protocol Manager can optimize memory and can be set to 'YES' or 'NO'. If the keyword is not used a default of 'NO' is assumed.

The second communications statement included in a CONFIG.SYS file for NDIS operations invokes the network adapter card driver. For example, if you were using the Madge Token-Ring Smart Plus adapter you would include the following statement in the CONFIG.SYS file:

DEVICE=[drive:]\path\SMARTND.DOS

3.4.3 Non-NDIS operations

Although this section is about NDIS operations a digression to discuss the installation of device drivers for non-NDIS operations is warranted as a mechanism to facilitate proper workstation setup when using IBM hardware in that environment.

LAN Support Program

If your workstation is connected to a LAN using IBM's LAN Support Program a series of device driver statements with various parameters must be added to the CONFIG.SYS file. These 'DXM' drivers establish the interfaces to protocols used by IBM LAN software. Table 3.4 lists those 'DXM' device drivers in the order by which they are entered in a CONFIG.SYS file. The entries in Table 3.4 are applicable for IBM's PC Adapter, PC Adapter II and the Adapter/A Token-Ring cards.

Device drivers

The DXMA0MOD.SYS device driver serves as an interrupt arbitrator. The device driver DXMAC0MOD.SYS loads the Token-Ring network adapter support driver for IEEE 802.2 program support, while the device driver DXMC1MOD.SYS adds support for the IBM 3270 Workstation program. If you want to

Table 3.4 IBM non-NDIS 'DXM' device drivers

Software interface supported	Token-Ring network device driver required[a]		
IEEE 802.3	AO	CO	
IEEE 802.3 and NetBIOS	AO	CO	TO
IEEE 802.3 and 3270 Workstation Program	AO	C1	
IEEE 802.3, NetBIOS and 3270 Workstation Program	AO	C1	TO

[a] AO = DXMA0MOD.SYS, CO = DXMC0MOD.SYS, C1 = DXMC1MOD.SYS, TO = DXMT0MOD.SYS.

support NetBIOS you must also load the DXMT0MOD.SYS device driver which adds support for that network transport protocol.

Protocol stack

Figure 3.6 illustrates the protocol stacks for operating three different IBM Token-Ring adapter cards with either IEEE 802 or NetBIOS interface application programs. Since Figure 3.6 represents non-NDIS operations, although you can support multiple protocol stacks, they are limited to operation on IBM adapter cards that are tailored to work with the interrupt arbitrator. To set up a stack you would load the appropriate device drivers through the inclusion of appropriate lines in the CONFIG.SYS file. For example, to support IEEE 802.2 and NetBIOS you would insert the following statements in your CONFIG.SYS file:

```
DEVICE=C:\path\DXMA0MOD.SYS
DEVICE=C:\path\DXMC0MOD.SYS
DEVICE=C:\path\DXMT0MOD.SYS
```

Driver parameters

There are three parameters that can be coded with DXMC0MOD.SYS and DXMC1MOD.SYS device drivers. Those parameters control the adapter address, the adapter's shared RAM address and early Token Release, the latter only applicable for 16 Mbps network operations. Common errors resulting from

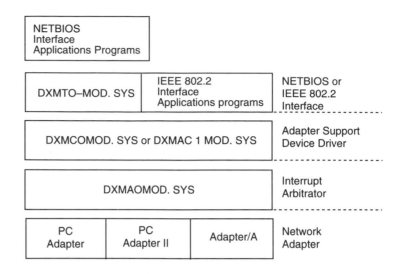

Figure 3.6 IBM non-NDIS protocol stack

improper parameters can include duplicate station addresses, memory conflicts or the failure of a station to use the early token release option. Thus, you should carefully verify the use of device driver statement parameters.

While the DXMC0MOD.SYS and DXMC1MOD.SYS drivers only support three optional parameters the DXMT0MOD.SYS driver supports a large number of parameters. Although most if not all default parameters are suitable for a workstation, when used with a gateway, server or a workstation using multiple applications, such as 3270 emulation and NetBIOS, you will probably have to adjust one or more parameters. Some of the key parameters that will more than likely require adjustment include the number of sessions, SAPs, link stations and names.

A session represents a logical connection between two NetBIOS names. If your computer is a gateway the session value setting limits the number of stations that can use the resources of the gateway.

A Service Access Point (SAP) can be considered to represent a mailbox used for communications between the data link layer and higher layer services. The number of SAPs required is usually based upon the transport protocols used. Thus, you will probably use one or more IBM manuals to determine an appropriate SAP value.

A link station represents one end of a formal connection between two devices via a local area network. You can consider the link station to reside above the SAP, enabling a SAP to support multiple link stations.

Each application using a link station needs to be separately addressable and requires a distinct subaddress to be associated with a link station. This subaddress is referred to as a name and provides a unique path between multiple sessions occurring on separate link stations. Figure 3.7 illustrates the relationship between service access points, link stations and NetBIOS names. By carefully reviewing the values associated with DXMT0MOD.SYS device driver parameters you may be able to avoid future problems that only become apparent as the workload on the network increases. Now that we have an appreciation for the device drivers required for non-NDIS adapter support, let's turn our attention back to the topic of this section, NDIS adapter support.

NDIS adapter support

The device driver which is compatible with the NDIS protocol manager is referred to as an NDIS MAC driver. The NDIS MAC driver is normally contained on a diskette that is included in the box in which your NDIS compatible network adapter card is packaged. If you are using the IBM LAN Support Program which supports both the IEEE 802.2 logical link control and NetBIOS transport

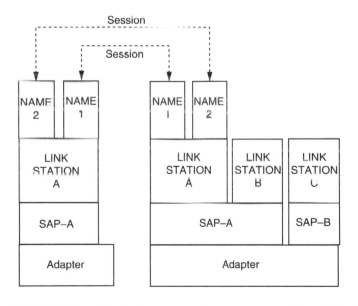

Figure 3.7 Relationship between service access points, link stations and NetBIOS names

protocols, there are a number of NDIS MAC drivers supported by that program, such as IBM's IBMTOK.DOS which supports IBM Token-Ring Network Adapters, MACETH.DOS for IBM PS/2 Adapter/A used on an Ethernet network, and ELNKII.DOS and SMCMAC.DOS for 3Com Etherlink II and Western Digital Ether-Card, EtherCard PLUS/A, SMC EtherCard Plus and several other types of Ethernet adapters. In addition to the NDIS MAC driver you will require a protocol driver as well as the files PROTMAN.DOS, PROTOCOL.INI and NETBIND.COM.

The protocol driver DXME0MOD.SYS is used if you require an IEEE 802.2 interface, while DXMJ0MOD.SYS should be used for a NetBIOS interface. When the IEEE 802.2 interface is required and the DXME0MOD.SYS device driver is used you must also use the interrupt arbitrator device driver, DXMA0MOD.SYS. You can also use that device driver as a mechanism to use the DXMT0MOD.SYS device driver in place of the DXMJ0MOD.SYS device driver. This is illustrated in Figure 3.8 which visually indicates the NDIS interfaces supported by the IBM LAN Support Program.

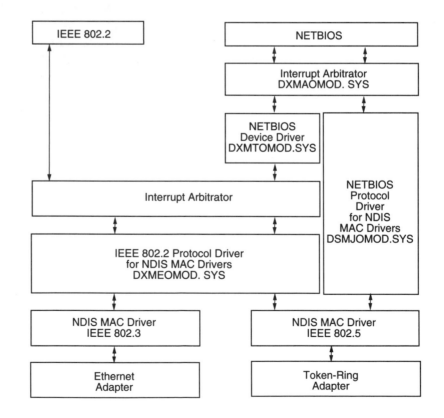

Figure 3.8   Support Program NDIS support interface

3.4.4 CONFIG.SYS statements

As previously discussed, the operation of NDIS is based upon the use of device drivers which are invoked through the use of statements in your CONFIG.SYS file. The first statement will always invoke the protocol manager. Thus, in a DOS environment you would enter the following statement in your CONFIG.SYS file:

DEVICE=C:\path\PROTMAN.DOS

When using the IBM LAN Support Program, PROTMAN.DOS by default looks for the PROTOCOL.INI file in a directory named LANMAN. To override this default you should include the /I: parameter in the statement followed by the drive and directory where the file PROTOCOL.INI actually resides. Thus, if you placed the file in the directory NETWORK you would enter the device driver statement in your CONFIG.SYS file as follows:

DEVICE=C:\path\PROTMAN.DOS /I:C:\NETWORK

If you elected to use an NDIS adapter with only NetBIOS your CONFIG.SYS statements would be as follows:

DEVICE=C:\path\PROTMAN.DOS /I:C:\NETWORK
DEVICE=C:\path\NDIS-MAC-DRIVER
DEVICE=C:\path\DXMA0MOD.SYS
DEVICE=C:\path\DXMJ0MOD.SYS

In the preceding example note that NDIS-MAC-DRIVER is replaced by the file name of the NDIS MAC driver. Also note that the above CONFIG.SYS sequence of commands corresponds to the rightmost protocol stack illustrated in Figure 3.8. Although the interrupt arbitrator is shown above the NetBIOS protocol driver it is loaded prior to the loading of the NetBIOS protocol driver. To support both IEEE 802.2 and NetBIOS you would enter the following sequence of statements in the CONFIG.SYS file, again assuming that the PROTOCOL.INI file resides in the directory NETWORK.

DEVICE=C:\path\PROTMAN.DOS /I:C:\NETWORK
DEVICE=C:\path\NDIS-MAC-DRIVER
DEVICE=C:\path\DXMA0MOD.SYS
DEVICE=C:\path\DXME0MOD.SYS
DEVICE=C:\path\DXMT0MOD.SYS

3.4.5 NETBIND.COM

The one exception to the use of the CONFIG.SYS file concerns the execution of the NDIS protocol binding utility program. This program must be executed before any network activity is started and is normally invoked through a statement in the AUTO-EXEC.BAT file. You should place the following statement in the AUTOEXEC.BAT file following any statements for terminate and stay resident (TSR) programs but prior to any statements required for LAN Support Program application program:

C:\path\NETBIND

3.4.6 PROTOCOL.INI modifications

There are a large number of parameters in the MAC section of the PROTOCOL.INI file that can be changed to customize a protocol driver to work with network application programs. Some parameters are used to set timer values that govern the delay prior to requiring acknowledging a received frame or transmitting a frame again when an acknowledgement is not received within the timer value. Normally, you can accept the default values for those parameters. Other parameters, such as NETADDRESS, must be entered or modified. For example, NETADDRESS is used to specify a locally administered address for an NDIS MAC driver that is bound to the DXMJ0MOD.SYS device driver. When you want to use the LAN Support Program with multiple protocol drivers and NDIS adapters you will have to modify the PROTO-COL.INI file. This modification is required to specify the second protocol driver and you should carefully read the manual as some protocol drivers are provided as a Terminate and Stay Resident (TSR) program. Those drivers must be invoked by a statement in the computer's AUTOEXEC.BAT file but must be placed before the NETBIND statement in that file. Based upon the preceding you should carefully review the PROTOCOL.INI settings supported by the device drivers you intend to use. The correct use of those settings may enable you to avoid a variety of network problems. In addition, some parameters can be used to improve LAN performance which may alleviate response time problems as well as possibly enable you to avoid network segmentation due to a high level of network utilization. Among performance tuning parameters you may wish to consider are those that adjust the frame size, increase the number of outstanding frames and increase the number of frames that are received prior to an acknowledgement being transmitted. By adjusting those parameters you may be able to reduce or eliminate network bottlenecks as well as reduce the perception of network problems by network users.

3.4.7 Using other adapters

Until now we have focused upon non-NDIS and NDIS statements required for use with IBM's LAN Support Program using IBM adapter cards. The use of adapter cards from other manufacturers for NDIS operations may be significantly easier to set up. For example, Madge Systems manufactures a 'smart' Token-Ring adapter card that requires you to load only one device driver. To generate a TCP/IP protocol stack using the NetManage Chameleon product with the Madge adapter only requires the following three statements in your CONFIG.SYS file:

```
DEVICE=C:\NETMANAG\PROTMAN.DOS /i:c:\netmanag
DEVICE=C:\MADGE\SMARTND.DOS
DEVICE=C:\NETMANAG\NETMANAG.DOS
```

Although the use of dual stacks can facilitate many network operations you should only consider their use when necessary. This is because their setup requires the use of additional computer memory which reduces the amount of memory available for executing application programs.

CABLE TESTING

One of the most appropriate locations to commence testing and troubleshooting local area network problems is the network's cable infrastructure. Many times, improper wiring and wiring problems can be directly identified as the cause of specific local area network transmission problems. Other times, a series of cable tests may provide an insight to problems and permit corrective actions to be identified.

In this chapter I will examine the characteristics of twisted-pair, coaxial and fiber optic cable. However, as the majority of current and emerging LAN technologies are based upon the use of twisted-pair cable I will devote most of my effort to twisted-pair. In addition to examining the characteristics of different types of cable I will note a popular 'defacto' as well as the 'dejur' cabling standards. Other topics covered in this chapter include a review of cable specifications, basic test measurements and cable tests, as well as a discussion of equipment you can consider using to perform the tests discussed in this chapter. From the information presented in this chapter you should obtain a detailed understanding of the value of different cable tests for isolating network problems as well as how those tests should be performed.

4.1 TEST EQUIPMENT

Test equipment manufactured for examining LAN cabling has its roots in equipment developed for testing telephone wiring. Devices to include tone generators and detectors and cable continuity testers were originally developed to test as well as verify the correct installation of telephone wiring from offices to wiring blocks in wiring closets. Tone generators were used to

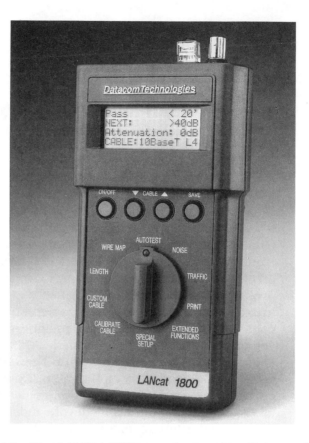

Figure 4.1 The LANCat 1800 manufactured by Datacom Technologies includes built-in specifications for several categories of LAN cables, permitting the tester to compare test results against the specifications and indicate a 'Pass' or 'Fail' test condition. (Photograph courtesy of Datacom Technologies, Inc.)

trace twisted-pair cabling as it is easy for a technician to connect the wire pair to an incorrect position on a wiring block in a typically cramped wiring closet. Cable continuity testers provide a mechanism to determine if a cable has a 'short' (a connection between conductors), an 'open' (a break in a conductor) or continuity enabling transmission to flow from end to end. Although you can still purchase equipment designed to perform a specific type of cable test, many manufacturers of cable test equipment combined a variety of cable tests into hand-held cable testers. Two popular hand-held cable testers are illustrated in Figures 4.1 and 4.2.

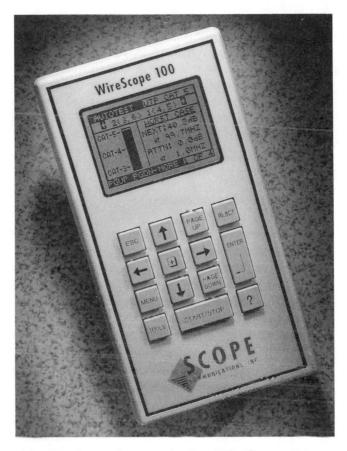

Figure 4.2   The Scope Communications WireScope 100 provides a graphic display of the results of different cable tests. (Photograph courtesy of Scope Communications, Inc.)

4.1.1 Hand-held cable testers

Figure 4.1 illustrates the LANCat 1800 LAN cable and activity tester manufactured by Datacom Technologies, Inc. of Everett, WA. This tester can be used to measure cable length, determine near end crosstalk (NEXT), measure attenuation, display a wire map and display network activity as a percentage of network utilization of IEEE 802.3 and 802.5 networks. In addition, the LANCat 1800 includes built-in specifications for several types of cable categories permitting a comparison of tests against stored parameters. This explains why the LANCat 1800 test display illustrated in Figure 4.1 can generate 'Pass' for a test.

The WireScope 100 manufactured by Scope Communications, Inc. of Northboro, MA which is illustrated in Figure 4.2 adds an ambient noise test and a graphic display of test results capability. The ambient noise test capability can be used over a period of time to determine if impulse noise spikes caused by internal machinery or external sources are the cause of periodic network error bursts. The WireScope 100 also contains a built-in clock which can be used to time-stamp tests.

4.1.2 Time domain reflectometer

A time domain reflectometer (TDR) is a cable fault locator which operates similar to radar, generating a pulse of energy and examining its reflection to determine the distance to a fault and to identify the type of fault. Although a TDR capability is built into most hand-held cable testers, the functionality of that type of TDR is usually limited to determining the distance to a fault and identifying two or three common faults. A stand-alone TDR which provides a graphical display of pulse reflections is usually required to obtain the ability to identify other types of cable problems. Later in this chapter I will examine the functionality of TDRs to include how they can be used to identify common cable faults as well as to denote other cable problems.

4.2 TYPES OF CABLE: TWISTED PAIR

There are three general types of cable commonly used to provide an intrabuilding wiring infrastructure for the construction of local area networks. Those cable types include twisted-pair, coaxial cable and optical fibers. This section and the next deal with twisted-pair cable; coaxial and fiber optic cable are covered briefly in Sections 4.4 and 4.5.

Twisted-pair cable, as its name implies, consists of one or more pairs of insulated wire twisted together in a regular geometric pattern. Since a length of wire functions as an antenna and can pick up electromagnetic emissions the wire pair would act similarly to a radio receiver. However, the twists are designed to produce a counterbalance to the receipt of such emissions since the electromagnetic fields of the pair of wires have opposite polarities and intensities and cancel each other out, reducing their potential to cause transmission errors.

4.2.1 UTP and STP

Twisted-pair cables usually consist of four, eight or 12 wires producing two, four or six pairs. A common 25-pair cable used to consolidate smaller pair bundles is primarily used for telephone wiring and is normally unsuitable for LAN applications. When twisted-pairs are shielded with foil or another substance to reduce the effect of electromagnetic emissions the wiring is referred to as shielded twisted-pair (STP). Thus, non-shielded twisted-pair is referred to as unshielded twisted-pair (UTP).

4.2.2 Conductors

The conductors in twisted-pair wiring are referenced with respect to their thickness using American Wire Gauge (AWG) numbering. The most common AWG conductors used in twisted-pair are 19, 22, 24 and 26; however, the AWG number is inversely proportional to the thickness of the conductor. As you might expect, a thin conductor has more resistance to data flow than a thicker wire. This is illustrated by the entries in Table 4.1 which denote the resistance for four common AWG cable pairs. As expected, a lower wire gauge has a thicker conductor which results in a lower resistance.

4.2.3 Cabling standards

There are two general types of cabling standards by which many types of twisted-pair wiring can be categorized – 'defacto' and 'dejur'.

Defacto standards represent a commonly used set of cabling rules and requirements which were developed by one or more vendors and do not carry the backing of a standards-making organization. Examples of defacto cabling 'standards' include the

Table 4.1 American wire gauge vs resistance

AWG	Ohms/1000 feet
19	16.1
22	32.4
24	51.9
26	83.5

original Ethernet cabling which specified the type of coaxial cable to be used in developing a LAN, and IBM's cabling system. The latter specifies a variety of twisted-pair and optical cables for use with the development of Token-Ring networks.

A dejur standard represents a standard developed by a standards-making organization. In the area of twisted-pair cabling the Electronics Industry Association and the Telecommunications Industry Association (EIA/TIA) working together developed several standards which have also been adopted by the American National Standards Institute (ANSI). Probably the most important standard is EIA/TIA-568, Commercial Building Telecommunications Wiring Standard. This standard contains detailed specifications on the electrical and physical characteristics of twisted-pair coaxial and optical fiber cable as well as guidelines concerning the cabling of new and existing buildings. In Sections 4.2.4 and 4.2.5 I will review the characteristics of IBM's cabling system and the TIA/EIA-568 standard, focusing my discussion towards the twisted-pair cabling used by each standard.

4.2.4 IBM cabling system

The IBM cabling system was introduced in 1984 as a mechanism to support the networking requirements of office environments. By defining standards for cables, connectors, faceplates, distribution panels and other facilities, IBM's cabling system is designed to support the interconnection of personal computers, conventional terminals, mainframe computers and office systems. In addition, this system permits devices to be moved from one location to another or added to a network through a simple connection to the cabling system's wall plates or surface mounts.

The IBM cabling system specifies seven different cabling categories. Depending upon the type of cable selected you can install the selected wiring indoors, outdoors, under a carpet, or in ducts and other air spaces.

The IBM cabling system uses wire which conforms to the American Wire Gauge or AWG. AWG is a unit of measurement with respect to the wire diameter. As previously discussed, as the wire diameter gets larger the AWG number decreases, in effect resulting in an inverse relationship between wire diameter and AWG. The IBM cabling system uses wire between 22 AWG (0.644 mm) and 26 AWG (0.405 mm). Since a larger diameter wire has less resistance to current flow than a smaller diameter wire, a smaller AWG permits cabling distances to be extended in comparison to a higher AWG cable.

Type 1

The IBM cabling system Type 1 cable contains two twisted pairs of 22 AWG conductors. Each pair is shielded with a foil wrapping and both pairs are surrounded by an outer braided shield or with a corrugated metallic shield. One pair of wires uses shield colors of red and green, while the second pair of wires uses shield colors of orange and black. The braided shield is used for indoor wiring, while the corrugated metallic shield is used for outdoor wiring. Type 1 cable is available in two different designs – plenum and non-plenum. Plenum cable is installed without the use of a conduit while non-plenum cable requires a conduit. Type 1 cable is typically used to connect a distribution panel or multistation access unit and the faceplate or surface mount at a workstation.

Type 2

Type 2 cable is actually a Type 1 indoor cable with the addition of four pairs of 22 AWG conductors for telephone usage. Because of this, Type 1 cable is also referred to as data-grade twisted-pair cable, while Type 2 cable is known as two data-grade and four-grade twisted pair. Due to its voice capability, Type 2 cable can support PBX interconnections. Like Type 1 cable, Type 2 cable supports plenum and non-plenum designs. Type 2 cable is not available in an outdoor version.

Type 3

Type 3 cable is conventional twisted-pair, telephone wire, with a minimum of two twists per foot. Both 22 AWG and 24 AWG conductors are supported by this cable type. One common use of Type 3 cable is to connect PCs to hubs in a Token-Ring network.

Type 5

Type 5 cable is fiber optic cable. Two $100/140 \mu$m optical fibers are contained in a Type 5 cable. This cable is suitable for indoor, non-plenum installation or outdoor aerial installation. Due to the extended transmission distance obtainable with fiber optic cable, Type 5 cable is used in conjunction with the IBM 8219 Token-Ring Network Optical Fiber Repeater to interconnect two hubs up to 6600 feet (2 km) from one another.

Type 6

Type 6 cable contains two twisted pairs of 26 AWG conductors for data communications. It is available for non-plenum applications only and its smaller diameter than Type 1 cable makes it slightly more flexible. The primary use of Type 6 cable is for short runs as a flexible path cord. This type of cable is often used to connect an adapter card in a personal computer to a faceplate which, in turn, is connected to a Type 1 or Type 2 cable which forms the backbone of a network.

Type 8

Type 8 cable is designed for installation under a carpet. This cable contains two individually shielded, parallel pairs of 26 AWG conductors with a plastic ramp designed to make undercarpet installation as unobtrusive as possible. Although Type 8 cable can be used in a manner similar to Type 1, it only provides half of the maximum transmission distance obtainable through the use of Type 1 cable.

Type 9

Type 9 cable is essentially a low-cost version of Type 1 cable. Like Type 1, Type 9 cable consists of two twisted pairs of data cable; however, 26 AWG conductors are used in place of the 22 AWG wire used in Type 1 cable. As a result of the use of a smaller diameter cable, transmission distances on Type 9 cable are approximately two-thirds those obtainable through the use of Type 1 cable. The color coding on the shield of Type 9 cable is the same as that used for Type 1 cable.

Summary of cable types

All seven types of cables defined by the IBM cabling system can be used to construct Token-Ring networks. However, the use of each type of cable has a different effect upon the ability to connect devices to the network, the number of devices that can be connected to a common network, the number of wiring closets in which hubs can be installed to form a ring, and the ability of the cable to carry separate voice conversations. The latter capability enables a common cable to be routed to a user's desk where a

Table 4.2 IBM cabling system cable performance characteristics

Performance characteristics	Cable type						
	1	2	3	5	6	8	9
Drive distance (relative to type 1)	1.0	1.0	0.45	3.0	0.75	0.5	0.66
Data rate (Mbps)	16	16	4^a	250	16	16	16
Maximum devices per ring	260	260	72	260	96	260	260
Maximum closets per ring	12	12	2	12	12	12	12
Voice support	no	yes	yes	no	no	no	no

^{a}Although 16-Mbps operations are not directly supported by Type 3 cable, its use is quite common when drive distances are very short.

portion of the cable is connected to their telephone while another portion of the cable is connected to their computer's Token-Ring adapter card.

Table 4.2 summarizes the performance characteristics of the cables defined by the IBM cabling system. The drive distance entry indicates the relative relationship between different types of cables with respect to the maximum cabling distance between a workstation and a hub as well as between hubs. Type 1 cable provides a maximum drive distance of 100 m between a workstation and a hub and 300 m between hubs for a network operating at 4 Mbps. Other drive distance entries in Table 4.2 are relative to the drive distance obtainable when Type 1 cable is used.

Connectors

The IBM cabling system includes connectors for terminating both data and voice conductors. The data connector has a unique design based upon the development of a latching mechanism which permits it to mate with another, identical connector.

Figure 4.3 illustrates the IBM cabling system data connector. Its design makes it self-shorting when disconnected from another connector. This provides a Token-Ring network with electrical continuity when a station is disconnected. Unfortunately, the data connector is expensive in comparison to RS-232 and RJ telephone connectors, with a typical retail price between $3 and $5, whereas RS-232 connectors cost approximately $2 and an RJ telephone connector can be purchased for 10 cents or so.

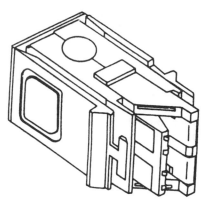

Figure 4.3   Cabling system data connector

Due to the cost of data connectors and cable, the acceptance of the IBM cabling system by end-users has been slow to materialize. Instead of being designed for IBM data connectors, many hub vendors as well as network adapter manufacturers design their products to use less expensive and far more available RJ connectors. Other vendors provide both an IBM data connector and an RJ telephone connector on their hubs, permitting users to select the type of connector they wish to use.

4.2.5   EIA/TIA-568 standard

The Electronics Industry Association/Telecommunications Industries Association 'Commercial Building Telecommunications Standard', commonly referred to as EIA/TIA-568, was ratified in 1992. This standard specifies a variety of building cabling parameters, ranging from backbone cabling used to connect a building's telecommunications closets to an equipment room, to horizontal cabling used to cable individual users to the equipment closet. The standard defines the performance characteristics of both backbone and horizontal cables as well as different types of connectors used with different types of cable.

Backbone cabling

Four types of media are recognized by the EIA/TIA-568 standard for backbone cabling. Table 4.3 lists the media options supported by the EIA/TIA-568 standard for backbone cabling.

Table 4.3   EIA/TIA-568 backbone cabling media options

Media type	Maximum cable distance
100 ohm UTP	800 meters (2624 feet)
150 ohm	STP 700 meters (2296 feet)
50 ohm thick coaxial cable	500 meters (1640 feet)
62.5/125 μm multimode optical fiber	2000 meters (6560 feet)

Horizontal cabling

As previously indicated, horizontal cabling under the EIA/TIA-568 standard consists of cable which connects equipment in a telecommunications closet to a user's work area. The media options supported for horizontal cabling are the same as those specified for backbone cabling with the exception of coaxial cable for which 50 ohm thin cable is specified; however, cabling distances are restricted to 90 meters in length from equipment in the telecommunications closet to a telecommunications outlet. This permits a patch cord or drop cable up to 10 meters in length to be used to connect a user workstation to a telecommunications outlet, resulting in the total length of horizontal cabling not exceeding the 100 meter restriction associated with many LAN technologies that use UTP cabling.

UTP categories

One of the more interesting aspects of the EIA/TIA-568 standard is its recognition that different signaling rates require different cable characteristics. This resulted in the EIA/TIA-568 standard classifying UTP cable into five categories. Those categories and their suitability for different type of voice and data applications are indicated in Table 4.4

Table 4.4   EIA/TIA-568 UTP cable categories

Category 1	Voice or low speed data up to 56 kbps; not useful for LANs
Category 2	Data rates up to 1 Mbps
Category 3	Supports transmission up to 16 MHz
Category 4	Supports transmission up to 20 MHz
Category 5	Supports transmission up to 100 MHz

In examining the entries in Table 4.4 note that categories 3, 4 and 5 support transmission with respect to indicated signaling rates. This means that the ability of those categories of UTP to support different types of LAN transmission will depend upon the signaling method used by different LANs. For example, consider a LAN encoding technique which results in six bits encoded into four signaling elements that have a 100 MHz signaling rate. Through the use of category 5 cable a data transmission rate of 150 Mbps ((6/4) × 100) could be supported.

Category 3 cable is typically used for Ethernet and 4 Mbps Token-Ring LANs. Category 4 is normally used for 16 Mbps Token-Ring LANs, while category 5 cable supports emerging 100 Mbps Ethernet LANs, such as 100VGAny-LAN and 100Base-T, and will support ATM to the desktop at a 155 Mbps operating rate.

UTP specifications

The requirement to qualify a segment of installed cable and attached connectors resulted in the EIA/TIA-568 standard defining a series of link performance parameters. Those parameters cover attenuation and Near End CrossTalk (NEXT) (see Sections 4.3.1 and 4.3.2) and are specified for UTP cable categories in Annex E to the standard. In the next section in this chapter I will examine cable tests designed to verify EIA/TIA-568 performance parameters, isolate Ethernet and Token-Ring cabling problems, and perform additional tests that can provide you with an insight to several types of cabling problems not directly covered by the previously referenced standard.

4.3 CABLE TESTS

In this section I will focus my attention upon a variety of cable tests to include those that can be used to verify EIA/TIA performance parameters as well as tests that can be used to verify the structure of installed cabling and obtain other cabling measurements beyond the EIA/TIA-568 standard. In examining tests designed to verify EIA/TIA-568 performance parameters I will also note the performance limits specified by that standard for different types of UTP wiring.

4.3.1 Attenuation

Attenuation represents the loss of signal power as a signal propagates from a transmitter at one end of the cable toward a receiving device located at the distant end of the cable. Attenuation is measured in decibels (dB) as indicated below:

$$\text{Attenuation} = 20 \log_{10}\left(\frac{\text{transmit voltage}}{\text{receive voltage}}\right)$$

For those of us a little rusty with logarithms let's examine a few examples of attenuation computations. First, let's assume the transmit voltage was 100, while the receive voltage was 1. Then,

$$\text{Attenuation} = 20 \log_{10}\left(\frac{100}{1}\right) = 20 \log_{10} 100$$

The value of $\log_{10} 100$ can be obtained by determining the power to which 10 should be raised to equal 100. Since the answer is 2 ($10^2 = 100$), $\log_{10} 100$ has the value of 2 and $20 \log_{10} 100$ then has a value of 40.

Now assume the transmit voltage was 10 while the receive voltage was 1. Then,

$$\text{Attenuation} = 20 \log_{10}\left(\frac{10}{1}\right) = 20 \log_{10} 10$$

Since the value of $\log_{10} 10$ is 1 ($10^1 = 10$), then $20 \log_{10} 10$ has a value of 20. Note that a comparison of the two examples indicates that a lower level of signal power loss results in a lower level of attenuation. Thus, the lower the attenuation the lower the signal loss. To facilitate the computation of attenuation and other cable test measurements, Table 4.5 presents the values of 16 common logarithms.

Table 4.5 Common logarithm values

Log	Value	Log	Value
Log 1	0.000	Log 9	0.954
Log 2	0.301	Log 10	1.000
Log 3	0.477	Log 20	1.301
Log 4	0.602	Log 30	1.477
Log 5	0.699	Log 40	1.602
Log 6	0.778	Log 100	2.000
Log 7	0.845	Log 1000	3.000
Log 8	0.903	Log 10000	4.000

One Way Attenuation Measurement   Meter

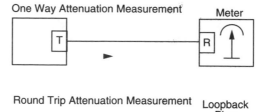

Round Trip Attenuation Measurement   Loopback
                                      Plug

A one way attenuation measurement requires the use of a meter
or trip measuring device at the distant end. In comparison, a round
trip attenuation measurement can be accomplished through
the use of a loopback plug at the distant end which ties transmit
(T) and receive (R) wire pairs together.

Figure 4.4   Measuring attenuation

There are two methods by which attenuation can be measured–
one way and round trip. Figure 4.4 compares each method of
attenuation measurement.

Most modern cable testers are sold with a remote unit, a stand-
alone device that is cabled to the distant end of a cable. The
remote unit functions as a loopback plug illustrated in the lower
portion of Figure 4.4, permitting one tester to be used. Without a
loopback plug or remote unit you would require a second cable
tester to be placed at the distant end as illustrated in the top
portion of Figure 4.4. Readers are referred to Table 4.6 which
contains attenuation and Near End CrossTalk limits for the three
types of UTP cabling specified by the EIA/TIA-568 standard for a
100 meter cable length between a wall plate and a telephone
closet, as well as for IBM cabling system type 1, 2, 6 and 9 cable.
Testers that have limits associated with those types of cable built
into the device will generate a 'Pass' or 'Fail' message when
testing those cables. If you test other types of cables you may have
to refer to an appropriate cable specification to determine if the
wiring is 'within spec' for the cable being tested.

4.3.2 Near End CrossTalk (NEXT)

Crosstalk represents the electromagnetic interference caused
by a signal on one wire pair being emitted onto another wire
pair, resulting in noise. Figure 4.5 illustrates the generation of

Table 4.6 Attenuation and NEXT limits in dB

(a) EIA/TIA-568

Frequency (MHz)	Category 3		Category 4		Category 5	
	Attenuation	NEXT	Attenuation	NEXT	Attenuation	NEXT
1.0	4.2	39.1	2.6	53.3	2.5	60.3
4.0	7.3	29.3	4.8	43.3	4.5	50.6
8.0	10.2	24.3	6.7	38.2	6.3	45.6
10.0	11.5	22.7	7.5	36.6	7.0	44.0
16.0	14.9	19.3	9.9	33.1	9.2	40.6
20.0	—	—	11.0	31.4	10.3	39.0
25.0	—	—	—	—	11.4	37.4
31.2	—	—	—	—	12.8	35.7
62.5	—	—	—	—	18.5	30.6
100.0	—	—	—	—	24.0	27.1

(b) IBM cabling system

Frequency (MHz)	Attenuation (dB/km) Type of cable[a]				NEXT (dB/km) Type of cable[a]			
	1P/2P	6P/9P	1/2	6/9	1P/2P	6P/9P	1/2	6/9
4	22	33	22	33	−58	−52	—	—
8	31.1	46.7	N/S	N/S	−54.9	−48.9	—	—
10	34.8	52.2	N/S	N/S	−53.5	−47.5	−40[b]	−34[b]
16	44.0	66.0	45	66	−50.4	−44.4	N/S	N/S
20	49.2	73.8	N/S	N/S	−49.0	−43.0	N/S	N/S
25	61.7	93.3	N/S	N/S	−47.5	−41.5	N/S	N/S
31.25	68.9	104.3	N/S	N/S	−46.1	−40.1	N/S	N/S
62.5	97.5	147.5	N/S	N/S	−41.5	−35.5	N/S	N/S
100.0	123.3	186.6	128	N/S	−38.5	−32.5	N/S	N/S
300.0	209.2	323.2	N/S	N/S	−31.3	−25.3	N/S	N/S

[a] For the IBM cabling system a cable type of P denotes plenum.
[b] 12–20 MHz.
[c] N/S – Not supported.

crosstalk due to the flow of current on one wire pair resulting in the creation of a magnetic field. The magnetic field induces a signal on the adjacent wire pair which represents noise. Since transmit and receive pairs are twisted and the transmit signal is strongest at its source, the maximum level of interference occurs at the cable connector and decreases as the signal traverses the

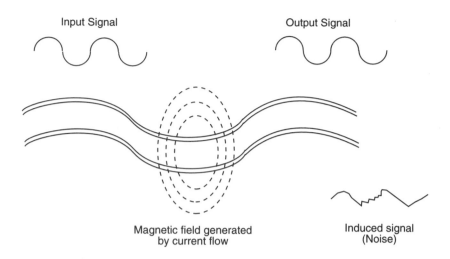

Figure 4.5 Crosstalk

cable. Thus, crosstalk is measured at the near end, hence the term NEXT.

NEXT results in an induced or coupled signal flowing from the transmit pair to the receive pair even though both pairs are not interconnected. Mathematically, NEXT is defined in decibels (dB) as follows:

$$\text{NEXT} = 20 \log_{10}\left(\frac{\text{transmit voltage}}{\text{coupled voltage}}\right)$$

Here the transmit voltage represents the power placed on the transmit pair, while the coupled signal is measured on the receive pair at the location where the transmit voltage was generated. Note that a larger dB NEXT measurement is better as it indicates a lower level of crosstalk. This is the opposite of attenuation, since a lower attenuation reading indicates less signal loss and is better than a higher reading for that parameter.

Table 4.6 indicates the EIA/TIA-568 specification limits for categories 3, 4 and 5 UTP cable and for IBM cabling system type 1, 2, 6 and 9 cable. Those categories represent the primary types of UTP and STP cable used for local area network data transmission.

In examining the entries in Table 4.6 note that the attenuation and NEXT of a cable must be measured over a range of frequencies. That range is based upon the cable category. For example, since category 3 cable is designed to support signaling rates up to 16 MHz, attenuation and NEXT should be measured up to and including the highest signaling rate supported by that type of cable.

Minimizing NEXT

There are several techniques you can consider to minimize NEXT. First, ensure the pair twisting in cable you are using was not altered by pulling the cable. Another method you can consider is to replace existing cable with cable that has more twists per foot; however, this technique can obviously be expensive in comparison to simply retwisting an existing cable. Another technique you can consider is to use a modular jack with a built-in miniature capacitor. Such jacks minimize the effect of the magnetic field thus reducing induced noise.

4.3.3 Using an AC voltmeter

In addition to using hand-held general purpose cable testers you can use an AC voltmeter to measure attenuation. To do so you would connect the voltmeter to the disturbed pair and connect a frequency generator to the disturbing pair, terminating both pairs in resistances equivalent to the cable's characteristic impedance. For example, if you were measuring NEXT for a 100 ohm UTP cable you would terminate each pair using a 100 ohm resistor.

By moving the frequency generator through a range of frequencies associated with the cable under test you can obtain an appropriate set of measurements. However, when using a voltmeter the measurements will be expressed in millivolts (mV),

Table 4.7 Decibel (dB) and millivolt (mV) equivalence

dB	mV
0	500.000
−3	375.000
−6	250.000
−9	187.500
−12	125.000
−18	62.500
−24	31.250
-30	15.625

requiring a conversion to dB to compare against the cable limits for the type of cable being tested. To facilitate that conversion Table 4.7 provides an equivalence chart between decibels and millivolts.

4.3.4 Other cable measurements: summary

In addition to attenuation and NEXT there are other cable measurements that can provide an insight to potential or existing cable problems. Those measurements include Capacitance, Impedance, Ambient Noise, Signal-to-Noise Ratio (SNR) and the Attenuation to Crosstalk Ratio (ACR). In addition to those measurements there are additional tests you can perform with certain types of test equipment that can be used to isolate cabling problems. Those tests include the determination of cable length to verify that a LAN cable segment is within specification, a wire map which indicates if a cable is correctly wired for a specific type of local area network, and a split pair wiring test developed to identify a split pair wiring error condition. All these techniques are covered in Sections 4.3.5–4.3.13.

4.3.5 Capacitance

Capacitance provides a measure of a cable's ability to store an electrical charge. The amount of capacitance in a cable depends upon the cable's dielectric constant, the distance between cable conductors, and the length of the cable. Capacitance occurs between different pairs of wires, between two wires of the same pair (known as mutual capacitance), and between the inner and outer conductors of a coaxial cable.

Capacitance is measured in picofarads (pF) and causes a digital signal to have its trailing edge, leading edge, or both edges bent based upon its strength. The lower the capacitance of a cable the greater the ability of a signal to retain its original form. Thus, low capacitance shielded cable is commonly used to extend transmission distances. Figure 4.6 illustrates the effect of mutual capacitance upon a digital signal while Table 4.8 lists mutual capacitance specifications for five common types of cable used for constructing LANs.

Many cable testers do not provide the ability to determine mutual capacitance. Instead, a capacitance meter is normally used to measure the effect of a low frequency signal injected into a

Figure 4.6   Effect of mutual capacitance on a digital signal

Table 4.8   Mutual capacitance specifications

Cable type	Mutual capacitance (Pf/foot)
IBM Type 1	9
TIA/EIA Category 3	20
TIA/EIA Categories 4,5	17
RG-58/U (coaxial)	28–30

cable. Prior to using a capacitance meter, you would measure the length of the cable to be tested. Next, you would measure the mutual capacitance at the cable end and divide that value by the cable length to determine the mutual capacitance per foot. Although a variation of ±1 to 2 pF/foot can be expected, higher deviations can indicate an improper termination at a punch down block, while a reading below the normal range can indicate either a split pair wiring error or another type of miswiring. I will discuss split pair wiring errors in Section 4.3.11.

4.3.6 Characteristic Impedance

The characteristic impedance of a wire represents its opposition to the flow of alternating current and is commonly denoted by the symbol Z_0. Impedance is a function of signal frequency and other electrical proportion and is measured in ohms. A linear level of impedance over a range of frequencies minimizes energy loss due to the resistance of a cable to the flow of electrons and provides a more suitable medium for data transmission.

Although impedance is not normally measured by many cable testers a situation known as impedance mismatch is a common cabling problem. This problem results from the connection of two cables with different impedance levels, resulting in part of a signal being reflected. The solution to this problem is to avoid mixing different types of cables.

4.3.7 Ambient noise

Ambient noise represents signal interference caused by a nearby electrical device, such as a radio, a television or even an electronic pencil sharpener. Ambient noise is measured using a narrow- or wide-band receiver; however, the use of a narrow-band receiver is normally not as effective as a wide-band receiver for detecting intermittent radio frequency (RF) signals. Ambient noise is measured in millivolts (mV) and test equipment normally measures both current and peak noise over a test period. Excessive noise indicates the nearby presence of electromagnetic interference, which may be easily compensated for by moving equipment away from the cable.

4.3.8 Signal-to-noise ratio

The signal-to-noise ratio (SNR) provides a measure of the quality of a signal. As the SNR decreases the probability of noise interfering with the signal increases, resulting in an increase in transmission errors.

Since the movement of electrons causes a fixed minimum level of noise, referred to as white or thermal noise, a minimum signal level is required to overcome the effect of that source of noise. In addition, a higher signal level is required to overcome a reasonable level of ambient noise caused by the operation of normal office equipment. Mathematically, SNR is defined as:

$$\text{SNR (dB)} = 20\log_{10}\left(\frac{\text{signal voltage}}{\text{noise voltage}}\right)$$

For IEEE 802.3 (Ethernet) and 802.5 (Token-Ring) LANs a SNR limit of 12 dB is specified, with higher SNRs providing a better level of performance. If the channel background noise level is low the SNR can be expressed as NEXT (dB) – attenuation (dB). To illustrate this assume a workstation is transmitting and receiving at the same time. Then, at the workstation's receiver the receive signal is equal to the transmit signal strength less attenuation, or

$$\text{Receive signal} = \text{transmit signal} - \text{attenuation}$$

The noise at the receiver then becomes

$$\text{Noise} = \text{transmit signal strength} - \text{NEXT}$$

Since

$$\text{Attenuation (dB)} = 20 \log_{10} \left(\frac{\text{transmit voltage}}{\text{receiver voltage}} \right)$$

and

$$\text{NEXT (dB)} = 20 \log_{10} \left(\frac{\text{transmit voltage}}{\text{coupled voltage}} \right)$$

then, since the properties of logarithms result in gains and losses being reduced to arithmetic addition and subtraction operations the SNR can be expressed as follows:

$$\text{SNR} = \text{Receive signal (dB)} - \text{noise (dB)}$$

Substituting the receive signal and noise values, we obtain:

$$\text{SNR} = \text{Transmit signal strength} - \text{Attenuation}$$

$$- (\text{transmit signal strength} - \text{NEXT})$$

Thus,

$$\text{SNR} = \text{NEXT (dB)} - \text{attenuation (dB)}$$

4.3.9 Attenuation-to-crosstalk ratio

The Attenuation-to-crosstalk ratio (ACR) functions as an alternative to SNR measurements. Attenuation governs the strength of the received signal, while crosstalk is normally the major source of noise. Thus, when NEXT is the only source of noise ACR is the same as the signal-to-noise ratio, since both parameters are referenced to the level of the transmit signal. However, when ambient noise is present on a cable ACR is not equivalent to the SNR, thus the SNR is a preferred measurement since it considers cumulative noise.

4.3.10 Jitter

Jitter is the displacement of a signal from its expected position. Both crosstalk and noise contribute to jitter, causing a signal to arrive either too early or too late at a receiver. Too much jitter results in an adapter card recognizing either a prior bit for the current bit or the following bit for the current bit, causing a transmission error to occur.

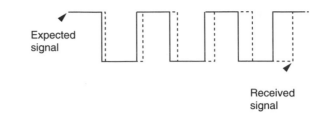

Expected
signal

Received
signal

Figure 4.7   Effect of jitter on a signal

Figure 4.7 illustrates how jitter can build up as a signal traverses a LAN. Note that a low amount of jitter which may take a while to build up cumulatively to cause an error is referred to as wander.

One common cause of jitter is from mixing shielded and unshielded twisted-pair cable. The difference in the electrical property of those cables will cause a degree of noise and signal distortion which will normally delay portions of the signal as it propagates down the media.

4.3.11 Split pair wiring

A split pair wiring test is used to detect a split pair wiring error. This error occurs when a two-wire circuit does not use a single twisted-pair cable. Instead, one wire from one pair and another wire from a second pair are used to form a two-wire circuit. Figure 4.8 illustrates an example of a split pair wiring error. Although the resulting two-wire circuit provides DC continuity for the circuit, the twisted pairs used to form the circuit are not correctly crossed. This results in the inability of the twists to cancel out electromagnetic interference.

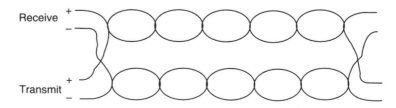

Receive

Transmit

Figure 4.8   Split pair wiring error

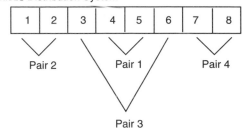

AT & T Premises Distribution System

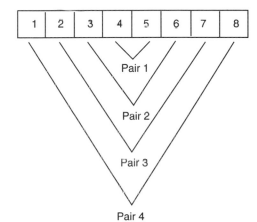

Universal Service Order Code

Figure 4.9   RJ-45 pin utilization

One common cause of split pair wiring errors is differences between different wiring schemes. For example, the Universal Service Order Code (USOC) wiring scheme uses similar wire to the AT&T Premises Distribution System (PDS); however, pair designations and terminations at the modular jack differ.

Figure 4.9 illustrates the RJ-45 pin utilization for AT&T's Premises Distribution System and for the Universal Service Order Code. Although both wiring schemes use pins 4 and 5 for pair 1, thereafter the wiring schemes differ. If your physical layer implementation is designed for PDS wiring while the actual wiring is performed to the USOC standard the end result is a split pair wiring error. Figure 4.10 illustrates the 8-pin RJ-45 connector assignments for 10Base-T, Token-Ring and EIA/TIA-568A cable. Note that the differences in pin connector assignments can easily result in wiring errors, especially when changing a LAN infrastructure.

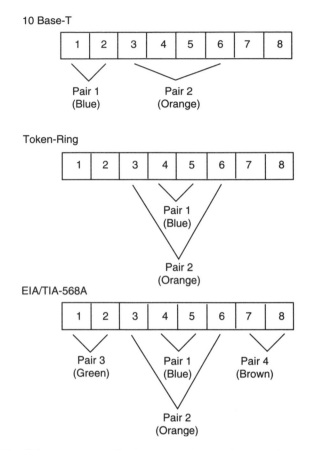

Figure 4.10   Other common 8-pin connector assignments

4.3.12 Wire map

Although some cable testers will display a split pair wiring error, other testers may not directly do so. Instead, the tester may be limited to displaying the results of a wire map test which indicates the wiring of a cable from end to end. Other testers will perform a wire map test and automatically display any problems encountered as well as the results of the test.

A wire map test requires the use of a remote unit connected to the opposite end of the cable to be tested. As a minimum, most cable testers will indicate by cable pairs opens, shorts, cross, reversed and straight-through connections. Although the terms 'cross' and 'reversed' may appear to have similar meanings, when applied to twisted-pair a 'reverse' means that each wire in a pair is crossed, while the term 'cross' means wires in one pair are crossed to wires in another pair. For example, if wires 1 and 2 form a wiring pair, a reversed pair would have wire 1 connected at one end to wire 2 at the other end and vice versa. If wires 3 and 6 form a second pair, then connecting wires 1 and 2 at one end to 3 and 6 at the distant end would represent an example of crossed pairs.

In addition to indicating how wires are connected the wire map indirectly provides one of the most basic tests you can use to verify cabling. That test is a continuity test, which indicates that a signal can flow from end to end. Without continuity the cable cannot be used and you will not be able to obtain other measurements. Thus, many persons on a routine basis prefer to perform a wire mapping prior to performing other tests.

4.3.13 Cable length verification

One of the most common cable tests that should be at the top of your LAN infrastructure is the verification of cable length. Measuring the length of a cable is important as the performance of a LAN highly depends upon staying within cable length specifications.

Most modern twisted-pair cabling is limited to 100 meters (328 feet) in length, to include patch cables from a workstation to a wall mount and from the wall mount to a hub. As cabling extends beyond the maximum cable length the degree of signal distortion rapidly increases, resulting in the inability of a receiver to recognize the transmitted signal.

The length of a cable is normally measured through the use of a Time Domain Reflectometer (TDR). Based upon principles similar to those used in the operation of a radar gun, the TDR transmits a pulse onto a pair of conductors. The pulse traverses the medium until it encounters either a short or an open circuit, which is hopefully at the end of the cable and not in the middle of a conduit. If the cable end has an open termination, the pulse is reflected back in its original format, while a short termination results in an inverted pulse being reflected.

NVP

The time between the transmission of a pulse and the receipt of its reflection forms the basis for computing the cable length. However, since the speed of electrons varies with the type of cable being tested, another cable parameter, referred to as the Nominal

Velocity of Propagation (NVP), must be known or determined to calculate the cable length correctly.

The NVP represents the speed at which electrons flow on a cable, expressed as a percentage of the speed of light. The speed of light in a vacuum is 186 000 miles per second and is commonly referred to as 1.00c. Some TDRs can automatically determine the NVP of a cable if you first enter the length of a segment and then use the TDR to compute the NVP. Other TDRs require the user to either select a specific cable type from a menu or enter a NVP value. NVP values range from approximately 0.60c for certain types of flat ribbon cable to over 0.90c for a few types of coaxial cable.

When using a known length of cable to determine its NVP it is important to use a reasonable length of cable, typically 100 feet or more, to obtain an accurate measurement. In fact, most TDRs cannot be used to determine cable lengths under 20 feet as those distances preclude the receipt of a valid reflection. A common error generated by TDRs is 'No Cable Found' when attempting to measure a cable whose length is under 20 feet.

TDR operation

Figure 4.11 illustrates the operation of a cable length test. Note that when a cable is properly terminated the pulse is absorbed and no reflection will be returned. This condition typically results in the TDR displaying the message 'No End Found'. Although a positive pulse is shown being injected into the cable, the start pulse can be either positive or negative, since the TDR compares the reflected pulse to the original to determine if the end is a short or open and uses round trip pulse time to determine cable length. The TDR computes the length of the cable as follows:

$$\text{Cable length} = \frac{\text{elapsed time} \times \text{NVP}}{2}$$

Although several vendors manufacture hand-held TDRs, many cable testers perform TDR operations as one of a series of built-in cable tests. As previously explained earlier in this section, the use of a stand-alone TDR may provide you with the ability to denote other types of faults beyond shorts and opens. To do so the TDR examines the returned waveform. Since literally thousands of different waveforms are possible, most TDRs that provide you with the ability to denote additional cable faults do so by providing a graphical display of the returned waveform. Then

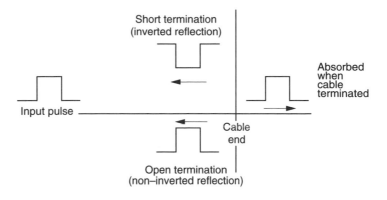

Figure 4.11 Using a Time Domain Reflectometer (TDR) to determine the length of a cable

you can use the TDR's manual to compare the reflected waveform against a series of printed waveforms that indicate a number of cable faults, such as corroded connector, cable splice and bridge tap.

4.4 COAXIAL CABLE TESTING

Coaxial is a term used to reference a type of cable which has several layers of material surrounding a common axis or 'coax'. Although coaxial cable was the primary transmission medium used for LANs through the 1980s, today the vast majority of new cabling uses twisted-pair wiring. However, in spite of the decline in the use of coaxial cable its installed base is considerable and in many organizations it serves as a backbone for interconnecting more modern Ethernet 10Base-T hubs.

Figure 4.12 illustrates the composition of a typical coaxial cable. Note that the center conductor, which is usually either solid copper or copper-clad aluminum, is surrounded by a non-conductive material referred to as the dielectric. The dielectric, in turn, is covered by a shield, usually a foil or wire braid. An outer covering, usually PVC, protects the shield, dielectric and center conductor.

The shield functions as a second conductor which is normally grounded and separated from the inner conductor by the dielectric material. Although there are many types of coaxial cable, they can be categorized by the type of transmission they are designed to support – baseband or broadband.

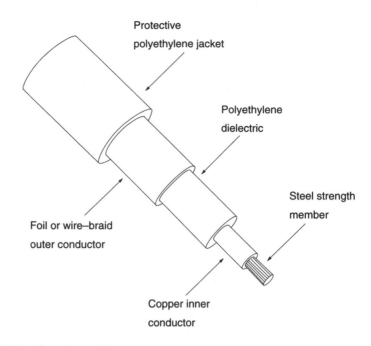

Figure 4.12 Coaxial cable

Baseband cable has a characteristic impedance of 50 ohms and is designed to support the transmission of one signal. Baseband cable uses a center conductor consisting of solid copper and its diameter can vary between 3/16 inch (4.75 mm) and 3/8 inch (9.5 mm). The larger diameter cable is typically used for a 10Base-5 network, while the thinner cable is used for a 10Base-2 network.

Broadband cable is designed for supporting multiple concurrent signals modulated through the use of RF modems. This results in broadband coaxial cable being the same type of cable used for Community Antenna Television (CATV) system. That is, broadband cable is 75-ohm cable which normally uses a center conductor of copper-clad aluminum. The cladding reduces the cost of the cable which is important for CATV systems where cabling distances can be extensive. However, signals transmitted on copper-clad aluminum tend to migrate to the surface of the conductor as frequencies increase, a phenomenon referred to as 'skin effect'. This makes the ability of the dielectric material to withstand cracking or separation when a cable is bent more important.

Most hand-held cable testers, similar to those illustrated in Figures 4.1 and 4.2, include a coax adapter which permits the device to be used to perform a variety of tests upon coaxial cable terminated with a BNC connector. Although you might expect those testers to perform certain tests, such as determining signal loss or attenuation, most hand-held testers unfortunately cannot be used to perform this test. This is because most hand-held testers are designed to work with a remote unit or loop-back plug which ties the transmit connector to the receive connector, enabling the tester to measure round trip attenuation and divide by two to determine one way attenuation. Since this trick cannot be performed with coaxial cable, most hand-held testers will not provide you with the ability to measure attenuation on coaxial cable. However, some testers can be used as a pair, with one tester transmitting a known signal at one end of the cable while the second tester is used as a meter or gauge at the opposite end of the cable to obtain the attenuation measurement.

Table 4.9 lists common coaxial cable performance characteristics for IEEE 802.3 local area network cable. 10Base-5 is commonly referred to as thick Ethernet cable while 10Base-2 is referred to as thin Ethernet (or colloquially by some people as Cheapnet because of its lower cost). Since 10Base-2 cable is thinner than 10Base-5 cable, as you might expect and as indicated in Table 4.9, the resistance of 10Base-2 cable exceeds that of 10Base-5 cable. This results in more attenuation occurring on 10Base-2 cable than on 10Base-5 cable.

Although a wire map test is not directly applicable to coaxial cable, that test can be used to denote open and short conditions as well as continuity which are applicable to coax. Other tests that most hand-held test equipment can perform on coaxial cable include testing ambient noise levels, cable length, signal-to-noise ratio and characteristic impedance. For a coaxial cable the measurement of characteristic impedance is a function of the resistance, capacitance and inductance of the cable. Although the characteristic impedance of coaxial cable is fairly constant over a wide frequency range, mixing cables from different manufacturers can result in an impedance mismatch. This can result in a

Table 4.9 IEEE 802.3 coaxial cable performance characteristics

Characteristic	10Base-5	10Base-2
Attenuation (dB/1000 kft):		
5 MHz	3.7	9.9
10 MHz	5.2	14.0
Capacitance (pF/ft)	26	25
Impedance (ohms)	50	50
Resistance (ohms/1000 kft)	1.43	10

degraded signal owing to reflections occurring where the cables connect. Fortunately, cable manufacturers publish the characteristic impedance of their cable which provides you with the ability to avoid the problems associated with signal reflections resulting from an impedance mismatch condition.

4.5 FIBER OPTIC CABLE TESTING

Unlike twisted-pair and coaxial cable which carries electrons, fiber optic cable transports light pulses generated by electrical-to-optical converters. Thus, the testing of fiber optic cable requires the use of equipment that generates and measures light.

Test equipment that can be used with fiber optic cable includes an optical power meter and an optical time domain reflectometer. A power meter is a hand held device used in conjunction with a light generator to verify optical continuity as well as measure optical attenuation. The light generator injects a known signal at one end of the cable while the power meter is connected to the opposite end of the cable.

An optical time domain reflectometer functions similarly to its magnetic media cousin; however, the optical TDR is normally a more sophisticated device and provides users with the ability to measure optical loss and reflections as well as determine the length of an optical cable.

5

WORKING AT THE DATA
LINK LAYER

Once you verify the workstation configuration and test the cable a logical progression of network testing is to work with transmission at the data link layer. In this chapter I will focus my attention upon this topic, using a commercially available software program as well as discussing the use of hardware products to observe the flow of frames on a local area network.

Observing the flow of frames at the data link layer can provide statistics that may serve as a clue for resolving network problems. Transmitting test messages encapsulated in a frame may shed light on whether or not a distant device is operational and provide the response time between transmitting a frame and receiving a response to the transmission. When applied to an internetwork the examination and comparison of response time to a sequence of network addressable devices may be useful for isolating network delays to specific hardware. In addition, frame monitoring can provide information concerning network error events which can be used to pinpoint the cause of many network related problems. Since the observation of frame flow requires the use of specialized hardware or software, I will discuss the use of two products to facilitate my investigation of the data link layer as a tool for testing and troubleshooting a LAN.

5.1 HARDWARE ANALYZERS

There are a number of hardware based network analyzers that can be used to examine the flow of data on Ethernet and Token-Ring LANs. Some analyzers are constructed using a laptop or notebook computer as the hardware platform and use special software to decode frames flowing on the network.

5.1.1 Laptop and notebook platforms

Through the insertion of a network adapter card the laptop or notebook becomes a participant on the LAN. Most analyzers that fall into this category include a network transmission facility which enables the device to transmit test frames and observe the reaction of different network nodes to those frames. Another common feature built into laptop and notebook based network analyzers is the ability to decode the contents of each frame, providing you with the ability to examine upper layer processes. I will temporarily defer a discussion of frame content decoding until later in this book as it more logically falls into a subsequent troubleshooting methodology.

A second type of hardware based network analyzer is similar in size to the hand-held cable testers which were previously discussed in Chapter 4. Thus, a popular term used to reference this class of network analyzers is, as you might expect, hand-held network analyzers.

5.1.2 Hand-held network analyzers: FrameScope echo tests

Figure 5.1 illustrates the Scope Communications FrameScope 802 network analyzer. This device can be used to analyze Ethernet coaxial, fiber and unshielded twisted-pair networks as well as unshielded and shielded twisted-pair Token-Ring networks. In addition to collecting a list of traffic and error statistics that can be used to identify stations or groups of stations that are introducing errors onto a network, you can use the FrameScope 802 to display frame counts and network utilization, identify the manufacturer of each network adapter active on the network, and perform several physical layer tests.

The FrameScope 802 also supports two interesting tests known as IP Echo and Novell Echo. Since I will discuss the different types of Token-Ring and Ethernet errors associated with each network, to include their probable causes, later in this chapter, for now I will focus my attention upon the two previously mentioned FrameScope 802 tests.

IP echo test

The IP echo test provides FrameScope users with the ability to generate an internet protocol (IP) PING. You would use this test to determine if an IP station at a given address is reachable and, if so, obtain the round trip request to response delay. Through the use of the IP echo test you can first determine if the distant

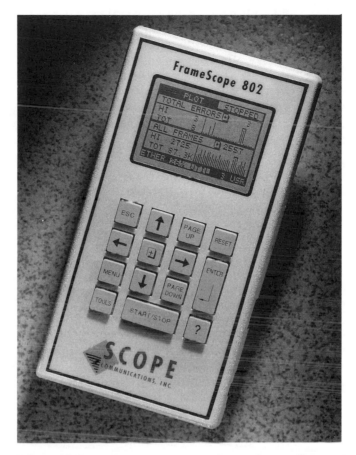

Figure 5.1   The Scope Communications FrameScope 802 is a hand-held network analyzer that can be used to examine the flow of frames on Ethernot and Token-Ring networks as well as to display a variety of network statistics. (Photograph courtesy of Scope Communications, Inc.)

location is active. If you receive more than one reply to the PING this would inform you that there are duplicate addresses on the network. By measuring the response delay between request and response you can determine if it is within an acceptable range or, if not, use it as an indicator for additional testing to determine the cause of response time problems.

To illustrate the versatility of an IP PING echo test, consider the internetwork illustrated in Figure 5.2. In this example let's assume the network technical control center receives a call stating that a user on the Token-Ring network located in Macon, GA, is experiencing a problem accessing a file server on the Ethernet LAN in Washington, DC. If the network control center is in Macon, GA, and a device capable of generating IP PINGs is available, let's assume each device between networks and the file server is PINGed. If the second router did not respond to the PING the cause of the problem could be either a line failure or the failure of the PINGed router. Similarly, if the file server did not respond we would note that the cause of the problem is either a failure, such as a cable cut on the Ethernet LAN, or a problem with the file server. If the user reported poor response instead of an inability to access the distant server, the sequence of PING round trip response times might isolate the cause of the poor response. For example, if the PING to router 2 indicated a two-second response time but PINGs to the hub and file server indicated response times of 2.01 and 2.06 seconds, respectively, either the router is overloaded or a marginal circuit between routers results in a large number of retransmissions that are adversely affecting response times when transmission flows between networks.

Novell echo test

The Novell echo test is similar to the IP echo test but is designed to determine if a Novell server or workstation is reachable and, if it is, displays the configuration of the server or workstation. This test can be used to determine software configuration incompatibilities between workstations and servers as well as to determine

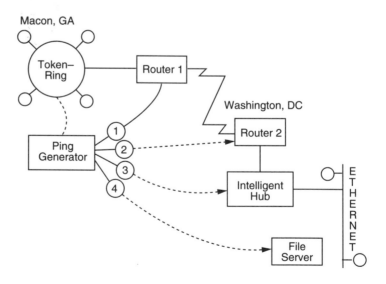

By transmitting PINGs to devices at locations 1, 2, 3 and 4 and noting response and response time you can isolate the location of many Internet problems

Figure 5.2 Using PING to isolate internetwork problems

if a particular workstation or server is active. By using this test you can note such problems as why a user cannot access a file server or why a user cannot print a job when sending the job to a print queue on a specific server.

The Novell echo test is similar to data available to NetWare users from the MONITOR utility program or through the use of the Frye Computer System NetWare Management program. Since the use of the Novell echo test is designed to test the network operating system, I will examine the use of the MONITOR utility program and Frye Computer Systems' NetWare Management program as a substitute for a Novell echo test in Chapter 6, which is focused upon Network Operating System testing.

5.2 SOFTWARE ANALYZERS – EXAMPLE: TokenVision

A software data link layer analyzer represents a computer program designed to operate on a computer connected to a local area network and which is used to obtain information about frame flow on the network. Frame flow information can include statistics concerning the activity of different network stations as well as the identification of frame errors based upon the observation of the flow of information on the data link layer. Another function available with some software analyzers is a frame generation capability. That capability can result in the IP and Novell echo tests discussed in the previous section in this chapter or other types of tests only limited by the ingenuity of the software developer. Since any discussion of software data link layer analysis requires the use of a product for demonstration purposes I will use a popular product known as TokenVision.

TokenVision is one of a series of network monitoring products developed by Triticom of Eden Prairie, MN, to provide data link layer information. Another product from Triticom is EtherVision, which provides monitoring and activity reports for Ethe-rnet local area networks. Since the two programs provide similar information concerning network activity by monitoring network frames, I will focus my attention upon the use of one program in this section. Using this information as a base will permit me to use the information presented in this section concerning Token-Ring network monitoring for an explanation of Ethernet monitoring.

5.2.1 Hardware considerations

To obtain the ability to read all network frames, TokenVision is similar to other data link layer monitoring programs in that it requires the use of a 'promiscuous' driver. The term 'promiscuous' refers to the fact that the driver is capable of receiving all frames transmitted on the network. In addition, since the TokenVision program must access registers on the LAN adapter card to read the contents of frames flowing to or through the network station operating the program, this requires the program to operate directly at the adapter cards' register level. Unfortunately, there are no standards governing the design of network adapter cards beyond their network functionality. Thus, vendors are free to implement different design techniques and indeed they do so. This means that TokenVision, like other programs that operate at the data link layer, must be programmed to work with specific adapter cards. Although Triticom supports more than 15 Ethernet and 20 Token-Ring adapter cards, the support is obviously not all-inclusive. Thus, you should check the adapter board supported by one or more data link layer monitoring programs prior to their acquisition. This will enable you to determine if you should acquire a new network adapter board and install that board in the workstation you wish to use for data link layer monitoring.

5.2.2 Program overview

Figure 5.3 illustrates the TokenVision main menu labeled 'Available Options'. This initial menu is similar across the Triticom product line and displays user selectable options as well as information concerning the configuration of the adapter card used in the workstation running the program. The latter is displayed in a horizontal window across the bottom of the display.

The first option in the Available Options menu, Monitor Traffic, is the key to the ability of the program to monitor frames. Activity can be monitored from the perspective of either the source or the destination address. Thus, once you select the Monitor Traffic entry in the Available Options menu the program will display a new menu labeled 'Station Address'. That menu will contain the selectable entries 'Source' and 'Destination', permitting you to control the manner by which station monitoring will occur. Selecting 'Source' results in the program reading the source address field in each frame flowing through or to the workstation. Similarly, selecting 'Destination' results in the program reading the destination field in each frame. Figure 5.4 illustrates the display of the 'Station Address' menu, which is superimposed over the 'Available Options' menu once you select the 'Monitor Traffic' option. Since the Source Address option is at the top of the

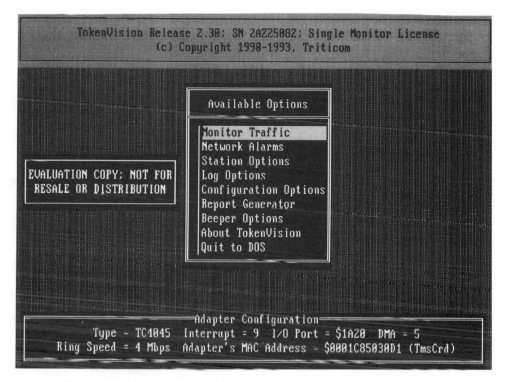

Figure 5.3 TokenVision 'Available Options' main menu

Station Address menu, let's select that option and examine how monitoring traffic at the data link layer can assist in isolating the potential cause of a range of local area network related problems.

5.2.3 Station monitoring

Figure 5.5 illustrates the TokenVision station monitoring display screen after the Source Address option was selected. As new stations are recognized by the program they are automatically displayed on the monitoring screen. In the 4-second period indicated by the elapsed time counter located at the lower left corner of the display a total of 46 stations were recognized. Note that the program counts the number of frames associated with each source address, providing you with the ability to determine network utilization by workstation. In the event that excessive network utilization is the cause of poor response you may be able to use this display as a tool to determine if some users are hogging network resources. This in turn may provide you with the ability to interview specific network users and determine if you should

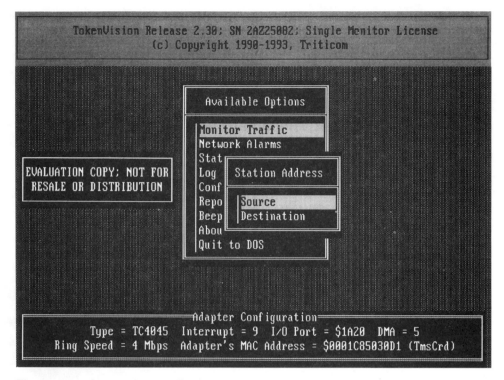

Figure 5.4 Once 'Monitor Traffic' is selected you can perform monitoring based upon either the source or destination address of frames flowing on the network

either segment an existing network or initiate another action to obtain a more reasonable level of network utilization. Obtaining additional information concerning network utilization requires the display of other program screens as we will shortly observe.

Concerning network users, in examining Figure 5.5 note that the identification for each station is denoted by the term 'Name?' followed by six hexadecimal digits. The term 'Name?' indicates that when the display occurred the TokenVision user had not assigned a logical name identification, such as Tom, Dick or Jane, to any workstation. The six hexadecimal digits represent a portion of the adapter card address for each station. By pressing the F2 key (Stn ID) you can toggle between different station address formats to include hexadecimal, assigned logical name and vendor ID, the latter resulting in the display of an abbreviation of the name of the manufacturer of the network adapter card. As you move the highlight bar over a particular station address information about the selected address is displayed in the first horizontal window while the lower window summarizes activity for all monitored stations. A quick glance at the right portion of the

```
Monitoring SRC Addr: Started Fri Dec 9, 1994 at 15:15:01              15:15:05
Name?-745003     51│Name?-E8C1BE      1│Name?-720000      1│
Name?-720002     20│Name?-F6B5BA     10│Name?-889BE8      1│
Name?-DE0F93     65│Name?-451000      9│Name?-8D196E      1│
Name?-0104E9     43│Name?-488038      1│Name?-DEC5AF      1│
Name?-230D17      6│Name?-318D64      1│Name?-3075FF      1│
Name?-00186B      3│Name?-0C82CB      1│Name?-FF9F11      1│
Name?-30BD4E      4│Name?-44D4C4      1│Name?-8870A5      1│
Name?-00423F      3│Name?-745002      1│Name?-0A7AD3      1│
Name?-0044A7     15│Name?-4D376D      1│Name?-2E2474      1│
Name?-1342B0      5│Name?-54276F      1│Name?-89AE28      1│
Name?-2E2401      7│Name?-745010 ·    1│Name?-2E29BE
Name?-2BF953      8│Name?-2E2C49      1│Name?-8D1BBE
Name?-3194FA      2│Name?-C8420D      1│
Name?-280001      1│Name?-740005      1│
Name?-6BD0D9      2│Name?-12E1E6      1│
Name?-0412D6      1│Name?-2E2C64      1│
Name?-E4D742      1│Name?-2E2C65      1│
┌Address────────Name────────Vendor-ID────────Frames────Bytes────%─Ave─Errors┐
 400031745003 Name?-745003 Vend?-745003        51       4015  18.1   78      0

┌Stns┬─Frames──Kbytes┬Bdcast┬Frm/S─Peak┬Hc/S─Peak┬SoftErr─Beacon┬MU┬─Elapsed┐
  46      281     21     84    35   142   18   18      0      0      │00:00:04
 F2-Stn ID  F3-Sort ID  F4 Sort Cnt  F5-Cnt/Kb/%/Av/Er  F6 Sky  F7-Stat  F8-Clr
```

Figure 5.5 The TokenVision station monitoring screen will display network frame activity based upon either source or destination address

lower window will denote total number of beacon frames that have been observed, the number of soft errors (SoftErr) and if a missed or unprocessed packet (MU) occurred. If you are using the firm's EtherVision product the first two error indicators would be replaced by cyclic redundancy check (CRC) and collision (Coll) error counters. In the next section in this chapter I will discuss in detail the types of Ethernet and Token-Ring network errors that may be detectable through the use of different hardware and software based network analyzers. In the interim, I will limit my discussion of network errors in this section to those that can be indicated by TokenVision and EtherVision.

Returning to Figure 5.5, if one or more error counters indicate a value you can move the highlight bar over different workstation addresses. Doing so will display errors associated with a particular workstation, enabling you to easily determine if a particular workstation is contributing to one or more network error events. Since the errors reported differ between Ethernet and Token-Ring networks, Table 5.1 describes the error events reported by EtherVision and TokenVision monitoring displays as

well as a description of what each error condition might indicate.
The only error events displayed by TokenVision and EtherVision
monitoring screens not included in Table 5.1 are MU errors.
Those errors indicate (M) the inability of the workstation
operating the program to keep up with network traffic, and (U)
that a frame was missed or software was unable to process a
frame. A mark under 'M' will indicate that all statistics may be
inaccurate, while a mark under 'U' indicates that individual
station statistics may no longer be accurate. Since both conditions have nothing to do with Ethernet or Token-Ring error
conditions they were not included in Table 5.1. Readers are
referred to Section 5.3 for a complete description of Ethernet and
Token-Ring errors that may be observable from data link layer
monitoring by the use of TokenVision, EtherVision and other
vendor products.

Once again returning to network traffic monitoring, let's extend
our monitoring period beyond the 4-second interval indicated in
Figure 5.5. Figure 5.6 illustrates the TokenVision source address
monitoring screen after a monitoring period of 6 minutes and 34
seconds. Note that the operator of the monitoring program
pressed the F2 key to toggle to the station address display
format in which the vendor of each adapter card is identified.

The IEEE assigns blocks of addresses for use by different
vendors, enabling the program to compare the first portion of
each source address read from the network to a table which
indicates the vendors assigned different address blocks. The

Table 5.1 EtherVision and TokenVision monitoring display errors

Error	Description
EtherVision	
CRC	Indicates the number of frames received that had a cyclic redundancy check (CRC) error. This error condition may indicate a cabling or transceiver problem.
Coll	Indicates the number of collision fragments detected when the complete source and destination addresses are recoverable from a fragment. If a collision occurs after the preamble was transmitted (late collision) this will result in a CRC error.
TokenVision	
SoftErr	Indicates the number of soft error Medium Access Control (MAC) frames that were observed.
Beacon	Indicates the number of beacon frames that were observed.

reason many vendor names are shown as 'Vend?' in Figure 5.6 results from the fact that the author's organization used a number of Token-Ring adapter cards acquired from a vendor that recently began manufacturing adapter cards. Consequently, the prefix address assigned to the vendor that manufactured those adapter cards was not included in the table maintained by the program version used by the author.

In examining Figure 5.6 note that there were a total of four soft errors observed. Soft errors can result from ring insertion and deinsertion, lost or multiple active monitors, lost or bad frame delimiters, multiple, corrupted or lost tokens, lost frames, line errors and the continuous circulation around the ring of the same frame. Since computers being powered on and off or rebooted are a common occurrence, you can normally expect a small number of soft errors. This is especially true for the situation illustrated in Figure 5.6 where 187 stations are now identified. If you note more than a few soft errors you would probably want to directly display TokenVision's MAC Statistics Display screen to determine where the errors originated and obtain additional information about

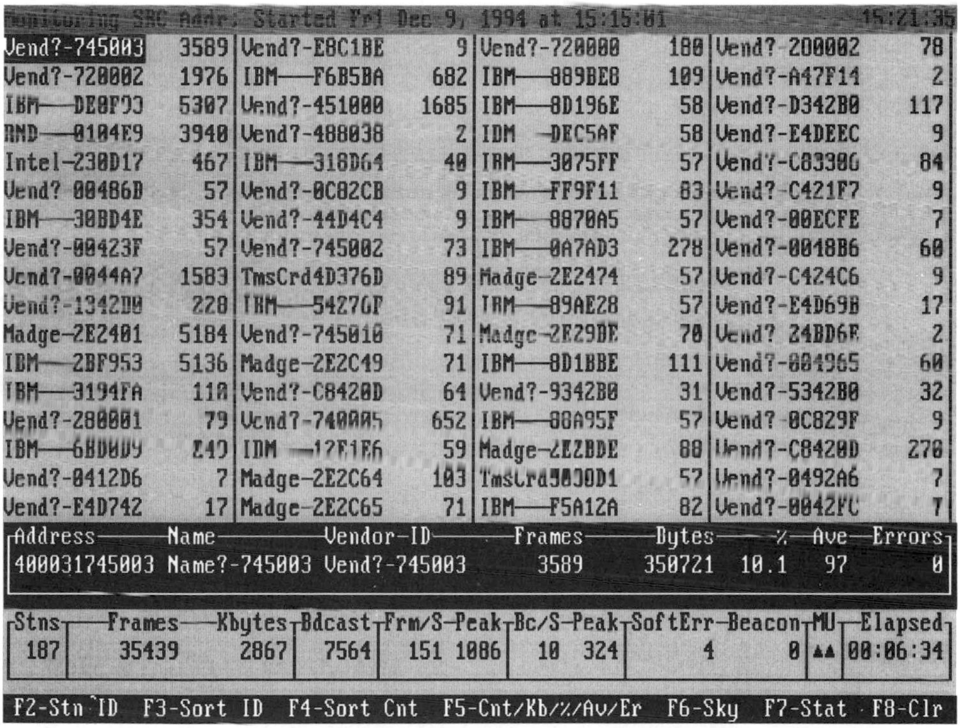

Figure 5.6 Extending the monitoring period can result in the identification of additional network stations as well as network error conditions

those errors. Later in this chapter I will view that display and examine its utilization as a tool to isolate network related problems.

5.2.4 Network utilization

Figure 5.7 illustrates the TokenVision skyline display indicating network utilization by time. As indicated in this display, network utilization is shown on a per second basis, resulting in the screen having the ability to show only one minute of network utilization. Since a one-minute period is normally insufficient to make a judgement about network utilization, you would probably press the F5 key if you were using this program to monitor the level of network traffic. This action would change the display period from seconds to minutes, permitting a one-hour view of network utilization. By itself this display can shed light on finger pointing between the network and file servers as the cause of poor response to interactive queries and prolonged file transfer times.

5.2.5 Network statistics

One of the more interesting screen displays of TokenVision and EtherVision with respect to isolating network problems is their network statistics display. Figure 5.8 illustrates the network statistics display for TokenVision; the EtherVision display is similar but tailored to Ethernet operating parameters, such as a frame length which does not exceed 1500 information bytes.

In examining the network statistics display illustrated in Figure 5.8 note that the Frame Counts window provides a characterization of network activity, while the Frame Size Distribution window provides a graphical and numeric breakdown of the length of observed frames. By comparing MAC and non-MAC frame counts you can obtain a general indication of internal Token-Ring administrative overhead.

The frame size distribution information can be useful as a general indicator of the relationship between interactive query–response and file transfer activity since file transfers have a large proportion of longer frames. Another area where the frame size distribution can be helpful is for determining if workstation configurations are correct for internetworking applications. For example, if you have bridged Ethernet and Token-Ring networks the largest Token-Ring frame should be less than or equal to 1500 information bytes, since that is the maximum supported by Ethernet. Otherwise, Token-Ring frames exceeding that length are not bridgeable onto an Ethernet network.

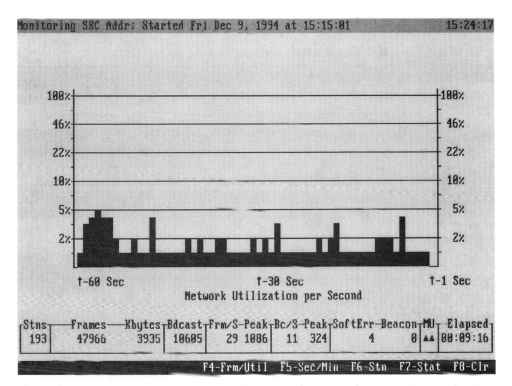

Figure 5.7 The TokenVision skyline display indicates network utilization by time

The upper Network Utilization window simply provides a graphical representation of the percentage of network utilization. Of far more interest are the three windows whose backgrounds appear in black, since those windows indicate peak levels of network utilization as a percentage as well as in bytes per second and frames per second. In addition, those windows indicate the time when peak activity occurred and the value of peak activity. Rather than periodically viewing the monitor screen, you can execute the program and view this screen at the end of the day to determine peak operating conditions and when they occurred.

The window labeled 'Source Route Frames' displays four types of routing frames whose presence applies only to IBM source routed networks.

The ARB entry represents the number of All Routes Broadcast (ARB) frames transmitted from a workstation along every route in an attempt to locate a path to a station on a different network. The transmission of ARB frames can result in the flooding of an internetwork when a large number of workstations operate applications that are used to set up a session with a computer on a different network. By comparing ARB frames to the total

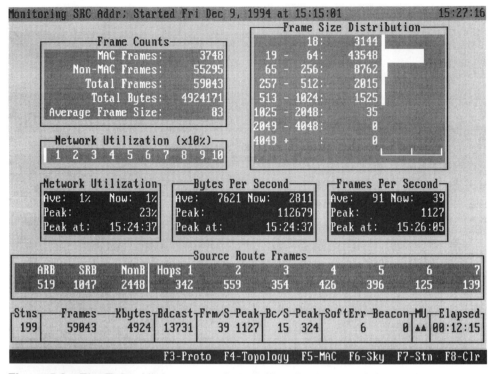

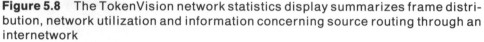

Figure 5.8 The TokenVision network statistics display summarizes frame distribution, network utilization and information concerning source routing through an internetwork

frame count you can obtain an indication as to whether or not your internetwork is being flooded.

The Single Route Broadcast (SRB) entry denotes the number of frames observed that were limited to flowing over only certain designated bridges during the route discovery process. Unlike an All Routes Broadcast frame, an SRB frame will only appear once on each network segment.

The NonB (Non-Broadcast) entry represents the number of frames that have a specific route in their Route Information Field. By comparing the total ARB, SRB and NonB entries to the total frames count you can determine internetwork traffic with respect to traffic on the network to which the workstation operating TokenVision is connected. The Hop field counts represent the number of bridges source routed frames were observed to 'hop' over. Although the hop entries should sum to the NonB frame count entry, Figure 5.8 does not show this. The reason for this apparent error is the setting of the 'M' and 'U' indicators, which indicates that some packets were missed and some were unprocessed. When the author later changed his computer platform from a 25 MHz 80486 based microprocessor to a 66M Hz based microprocessor the 'M' and 'U' indicators remained untagged during subsequent monitoring sessions.

5.2.6 Ring topology

Another TokenVision display screen that can facilitate the isolation of certain network errors is the ring topology map. This map, which is illustrated in Figure 5.9, shows the physical ordering of the active nodes in the ring to which the workstation operating TokenVision is connected. In this screen display note that the author located his workstation address and assigned his name to the station identifier.

As you move the highlight bar from station to station, its station identifier and its nearest active upstream neighbor's address (NAUN), either physical or logical assigned name, as well as transmission information for the selected station is displayed. Since the NAUN is the station that transmits all information to its

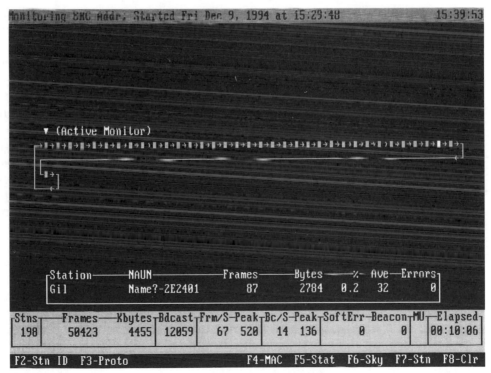

Figure 5.9 The TokenVision ring topology display can be used to locate a beaconing workstation

downstream neighbor, if a station detects an error condition, such as a beacon, the problem lies somewhere between that station and its NAUN. Thus, if a beacon was indicated in Figure 5.9 you would know station Gil received it from the station whose address is 2E2401.

5.2.7 MAC statistics

MAC or Medium Access Control frames are used on a Token-Ring network to transport ring management information. Thus, the MAC statistics screen display which is illustrated in Figure 5.10 provides a summary of Token-Ring management information.

The three windows in the MAC Statistics Display summarize Active Monitor, Ring Recovery and Soft Error frames during the monitoring period. The Active Monitor window indicates the number of Active Monitor Present frames observed since network monitoring commenced, the number of Active Monitor Error frames transmitted by the Active Monitor upon receipt of a Ring Purge or Claim Token frame, and the number of Neighbor Notification Incomplete frames sent by the Active Monitor.

The Active Monitor transmits an Active Monitor Present frame every 7 seconds. Thus, 297 Active Monitor Present frames represent a total of 297×7 or 2079 seconds, or 34 minutes and 39 seconds, which is almost identical to the elapsed time of 34 minutes and 37 seconds shown in the lower right corner of Figure 5.10. Since the commencement of monitoring can be within ± 7 seconds of viewing an Active Monitor Present frame, the 'M' and 'U' tags do not indicate any major problem with the statistics based upon Active Monitor Present frame monitoring.

If the Active Monitor workstation fails or is turned off a procedure is required for another workstation to become the Active Monitor. This process is known as Token-Claiming, in which a station recognizes that the Active Monitor is no longer present and issues a Claim Token MAC frame. Several additional conditions previously discussed in Chapter 2 can also result in the generation of a Claim Token and readers are referred to that chapter for information.

Although the Active Monitor and Ring Recovery windows keep a running total of the indicated frames they only display information about the last noted occurrence, such as the station address and its NAUN address. Similarly, the Soft Error window once filled will be scrolled upward, resulting in the oldest information being removed first. Fortunately, you can use the program's network event log to view previous events that were either covered by

```
Monitoring SRC Addr: Started Fri Dec 9, 1994 at 15:53:19              16:27:55
                        ┌Active Monitor MAC Frames┐
 Monitor Present:    297  Last: 16:27:54 Stn Name?-745002 NAUN Name?-451000
   Monitor Error:      0  Last: --:--:-- Stn ----------- NAUN -----------
 Neighbr Ntf Inc:      0  Last: --:--:-- Stn ----------- NAUN -----------

                        ┌Ring Recovery MAC Frames┐
    Claim Token:        0  Last: --:--:-- Stn ----------- NAUN -----------
     Ring Purge:        2  Last: 16:24:52 Stn Name?-745002 NAUN Name?-451000
        Beacon:         0  Last: --:--:-- Stn ----------- NAUN -----------

                        ┌Soft Error MAC Frame Report┐
 1 BrstErr                 16:02;36 Stn Name?-C8420D NAUN Name?-30BD4E
 1 ToknErr                 16:02:36 Stn Name?-745002 NAUN Name?-451000
 1 RcvrCon                 16:07:39 Stn Gil          NAUN Name?-2E2401
 1 ToknErr                 16:24:54 Stn Name?-745002 NAUN Name?-451000
 1 BrstErr                 16:24:54 Stn Name?-8D196E NAUN Name?-720000


┌Stns┬─Frames─┬─Kbytes┬Bdcast┬Frm/S─Peak┬Dc/S─Peak┬SoftErr┬Beacon┬MU┬Elapsed┐
 201   375946   28755   40848  42   1171  22   171    5      0  ▲▲ 00:34:37

 F2-Stn ID  F3 Proto              F4-Topology  F5-Stat  F6 Sky  F7-Stn  F8-Clr
```

Figure 5.10 The TokenVision MAC statistics display can be used to identify the cause of certain types of network errors

newer events or scrolled off the soft error window. Figure 5.11 illustrates the TokenVision Network Event Log window. Note that each event is time stamped and error events tracked by the program are identified by both their physical and, if assigned, their logical address. You can either scroll through the log or use another program option to generate a hard copy of the event log. In examining the events shown in the Network Display Log note that the program time stamps and enters into the log each new peak network utilization. By reviewing the contents of this log you can obtain an indication of how network activity increases as well as when each new peak utilization period occurred. This information could provide you with a different opinion concerning the need for network segmentation than from an examination of the MAC statistics display which is limited to indicating the current peak network utilization level.

The Soft errors shown in Figures 5.10 and 5.11 can be categorized as isolating errors, non-isolating errors and hard errors. An isolating error is an error which can be identified as occurring between a workstation and its NAUN. A non-isolating error is an error condition that could be caused by any adapter in the ring, while a hard error is an error condition which may not be recoverable and which could disrupt the operation of the network. In Section 5.3 I will focus my attention upon the types of Ethernet and Token-Ring errors observable from the use of different hardware and software network analyzers. Since the majority of this chapter is focused upon the use of EtherVision and TokenVision as tools to monitor traffic at the data link layer, the abbreviations used by those programs to indicate network errors will be identified. This will permit you to judge the comprehensiveness of those programs in providing network error information as well as for use in evaluating the comprehensiveness of different data link layer monitoring products with respect to their error identification capability.

5.3 DATA LINK LAYER ERRORS

Since I previously examined the use of a few hardware and software network analyzer tools to gather statistics and identify

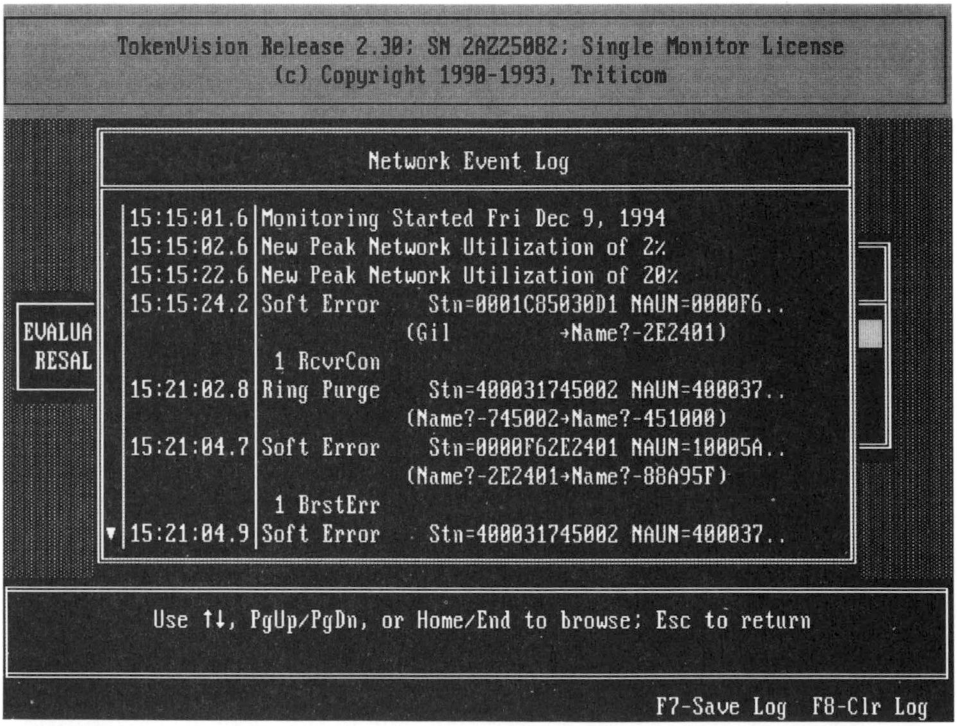

Figure 5.11   You can use the TokenVision Network Event Log to obtain a list of network events to include error conditions as well as when each new peak network utilization occurred

different network errors, a logical conclusion to this chapter is to note the different types of Ethernet and Token-Ring errors observable from data link monitoring. As no product examined by this author was found to be all-inclusive, the summary of network errors provides you with the ability to compare the capability of different vendor products.

5.3.1 Ethernet

Table 5.2 lists six common Ethernet errors that different types of network analyzers may be able to detect. Entries in the table also include a description of each error condition and its possible or probable cause as well as an abbreviation following the error condition used to denote those conditions tracked by EtherVision.

In examining the entries in Table 5.2 note that collisions do not actually represent Ethernet errors; however, since most network

Table 5.2 Ethernet errors reported by network analyzers

Error condition	Description and possible cause
Alignment	A received frame does not contain an integral number of octets or bytes. Possible cause can be cabling or adapter problem.
Collisions (Coll)	The number of collisions that occurred. This is a normal occurrence and should not be actually be considered an error.
Cyclic Redundancy Check (CRC)	The computed CRC does not match the CRC field contained in the frame. A CRC error indicates that data in the frame is corrupted. EMI, crosstalk and other cable problems are a common cause of CRC errors.
Late collision	A collision is detected later than 512 bits after the beginning of a transmitted frame. This error normally indicates that two or more stations are outside the distance limit specified by the IEEE 802.3 standard.
Long frame	A received frame exceeds the maximum allowable frame length of 1518 bytes. A failing adapter or a late collision could result in a long frame.
Short frame	A received frame is shorter than the minimum allowable frame length of 64 bytes. A failing adapter card or a collision could result in a short frame.

analyzers track this activity as an error it was listed in the table. In actuality, the frequency of collisions is closely tied to the level of network utilization, with higher levels of network utilization resulting in a higher collision count per unit time. Both long and short frames can represent a failing adapter or the effect of collisions upon a frame. Since collisions are random events, you can determine if an adapter is the problem by examining the source address associated with long and short error frames. If one adapter address is primarily associated with either error condition you should consider replacing the indicated adapter card.

5.3.2 Token-Ring

Token-Ring adapter cards are much more sophisticated than Ethernet adapters with respect to their network management capability. Each adapter card includes a set of built in counters used to keep track of critical soft errors. Most soft errors are recoverable, though an excessive number of such errors can considerably degrade network performance. As previously discussed, soft errors can be categorized as isolating errors, non-isolating errors and hard errors.

Isolating errors can be identified as occurring between a workstation and its NAUN, providing you with the ability to pinpoint the location of the problem. A non-isolating error could be caused by any adapter card in the ring, while a hard error is an error condition which may not be recoverable and which could disrupt the operation of the network.

In addition to MAC frames that transport adapter error counter information a Token-Ring network transports a number of ring management frames. By providing information about those frames, such as beacons, purges and claim tokens, you may be able to use a network analyzer to identify other types of network related problems.

Ring management

Table 5.3 describes three common ring management frames tracked by many network analyzers. The Claim Token frame can be placed on the network whenever one of the three conditions listed in Table 5.3 occurs. If a station cannot receive the claim token it generated, this results in an escalation of the failure to a beaconing state.

When in a beaconing state, both the station that generated the beacon frame and its NAUN briefly deinsert themselves from the ring and initiate a self-test operation. If either station detects a hard error when performing its self-test the station will remain deinserted, permitting the ring to recover.

Since a beacon frame contains both the address of the beaconing station and its NAUN you can use a network analyzer to isolate the location of a hard error. Thus, if both the beaconing station and its NAUN pass their self-test, you can use the address information as a clue for the manual inspection of wiring and connectors between stations that could be the cause of the beaconing condition.

Soft errors

Table 5.4 lists Token-Ring soft errors categorized by error type – isolating, non-isolating and hard error – lumps certain errors into an all-inclusive 'other' category. The abbreviation following the name of a line error indicates the mnemonic the TokenVision program, previously described in Section 5.2, uses to identify the error.

Line error

A line error can result from EMI, near end crosstalk, loss connectors or a faulty adapter card. Thus, the ability to note the

Table 5.3 Ring management frames

Frame type	Description
Claim token	Generated when: 1. A ring station inserts into the ring and does not detect an Active Monitor. 2. The current Active Monitor or a Standby Monitor detects a signal loss or has its internal timer expire, indicating too long an interval since a token was last seen. 3. Active Monitor does not receive ring purge frames back.
Beacon	Generated when: 1. Claim process fails to recover the ring, resulting in the ring station issuing beacon frames. 2. Ring station detects a hard error.
Purge	Generated by the Active Monitor when its timer expires prior to a token returning to the monitor.

source address and destination address of line errored frames provides you with a starting point for isolating the cause of the error. For example, you might check the cable at both source and destination addresses for pulls that reduce the twists per foot and could cause NEXT, resulting in line errors. You could also check the cable connectors at each station as well as perform a visual check of the wiring area to determine if a source of EMI, such as a copier, was recently placed near a cable.

Burst error

When examining the burst error count you should note that a few burst errors are usually reported when a station is inserted into the ring or deinserted from the ring. If a large number of burst errors is associated with a station this typically indicates an excessive lobe cable length.

Access control error

An access control error indicates that the reporting station receiving the error may have its NAUN operating in a marginal condition. Thus, a frequent place to start your investigation of access control errors is the NAUN of the station reporting those errors.

Abort delimiter error

An abort delimiter error is normally a very rare condition. If this error condition persists it can be used to identify a station on the verge of failure which has a large number of recoverable transient errors.

Lost frame error

The first non-isolating error listed in Table 5.4, lost frame error, can result from the corruption of a frame occurring during its traversal of the ring. This error condition can also indicate that the reporting station's receiver is operating at a marginal level.

Receiver congestion error

The receiver congestion error can be a common occurrence on heavily loaded file servers. Another cause of receiver congestion is

Table 5.4   Token-Ring soft errors

Error condition	Description
Isolating errors	
Line Error (LineErr)	Occurs when: 1. A token or frame is repeated by the ring station. 2. Ending delimiter error-detected bit is set to zero. 3. A code violation between starting and ending delimiters of a frame or token is detected. 4. Frame Check Sequence error is detected.
Burst Error (BrstErr)	Occurs when a ring station detects the absence of signaling transitions for a period equal to or greater than five half-bit times.
Access Control Error (A/CErr)	An access control error results from a ring station receiving a Standby Monitor Present frame prior to first receiving an Active Monitor Present frame.
Abort Delimiter (AbortDL)	An abort delimiter occurs when one of the following activities is detected by a ring station. 1. A recoverable transient error. 2. A non-recoverable hard error which results in the removal of the station from the ring. 3. A token which does not have an ending delimiter as its third byte.
Non isolating errors	
Lost Frame Error (LostFrm)	Occurs when a station's physical trailer timer expires while it is transmitting.
Receiver Congestion (RcvrCon)	Occurs when a station receives a frame but has no available buffer space to receive it.
Frame Copy Error (FCpyErr)	Occurs when a frame previously copied by one station is copied by another station. The occurrence of a Frame Copy Error may indicate that two or more stations have the same address.
Token Error (ToknErr)	Occurs when an Active Monitor recognizes an error condition which requires the monitor to transmit another token.
Hard error	
Internal Error (IntlErr)	Occurs when a ring station recognizes a recoverable internal error.
Frequency Error (FreqErr)	Occurs when a ring station detects an abnormal deviation from the Token-Ring signaling specification.
Other errors	
Multiple Monitors	Occurs when the Active Monitor detects the potential presence of another Active Monitor on the network.
Active Monitor	Occurs when the Active Monitor detects a Claim Token MAC frame which indicates that another station detected an error in the Active Monitor.
Duplicate Address	Occurs when a station detects the presence of another station with the same MAC address as its own.

a workstation using an adapter card that can be set in 16 kilobyte increments for memory sharing operations between the adapter and the computer it is inserted into. In this situation you might consider resetting the amount of adapter memory sharing to a higher value if the workstation continuously has a high level of receiver congestion.

Frame copy and token errors

In addition to indicating a duplicate address, a frame copy error can also indicate a line error affecting the frame's A bit. In comparison, a token error can result from a continuously circulating frame, a lost frame or token, or a circulating priority token. If this situation persists it could indicate that data is being constantly corrupted somewhere on the ring.

Internal error

The first hard error listed in Table 5.4, internal error, can be used to identify a station in a marginal operating condition.

Frequency error

The second error condition, frequency error, is normally generated by an Active Monitor when there is an excessive amount of jitter on the ring.

Other soft errors

The multiple monitors error can result from an improper hub switch operation, placing the active monitor present frame from one network onto another network. The Active Monitor error will be used to switch the Active Monitor function to a Standby Monitor. The third error in the 'other' category, duplicate address, indicates that two workstations were configured with the same locally administered address and the configuration of one station should be changed.

Through the use of a network analyzer you can identify and isolate many problems at the data link layer. Although this will not provide you with the ability to correct all network errors, it represents a good starting point for isolating and correcting network transport related problems.

6

CHECKING THE NETWORK OPERATING SYSTEM

For most local area networks the network operating system (NOS) resides on a server, resulting in an examination of the network operating system being equivalent to an examination of the operational characteristics of the file server. I say 'equivalent' instead of 'equal' as other portions of the network operating system must be installed on each workstation to provide a communications capability between client workstations and network servers. Thus, testing and troubleshooting of the network operating system in a client–server environment requires an examination of NOS modules operating on network servers and network clients.

Similar to testing and troubleshooting any network area, testing and troubleshooting a network operating system requires the use of one or more tools. Such tools can be a hardware or software product or a combination of hardware and software. Unfortunately most tools designed for testing and troubleshooting a network operating system are developed for use with a specific NOS. Since Novell NetWare currently represents over 70 percent of the installed base of network operating systems, it should come as no surprise that the majority of tools developed to assist in testing and troubleshooting network operating systems were developed for use with NetWare. In attempting to provide information useful to a majority of readers I will focus my attention upon NetWare in this chapter. In doing so I will examine the use of NetWare utility programs as well as products from Frye Computer Systems of Boston, MA, developed to provide users with the ability to control and manage NetWare based networks. Although not specifically developed as testing and troubleshooting products, Frye software provides this capability within Frye's series of software modules that can be obtained individually or as an integrated series of products. While the use of several Frye software products will be examined in this chapter, readers should note that similar but perhaps less comprehensive integrated products are obtainable from other vendors. Regardless of the product used, the important thing to note is how information provided by the product is used to facilitate testing and troubleshooting of the network operating system. Thus, my examination of the use of NetWare utility programs and several Frye Computer Systems software products will be focused upon the use of information they display rather than on how the product is installed.

6.1 SERVER OBSERVATION

There are certain network symptoms that can denote whether a problem is related to workstation, network or file server. For example, assume that a network user reports that the use of a server-based application for which queries previously resulted in a response within a few seconds now required 15 to 30 seconds or longer. Is the network overloaded? Is a configuration or other problem on the workstation due to the recent installation of new hardware or software causing the problem? If you're using an Ethernet network, is the utilization level at a point where a large number of collisions are resulting in a significant degradation in the ability of the network to transport information? Is the utilization level of the file server causing poor response? Or is the problem caused by a combination of workstation software, network traffic and server utilization?

To determine the cause or possible causes of a network problem requires an examination of the network transport infrastructure and the network file server and may require an examination of software used on the workstation. Since I previously examined the operation of the network transport infrastructure in Chapter 5, I will focus my attention in this chapter upon the network operating system to include client and server software.

6.1.1 NetWare management

At the time this book was written the Frye Utilities for Networks consisted of a series of eight programs that can be operated from an integrated menu. Figure 6.1 illustrates the Frye Utilities for Networks integrated menu. In Sections 6.1.2–6.1.5 I will focus my

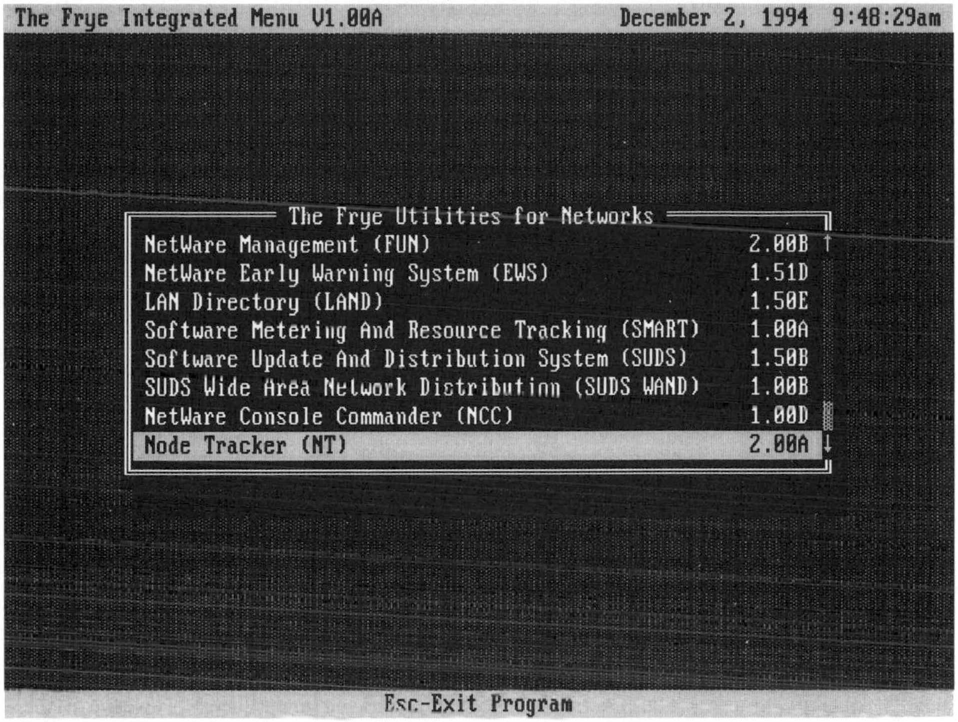

```
The Frye Integrated Menu V1.00A                 December 2, 1994  9:48:29am




            ┌──────── The Frye Utilities for Networks ────────┐
            │ NetWare Management (FUN)                   2.00B ↑│
            │ NetWare Early Warning System (EWS)         1.51D │
            │ LAN Directory (LAND)                       1.50E │
            │ Software Metering And Resource Tracking (SMART) 1.00A │
            │ Software Update And Distribution System (SUDS) 1.50B │
            │ SUDS Wide Area Network Distribution (SUDS WAND) 1.00B │
            │ NetWare Console Commander (NCC)            1.00D │
            │ Node Tracker (NT)                          2.00A ↓│
            └─────────────────────────────────────────────────┘




                         Esc-Exit Program
```

Figure 6.1   The Frye Utilities for Neworks Integrated Menu

attention upon the use of Frye Computer Systems' NetWare Management program which is the top entry in the menu illustrated in Figure 6.1, as well as on the NetWare MONITOR utility program. In Section 6.2 I will examine the use of the Frye Node Tracker and the Frye NetWare Early Warning System programs.

6.1.2 NetWare general server performance characteristics

The Frye Computer Systems' NetWare Management program consists of a series of modules that can be used to display information about the operation of the file server, workstations and print servers connected to a file server, data about users defined on a server, a variety of disk utilization information to include print job queues and the display of different reports. Since my primary objective is to examine the use of Frye Computer Systems' NetWare Management program as a tool for testing and troubleshooting network operating system problems,

I will primarily focus my attention upon the use of this program to diagnose network operating system related problems.

Figure 6.2 illustrates the NetWare Management Server: General display screen. The right side of this display indicates via a bar graph the percentage of server utilization for the past 30 seconds. The left side of the display indicates the current value for 12 server parameters as well as the serial number of the program. As I will later note in this section, many of the parameters displayed through the use of Frye software can also be obtained from the use of NetWare utility programs and other third-party products. What distinguishes Frye software is its comprehensive display capability as well as its integration and ease of use.

Server Utilization

The Server Utilization percentage displayed on the left side of Figure 6.2 indicates the numeric value of the file server's usage for the past second and corresponds to the rightmost graphical

```
The Frye Utilities - NetWare Management V2.00B    December 2, 1994  9:56:45am
        26 users on MDPC-1, up 11 days 11 hrs 21 mins 43 secs

========================= Server: General =========================
Server Utilization:   5%
Disk I/O Pending:     0                       ── Utilization % ──
Dirty Cache Buffers:  2              95-
Service Processes:    3              85-
Logins Allowed:       Yes           75-
Processor Speed:      915            65-
Total Server Memory:  9,984k        55-
Cache Buffers:        26%            45-
Maximum Connections:  50             35-
NetWare Version:      3.11A          25-
TTS Level:            1              15-
SFT Level:            2,              5-
NetWare Serial #:     06899489

General  Memory  Drivers  misC  Set  Resources  modUles  Io  stAts  sYsfiles
                    Press Ctrl for main menu
        F1-Help  F2-Server  F6-Freeze  F10-Commands  Esc-Main Menu
```

Figure 6.2 Frye Utilities NetWare Management Server: General display screen

display position. Although a high level of server utilization will serve to pinpoint network delays, this parameter can provide a false indication of a network operating system problem caused by hardware. For example, consider a file server which receives a large number of I/O requests but which uses a relatively slow-speed disk. Here the speed of disk I/O will limit the amount of work the file server can perform, resulting in the server's utilization being relatively low. Thus, an examination of file server performance will normally require an examination of a significant number of parameters as I will soon note.

Disk I/O Pending

The second entry in the left column of Figure 6.2, Disk I/O Pending, represents a method to distinguish between server processing and disk I/O problems resulting in network response time delays. When the Disk I/O Pending entry has a large value over a period of time this indicates that server performance is being degraded by the inability of the server's disk or disks to keep up with I/O requests. If utilization is high but the Disk I/O Pending value is low, this would indicate that an upgrade of the server processor, perhaps via an overdrive processor, or the replacement of the motherboard of the server with a new motherboard containing a faster microprocessor, is warranted instead of the replacement of the disk or disks.

Dirty Cache Buffers

The Dirty Cache Buffers entry indicates the number of disk cache buffers that contain information but have yet to be written to disk. If the number of dirty cache buffers consistently remains above 10 this commonly indicates that disk performance is adversely affecting file server performance.

Service Processes

The fourth parameter listed in the left column of Figure 6.2, Service Processes, indicates the number of tasks NetWare can work upon at one time. The Service Processes value is based upon the file server configuration. Normally, a server with less than three available service processes will perform poorly.

Logins Allowed

The Logins Allowed entry indicates whether or not new users and objects such as print servers can be attached to the file server. Simply viewing this entry can answer why some network users may report that they are unable to access the file server. When this entry is set to 'off', it indicates that either through a server console command or the use of a NetWare utility program or menu entry, a supervisor or person with supervisory rights disabled logins. Sometimes network administrators disable logins prior to performing a complete backup of the file server and a failure to enable logins is a common problem that a glance at Figure 6.2 can indicate.

Processor Speed

The Processor Speed entry displays the speed rating of the microprocessor in the file server. This entry reflects the rating NetWare assigns to the server's microprocessor based upon a test performed when the server is started. A 80386SX based computer running at 16 MHz should result in a processor speed entry rating of approximately 120. In comparison, a 80486 66 MHz based file server produced the processor speed rating of 915 illustrated in Figure 6.2.

Some computers contain microprocessors that can operate at one of two clock speeds. You can use this display or the NetWare SPEED console command to display the NetWare rating assigned to each speed to determine the potential effect of operating the microprocessor at a higher clock speed. Another use for the processor speed entry or the use of the console SPEED command is to observe the potential effect of replacing one server platform with another platform. Although the processor speed entry reflects the processing capability of the computer and does not consider its I/O capability, it can be used as an evaluation parameter when comparing server platforms.

Total Server Memory and Cache Buffers

The Total Server Memory entry indicates the amount of random access memory (RAM) installed in the file server; however, this entry does not include RAM reserved by your computer hardware. For example, shadow RAM would not be included in the Total Server Memory entry.

The amount of total server memory by itself can be useful to ensure your server has a sufficient amount of RAM based upon the Network Operating System specifications which are normally based upon the maximum number of connections to be supported. However, by itself the entry does not indicate the use of memory, nor indicate whether or not additional memory is warranted. Later in this section I will examine the use of another NetWare Management display and NetWare's MONITOR utility program which provide detailed information concerning the use of RAM.

The Cache Buffers entry indicates the percentage of total server RAM used as disk cache buffers. This storage area is used to hold the contents of the most frequently accessed files and a reduction in the percentage of RAM allocated to this function will adversely affect the performance of the file server with respect to the time required for network users to access information.

Maximum Connections

The Maximum Connections entry reflects the license restriction of the software in use. Thus, the entry of 50 in Figure 6.2 indicates that a maximum of 50 users can be logged onto the server at any point in time.

The remaining four entries on the left side of Figure 6.2 are not directly applicable to testing and troubleshooting the network operating system; however, they can assist you in determining the version of NetWare operating on a server to determine capability and related tasks.

6.1.3 Memory considerations

As previously discussed, the Total Server Memory entry in the Server: General display screen illustrated in Figure 6.2 by itself does not provide an indication of the use of memory, nor if memory should be allocated differently to enhance server performance. To obtain a better indication of server memory utilization you must examine the use of each 'NetWare memory pool'; this term is used to represent an area of RAM used by the file server for a specific function. For example, under NetWare version 3.1 five memory pools are used – permanent, alloc, cache buffers, cache movable and cache non-movable. Since an understanding of how each memory pool is used can facilitate the examination of memory use, let's turn our attention to the function associated with each memory pool. In doing so I will also focus my attention upon the Frye Utilities NetWare Management Server: Memory display screen which is illustrated in Figure 6.3 and the NetWare MONITOR utility program. The screen illustrated in Figure 6.3 is very similar to the Resource Utilization screen display you can obtain through the use of NetWare's MONITOR utility program. To use the MONITOR program you must either load it from the console or through the use of the RCONSOLE command. Thus, you must either be the network supervisor or have supervisory rights. Figure 6.4 illustrates the initial MONITOR utility program screen display while Figure 6.5 illustrates the results obtained from selecting the Resource Utilization entry from the Available Options menu in the initial MONITOR screen display. Note that the utilization percentage from Figure 6.4 represents the same utilization value used in the Frye Utilities screen display previously illustrated in Figure 6.1. Similarly, the top portion of Figure 6.5 presented by NetWare's MONITOR program which presents server memory statistics provides the basic information presented by the Frye Utilities NetWare Management Server: Memory display screen illustrated

```
The Frye Utilities - NetWare Management V2.00B    December 2, 1994  9:58:45am
         26 users on MDPC-1, up 11 days 11 hrs 23 mins 42 secs

============================= Server: Memory =============================
Name                        Size/Bytes   %   Allocated From

Permanent Memory             3,093,940   33  Total Server Work Memory
Alloc Short Term Memory        548,880    5  Total Server Work Memory
Cache Buffer Memory          2,413,840   26  Total Server Work Memory
Cache Movable Memory         1,692,220   18  Total Server Work Memory
Cache Non-Movable Memory     1,464,340   15  Total Server Work Memory
Total Server Work Memory     9,213,220  N/A  N/A

Directory Cache Buffer Memory  455,760   14  Permanent Memory
Used Permanent Memory        3,091,412   99  Permanent Memory
Used Alloc Short Term Memory   210,516   38  Alloc Short Term Memory

General  Memory  Drivers  misC  Set  Resources  modUles  Io  stAts  sYsfiles
                       Press Ctrl for main menu
           F1-Help  F2-Server  F6-Freeze  F10-Commands  Esc-Main Menu
```

Figure 6.3 Frye Utilities NetWare Management Server: Memory display screen

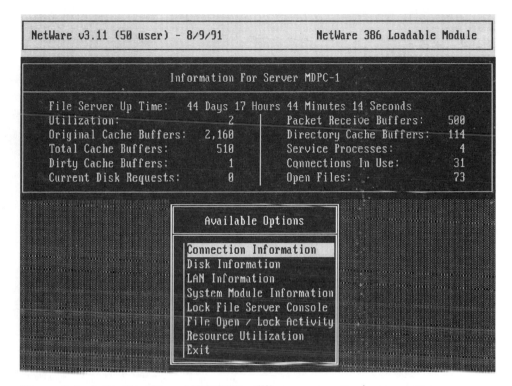

```
NetWare v3.11 (50 user) - 8/9/91          NetWare 386 Loadable Module

                    Information For Server MDPC-1

File Server Up Time:   44 Days 17 Hours 44 Minutes 14 Seconds
Utilization:              2         Packet Receive Buffers:   500
Original Cache Buffers: 2,160       Directory Cache Buffers:  114
Total Cache Buffers:    510         Service Processes:          4
Dirty Cache Buffers:      1         Connections In Use:        31
Current Disk Requests:    0         Open Files:                73


                        Available Options

                    Connection Information
                    Disk Information
                    LAN Information
                    System Module Information
                    Lock File Server Console
                    File Open / Lock Activity
                    Resource Utilization
                    Exit
```

Figure 6.4   Initial NetWare MONITOR utility program display screen

in Figure 6.3. In fact, many of Frye Computer Systems' screen displays are similar to displays obtainable from different NetWare utility programs. What distinguishes the two is the fact that the Frye Utilities NetWare Management program is an integrated product which provides users with the ability to display from one program information that would require the use of a number of NetWare utility programs.

Permanent memory pool

Under NetWare RAM is subdivided into two general areas – permanent or non-allocatable memory, and an area for file cache operations which can be allocated. Permanent memory is used for long-term operations, such as directory cache buffers and packet receive buffers. Directory cache buffers facilitate the expedient generation of network directory requests while packet receive buffers provide the server with a place to store information received from the LAN prior to its processing. Once allocated, permanent memory cannot be reallocated unless the server is rebooted.

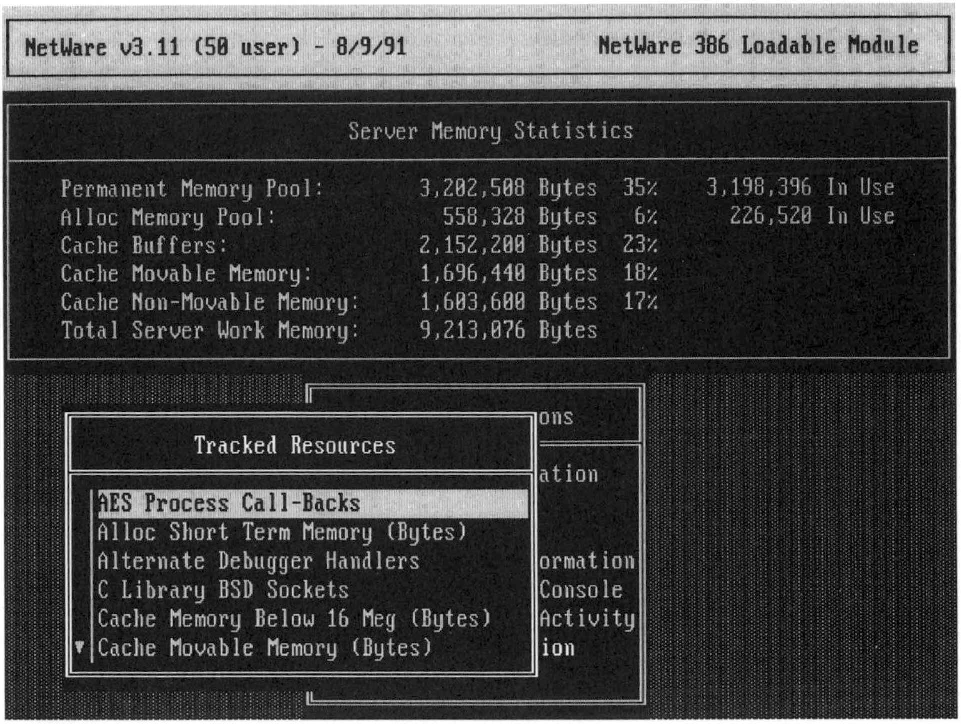

```
NetWare v3.11 (50 user) - 8/9/91          NetWare 386 Loadable Module

                        Server Memory Statistics

      Permanent Memory Pool:      3,202,508 Bytes   35%   3,198,396 In Use
      Alloc Memory Pool:            558,328 Bytes    6%     226,520 In Use
      Cache Buffers:              2,152,200 Bytes   23%
      Cache Movable Memory:       1,696,440 Bytes   18%
      Cache Non-Movable Memory:   1,603,600 Bytes   17%
      Total Server Work Memory:   9,213,076 Bytes

                                              ons

              Tracked Resources              ation

         AES Process Call-Backs
         Alloc Short Term Memory (Bytes)
         Alternate Debugger Handlers         ormation
         C Library BSD Sockets               Console
         Cache Memory Below 16 Meg (Bytes)   Activity
       ▼ Cache Movable Memory (Bytes)        ion
```

Figure 6.5 Server Memory Statistics displayed through the use of the NetWare MONITOR utility program

One common problem associated with an insufficient amount of permanent memory is the inability of the server to retrieve information destined to itself when a network becomes loaded. Here the solution to this problem is to increase the amount of RAM allocated to permanent memory.

Alloc memory pool

The Alloc memory pool is used to store loadable modules for temporary or short term use. Another use of the alloc memory pool is for holding drive mapping and user connection information. The alloc memory pool can be considered as semi-permanent memory as once memory is allocated to this pool it is not returned for use by file cache buffers. Instead, when a module is unloaded the freed memory returns to the alloc memory pool for use by other loadable modules.

By comparing the 'used alloc short term memory' value to the 'alloc short term memory' value you can determine if additional memory should be allocated to this memory pool. If more memory is required you can use the NetWare SET command to increase the amount of memory allocated to this memory pool. Later in this section I will examine the use of the NetWare SET command to alter certain memory allocations.

Cache buffer memory pool

The cache buffer memory pool consists of RAM used for data caching. In the example illustrated in Figure 6.3, 2.4 Mbytes or 26 percent of total server RAM is shown allocated for cache buffer operations. This RAM storage area is used to hold the contents of the most frequently accessed files and represents the storage area from which the two remaining memory pools, cache movable and cache non-movable, obtain additional memory.

Cache movable memory pool

The cache movable memory pool is used to store system tables that dynamically grow, such as directory tables and file allocation tables (FATs). Since this memory pool is movable the operating system can move unused areas of the cache movable memory so it can be used as a portion of the cache buffer memory pool.

Cache non-movable memory pool

Cache non-movable memory is used to provide storage for loadable modules. Although memory allocated to this pool is not movable, that memory can be expanded upon or returned for use by the file cache memory pool. When returned for use by the file cache memory pool memory blocks cannot be moved. Instead, pointers are established which expand the file cache memory pool by using a portion of cache non-movable memory.

Using SET commands

There are several NetWare SET commands you can consider using to directly or indirectly alter memory pool allocations. First, SET to set the cache buffer size can be used to control the block size of cache buffers. Although the default value of 4096 bytes under NetWare Version 3.X is normally sufficient for most organizations, this buffer size can be set up to 16 384 bytes per block. Regardless of whether or not you use the SET command to change the cache buffer size, there are several SET commands you can consider using to directly alter the allocation of memory and indirectly tune the server's performance with respect to different functions associated with certain memory pools.

If the file server is responding slowly to directory searches you should consider increasing the value for the maximum directory cache buffers through the use of a SET command. Another directory cache buffers setting that warrants attention is the minimum directory cache buffers value. If this value is set too high too much memory will always be reserved for directory searches, precluding the allocation of some memory that may be more productively assigned to file caching operations. Thus, you must carefully consider the values assigned for both the minimum and maximum number of directory cache buffers. Concerning file caching, you can use the SET command to specify the minimum number of file cache buffers used for file caching.

Under NetWare all memory which is not allocated for other purposes is used for file caching. However, when memory is used for other purposes, such as directory caching, the file server has less memory available for file caching. Thus, setting a minimum number of file cache buffers serves as a floor or limit at which the file server stops providing memory used for file caching for other functions. When considering changing the minimum file cache buffers value from its default setting, it's important to remember that as you increase this value you limit memory that can be allocated to other server functions. Thus, setting the value of the minimum number of file cache buffers can result in an inability to load one or more NetWare Loadable Modules (NLMs).

6.1.4 Using the NetWare MONITOR utility program

In examining the NetWare MONITOR utility screen display illustrated in Figure 6.4, note that the original cache buffers entry reflects the number of cache buffers that were available when the file server was brought up or booted. In comparison, the total cache buffers entry indicates the number of blocks currently available for file caching and decreases as modules are loaded. Assuming the default block size is 4 Kbytes, at the time MONITOR was used there were 510 buffers of 4 Kbytes/buffer or 2.04 Mbytes of server storage available for loading modules. As the number of total cache buffers decreases this can serve as a warning to reallocate or expand server memory.

The dirty cache buffers entry denotes the number of file blocks in memory awaiting transfer to disk. If this number gets too large interactive query/response applications will begin to notice delays, with the disk controller or disk more than likely functioning as a bottleneck.

The packet receive buffers entry denotes the number of buffers available to service workstation frames. If the server drops frames this would indicate that that value should be increased.

To determine if the server is dropping frames you would perform an analysis of network traffic as discussed in Chapter 5. As an alternative you can use several NetWare utility programs or a different Frye Computer Systems' program to determine if servers or workstations are dropping packets. Later in this chapter I will examine several display screens generated by the use of the Frye Node Tracker program to obtain information on the flow of packets between clients and servers on a NetWare LAN.

The directory cache buffers entry denotes the number of buffers available for directory caching. As previously discussed, you may wish to consider increasing this value if network users experience a slow response when using the Novell NetWare NDIR command to obtain a network directory listing or using the DOS DIR command with a network drive.

6.1.5 Tuning SETable parameters

NetWare supports approximately 75 parameters whose values can be reset from their default through the use of the SET command. You can view the present setting of setable parameters through the use of several NetWare utility programs and set or reset their values through the use of the console SET command. Unfortunately, some NetWare utility programs simply display current values for setable parameters, while other programs or commands may display the range of values that can be specified for some parameters.

By using the Frye Utilities NetWare Management program you can obtain a description of the function of each setable parameter as well as its current value, range of values supported and other information. This is indicated in Figure 6.6 which shows the use of the Frye Utilities NetWare Management program to view the current setting of the Delay Before First Watchdog Packet server setable parameter as well as other information concerning that

```
The Frye Utilities - NetWare Management V2.00B     December 2, 1994 10:13:07am
        26 users on MDPC-1, up 11 days 11 hrs 39 mins 48 secs
╔═══════════ Parameters ═══════════╗╔═══ Server: Setable Parameters ═══╗
║Allow Unencrypted Passwords       ↑║Name:                             ║
║Auto Register Memory Above 16 Megabyte║  Delay Before First Watchdog    ║
║Auto TTS Backout Flag             ║    Packet                         ║
║Cache Buffer Size                 ║ Description:                       ║
║CDDRV Bug                         ▓║   Amount of time the server will  ║
║CDDRV Debug                       ║    wait, without receiving a request║
║CDDRV dump DI errors              ║    from a workstation, before asking║
║CDDRV Dump IOs dequeued           ║    the workstation if it is still ║
║CDDRV Dump IOs queued             ║    attached to the file server    ║
║CDDRV Error report                ║ Category:                         ║
║CDDRV Max Threads per Device      ║    Communications (Advanced)      ║
║CDDRV XError report               ║ Current Value:                    ║
║Console Display Watchdog Logouts  ║    4 mins 56.6 secs               ║
║▓Delay Before First Watchdog Packet▓║ Limits:                         ║
║Delay Between Watchdog Packets    ║    15.6 secs To 20 mins 52.3 secs ║
║Directory Cache Allocation Wait Time║                                 ║
║Directory Cache Buffer NonReferenced D║ Special Notes:                 ║
║Dirty Directory Cache Delay Time  ↓║                                   ║
╚══════════════════════════════════╝╚══════════════════════════════════╝
   General  Memory  Drivers  misC  Set  Resources  modUles  Io  stAts  sYsfiles
                    Press Ctrl for main menu
         F1-Help  F2-Server  F6-Freeze  F10-Commands  Esc-Main Menu
```

Figure 6.6 Using the Frye Utilities NetWare Management program to obtain specific information on a server setable parameter

parameter. Although a detailed description of every server setable parameter is beyond the scope of this book you should periodically adjust these parameters, even when not experiencing any noticeable server problems. This is because the adjustment of many of those parameters can be used to enhance server performance, providing you with a tool for server tuning.

6.2 WORKSTATION OBSERVATION

In this section I turn my attention to observing NOS information relevant to client workstations. In doing so I will use the Frye Utilities NetWare Management and Node Tracker programs to observe certain activities. Although the title of this section is 'Workstation observation', certain key workstation parameters are actually stored on the file server while other parameters, such as the use of IPX and SPX, should be examined on both the workstation and the file server to isolate NetWare transmission problems. Therefore, when appropriate, I will examine certain network operating system parameters on both the client and the server in this section, in spite of its title.

There are several common workstation access problems that can be isolated through the use of NetWare's SYSCON utility program or the Frye Utilities NetWare Management program. Since the use of the latter many times results in a display that replaces two or more SYSCON displays, I will use the Frye Computer Systems' NetWare Management program to illustrate how you can examine certain network parameters to isolate the cause of common workstation network operating system related problems.

6.2.1 Network access

Figure 6.7 illustrates the NetWare Management General Information display for the user GXHELD. Many times the inability of a user to access the network can be traced to a NOS parameter

```
The Frye Utilities - NetWare Management V2.00B    December 2, 1994 10:42:06am
             26 users on MDPC-1, up 11 days 12 hrs 7 mins 11 secs
┌──────Users──────┐  ┌──────────────General Information──────────────┐
│ASYNCSVR        ↑│  │User Name: GXHELD                               │
│BRPEOPLE         │  │Full Name: Gilbert Held                         │
│CCAARON          │  │User ID: B000001                                │
│CLCHEEK          │  │Date of Last Login: December 2, 1994  10:15:30am│
│CO-OP            │  │Currently Logged In: Yes, at 1 station          │
│CONT             │  │Console Operator: Yes                           │
│COSTELLO         │  │Maximum Connections: 2                          │
│CWGOODRO         │  │Account Balance: 999,999                        │
│DCGUEST          │  │Credit Limit: Unlimited                         │
│ELPANCON         │  │Maximum Server Disk Space: See Disk screen      │
│EXMCDANI         │  │Account Disabled: No                            │
│FRED             │  │Date Account Expires: N/A                       │
│TTWARD           │  │Minimum Password Length: 5                      │
│FXRED            │  │Unique Password Required: No                    │
│GATEWAY          │  │Allow Password Change: Yes                      │
│GKWRIGHT         │  │Force Password Change: Yes                      │
│GUEST            │  │  Days Between Changes: 365 Expiration Date: 9/15/96│
│GXHELD          ↓│  │  Grace Logins Allowed: 6   Remaining: 6        │
└─────────────────┘  └───────────────────────────────────────────────┘
Info  Groups  Security  Managers  managEes  Login  Restrict  Pcon  Trustee  Disk
                         Press Ctrl for main menu
   F1-Help  F2-Server  F6-Freeze  F10-Commands  Ins  Del  Enter  Esc-Main Menu
```

Figure 6.7   The Frye Utilities NetWare Management General Information display or NetWare's SYSCON utility program can be used to determine many problems associated with the inability of a user to access a file server

setting. Thus, the use of the General Information display screen or a similar display may facilitate determining the cause of such problems and provide you with information required to initiate corrective action. In addition, the General Information display can provide other information that may be useful in isolating other problems.

In Figure 6.7 note that the Account Disabled entry indicates whether the supervisor or a person with supervisory rights previously disabled the selected user account. This is one of several entries in the General Information display that can shed light upon the inability of a user to log onto a file server. If your installation uses NetWare's accounting feature the Account Balance and Credit Limit entries should be examined. The Account Balance indicates the 'funds' available to the user for expenditure based upon connect time, server requests and disk usage. The Credit Limit entry indicates the amount of money the user can owe prior to losing access to the file server.

Other entries on the General Information display that can indicate the reason for a network user's inability to log onto a file server include the date the account expires, grace logins allowed and grace logins remaining. Here the term 'grace logins' refers to the number of times a user can log in after the password expired.

6.2.2 Time of day restrictions

Although the display shown in Figure 6.7 can be used to determine the cause of several problems associated with a user's inability to access a server, the display is not all-inclusive. NetWare supports time of day access restrictions. Thus, a user may have a valid account but not be able to log into the server due to previously established time of day restrictions. To determine if such restrictions are the cause of a user's login problem, you can use SYSCON or the Frye NetWare Management Restrictions display to view the restrictions associated with a user. Figure 6.8 illustrates the Frye Utilities NetWare Management Restrictions display. In this example there are no restrictions associated with the network user GXHELD.

6.2.3 Node configuration

A frequent problem associated with the use of a network operating system is the relationship between LAN hardware

```
The Frye Utilities - NetWare Management V2.00B     December 2, 1994 10:44:03am
          26 users on MDPC-1, up 11 days 12 hrs 9 mins 56 secs
┌══ Users ══╗┌════════════════════ Restrictions ════════════════════┐
│ASYNCSVR    ↑│              Allowed Login Times
│BRPEOPLE     │     1--------AM---------1-1-1--------PM----------1-1-
│CCAARON      │     2-1-2-3-4-5-6-7-8-9-0-1-2-1-2-3-4-5-6-7-8-9-0-1-
│CLCHEEK      │ Sun *************************************************
│CO-OP        │ Mon *************************************************
│CONT         │ Tue *************************************************
│COSTELLO     │ Wed *************************************************
│CWGOODRO     │ Thu *************************************************
│DCGUEST      │ Fri *************************************************
│ELPANCOA     │ Sat *************************************************
│EXMCDANI     │
│FRED         │              Allowed Login Stations
│FTWARD       │     Network:Node              Network:Node
│FXRED        │     No restrictions defined
│GATEWAY      │
│GKWRIGHT     │
│GUEST        │
│GXHELD      ↓│
└═════════════┘└═══════════════════════════════════════════════════┘
Info  Groups  Security  Managers  managEes  Login  Restrict  Pcon  Trustee  Disk
                       Press Ctrl for main menu
          F1-Help  F2-Server  F6-Freeze  F10 Commands  Enter  Esc-Main Menu
```

Figure 6.8 Viewing time of day restrictions can indicate why a user with a valid account cannot access a server

and software modules operating on a workstation. In my examination of the configuration of network nodes as well as NetWare IPX and SPX statistics, I will use Frye Computer Systems' Node Tracker program. Node Tracker is a separate program module which can be integrated into the Frye Utilities for Networks suite of pro-grams. Node Tracker was developed to provide network users with information primarily focused upon workstations or nodes to include network servers. Information provided by Node Tracker includes the display of node configurations, IPX, SPX and Shell statistics and the generation of a number of reports that provide information on packet level statistics for workstations, bridges and file servers. In addition, you can use Node Tracker to identify the versions of certain network and workstation software operating on each computer attached to a network.

Figure 6.9 illustrates the initial Node Tracker Node Configuration display with the highlighted bar on the left portion of the screen positioned over the top entry. Here the prefix and suffix

```
The Frye Utilities - Node Tracker V2.00A          December 2, 1994 10:59:46am
                          Current Server: MDPC-1
┌─── Nodes ───┐┌──────────────── Node Configuration ──────────View All┐
│----00000001----││Logical Nodes - All Unique Node IDs                    │
│0000007E41A1 FS ││Physical Nodes - RT/FS 1st LAN Node IDs + All WS Node IDs│
│0000007E41A2 FS ││                                                        │
│00008371A4C2 WS ││Logical Nodes      All Networks    Network 00000001     │
│00008371A787 FS ││     RT Nodes:          0                     0         │
│00008371D51D FS ││     FS Nodes:         61                    11         │
│00008371D6A6 FS ││     WS Nodes:        311                    39         │
│00008371D78F FS ││      Total:          372                    50         │
│0000837493F7 WS ││Physical Nodes     All Networks    Network 00000001     │
│0000837C697E FS ││     RT Nodes:          0                     0         │
│0000F61631FD FS ││     FS Nodes:         29                    11         │
│0001FA0004DC FS ││     WS Nodes:        311                    39         │
│08005A0A7D6E WS ││      Total:          340                    50         │
│08005A0A948E WS ││                                                        │
│08005A0A981E WS ││Last Mapping Type:         All Networks (34 Mapped)     │
│08005A0AA3C6 WS ││Licensed Physical Nodes:              50                │
│08005A0AA3D1 WS ││                                                        │
│08005A0AA42E WS ↓││Need Additional Server Licenses To View All Mapped Nodes│
└─────────────┘└────────────────────────────────────────────────────────┘
  Config  Ipx  Spx  sheLl  sHelldriver  shellTable  Router  routerDriver
                         Press Ctrl for main menu
       F1-Help F2-Server F4-Print F6-Freeze F8-Map F10-Cmds Esc-Menu
```

Figure 6.9   Initial display of Node Tracker Node Configuration screen

dashes indicate the network to which the file server is connected. By moving the highlighted bar downward over a specific node you can display specific information about the configuration of the node. That information includes the network adapter address, network user name, the versions of IPX, SPX, and the NetWare Shell, the version of the Operating System, and LAN board configuration information. Concerning the LAN board configuration, information displayed will include the LAN program being used on the node and, if applicable, the presence of such dual stack software as ODI and NDIS.

Figure 6.10 illustrates the Node Configuration display for a specific workstation node. Many times a glance at this screen can identify possible incompatibilities between different software modules or between software modules and a specific type of LAN adapter card. Although Figure 6.10 does not indicate the recognition of the LAN board, Node Tracker can often identify the specific type of adapter card. This information can be extremely helpful when compared against a list of known incompatibilities between hardware and software products. In addition, by

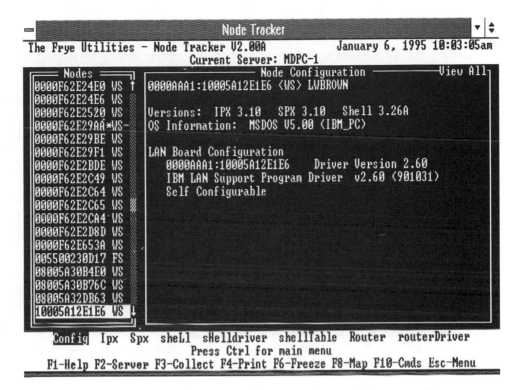

Figure 6.10 Examining the node configuration for a specific workstation

comparing the configuration of a workstation that has no reported problems to the configuration of a workstation whose user reports an initialization or operational problem, you may be able to rapidly note a problem resulting from incompatible software releases that can be easily corrected.

6.2.4 IPX statistics

One of the key features of Node Tracker is its display of a variety of statistics for selected nodes, ranging from workstations to bridges and file servers. Figure 6.11 illustrates the Node Tracker IPX Statistics display screen for a selected workstation. Node Tracker displays a total of 14 IPX related items, ranging from the length of time IPX was loaded through the number of open socket failures. In this section I will examine some of the IPX statistics tracked by the program and how they can provide assistance in troubleshooting certain types of network problems.

```
The Frye Utilities - Node Tracker V2.00A        January 6, 1995 11:07:40am
                          Current Server: MDPC-1
 ═══ Nodes ═══╗ ──────────── IPX Statistics ──────────Uiew All┐
----00000100----↑ 0000AAA1:0000F62E29AA <WS> GXHELD
0020AF3E1D64 WS
----0000AAA1---- Time Since IPX Loaded          1 hr 17 mins 45.3 secs
0000F62E23D4 WS ▌Packets Received                           55,450
0000F62E2401 WS  Packets Transmitted                        51,416
0000F62E24E0 WS  Packets Lost (No ECBs)                      3,950
0000F62E24E6 WS  Route Not Found Errors                          0
0000F62E2520 WS
0000F62E29AA*WS  Listen ECBs Posted                         51,112
0000F62E29BE WS  Malformed ECBs                                  0
0000F62E29F1 WS  ECBs Could Not Be Cancelled                     0
0000F62E2BDE WS
0000F62E2C49 WS  AES Events                                471,139
0000F62E2C64 WS  Postponed AES Events                            3
0000F62E2C65 WS
0000F62E2CA4 WS  Maximum Possible Sockets                       20
0000F62E2D8D WS  Peak Open Sockets                               9
0000F62E653A WS ↓ Open Socket Failures                          0

  Config  Ipx  Spx  sheLl  sHelldriver  shellTable  Router  routerDriver
                        Press Ctrl for main menu
       F1-Help F2-Server F3-Collect F4-Print F6-Freeze F8-Map F10-Cmds Esc-Menu
```

Figure 6.11   Examining a workstation's IPX statistics

Packets Lost

The Packets Lost entry indicates the number of times a packet arrived at the node but IPX could not supply a receive Event Control Block (ECB) to service the packet. Consequently the packet was lost.

Lost packets are a common occurrence when a workstation's processor or disk is unable to keep up with a sequence of received packets. Only if the lost packet count exceeds 10 percent of the total number of received packets should you consider probing deeper to determine if a faster processor or enhanced disk system is required for the application or mixture of applications being executed. A more serious error is a Route Not Found error.

Route Not Found

A Route Not Found error value indicates how many times IPX attempted to send a packet but could not find a route to the specified address. Common causes for a Route Not Found include a cabling problem or the failure of a server performing routing or of a router.

Event Control Blocks

The Listen ECBs Posted entry denotes the number of times programs operating on the node provided a listen ECB to IPX. In comparison, the Malformed ECBs entry indicates the number of times a defective ECB was passed to IPX by an application program. Theoretically this should never happen and a value for this parameter indicates either an application program problem or a problem in the NetWare shell. The third ECB entry, ECBs Could Not Be Cancelled, indicates how many times IPX could not cancel an Event Control Block. If the workstation commences a file service request which is aborted by a program prior to transmission the result is a canceled ECB. If IPX attempted to cancel an ECB that required cancellation an entry value could indicate that the request came too late. Thus, a small number for this parameter would not be a cause for alarm.

Asynchronous Event Scheduler

An Asynchronous Event Scheduler (AES) is a component of NetWare which is used to schedule events. Thus, the AES Events entry simply indicates the number of times AES was used to schedule a function to happen on either a workstation or server. In comparison, the Postponed AES Events entry indicates how many times IPX was too busy doing something else and could not act upon the event, requiring it to be processed later than expected. A small number of Postponed AES Events can normally be expected. As this number increases it indicates a higher level of network processing which may require a processor upgrade.

Sockets

In examining the last group of entries in Figure 6.11 I should again review the term socket. A socket represents the address of a process within a node. For example, service advertising (how a server broadcasts its location to other servers on a LAN), file service and routing information represent three processes on a file server that would have socket addresses. The Maximum Possible Sockets entry indicates the number of IPX sockets that can be open at one time. On a workstation this value is configurable through the use of an IPX SOCKETS statement in the SHELL.CFG file. On a server the operating system will allocate additional space for sockets on an as-required basis. However, if the server is unable to allocate a socket when needed this will result in an open socket failure. Here the Open Socket Failures entry indicates the number of times a NetWare file server or NetWare shell operating on a workstation attempted to open an IPX socket and failed. This should only happen when the Maximum Possible Sockets value is reached. For a workstation you can modify the SHELL.CFG file to alleviate this problem. For a file server additional memory may be required to alleviate this problem.

6.2.5 SPX statistics

Unlike IPX, SPX is a connection oriented guaranteed delivery protocol. This protocol is used by NetWare for running RCONSOLE where each keystroke must be received exactly as sent as well as by many third-party programs. By examining SPX statistics for both workstations and servers you may be able to isolate the cause of a variety of problems.

Bad Send Packet Requests

Figure 6.12 illustrates the Node Tracker SPX Statistics screen. Here the Bad Send Packet Requests entry indicates the number of times an invalid request to transmit a packet was passed to SPX. Typically, a bad send packet request results from the connection ID passed to SPX not representing the ID of a currently valid connection or an SPX header containing invalid information. When this error occurs it normally indicates a problem with a NetWare Loadable Module or an application on a node.

Send Packet Failures

The Send Packet Failures entry indicates how many times SPX was asked to send a packet but could not deliver the packet to the destination location. A value for this parameter can indicate the failure at the destination, a network wiring problem or the failure of a router or server performing routing.

```
The Frye Utilities - Node Tracker V2.00A        January 6, 1995 11:08:20am
                         Current Server: MDPC-1
┌══ Nodes ══┐┌══════════ SPX Statistics ══════════┐─View All┐
│----00000100----↑│0000AAA1:0000F62E29AA <WS> GXHELD
│0020AF3E1D64 WS  │
│----0000AAA1----│Send Packet Requests                        228
│0000F62E23D4 WS▐│Bad Send Packet Requests                      0
│0000F62E2401 WS  │Send Packet Failures                          0
│0000F62E24E0 WS  │No Remote Listen ECBs                         25
│0000F62E24E6 WS  │Listen Packet Requests                       351
│0000F62E2520 WS  │Malformed Listen ECBs                          0
│0000F62E29AA*WS  │Packets Received                             589
│0000F62E29BE WS  │Bad Packets Received                           1
│0000F62E29F1 WS  │Duplicate Packets Received                     0
│0000F62E2BDE WS  │No Listen ECBs                                  0
│0000F62E2C49 WS  │Maximum Possible Connections                  15
│0000F62E2C64 WS  │Peak Open Connections                          2
│0000F62E2C65 WS  │Aborted Connections                            0
│0000F62E2CA4 WS  │Watchdog Aborted Connections                   2
│0000F62E2D8D WS  │Establish Connections:  Requested  40  Failed  0
│0000F62E653A WS ↓│Listen For Connections: Requested   3  Failed  0
└═══════════┘└═══════════════════════════════════┘
   Config  Ipx  Spx  sheLl  sHelldriver  shellTable  Router  routerDriver
                        Press Ctrl for main menu
     F1-Help F2-Server F3-Collect F4-Print F6-Freeze F8-Map F10-Cmds Esc-Menu
```

Figure 6.12   Examining a workstation's SPX statistics

Event Control Blocks

The No Remote Listen ECBs entry indicates how many times SPX
tried to send a packet that was not received at the distant end.
This entry denotes that the computer at the other end of the
connection is falling behind in processing incoming information.

A Malformed Listen ECBs entry indicates the number of times
an application passed a defective listen ECB to SPX. Any value for
this parameter indicates a problem with an application.

Packets received

The Bad Packets Received entry indicates the number of defective
packets received by SPX, while Duplicate Packets Received
indicates that a packet was not acknowledged prior to the
packet timeout value expiring and a second packet was
transmitted and received. Since collisions on Ethernet or heavy

traffic on Token-Ring networks can result in delays that cause timeouts, a small number of duplicate packets received is no cause for alarm.

Connections

The largest number of SPX connections a node can establish is governed by an entry in the SHELL.CFG file on a workstation. In comparison, NetWare's operating system will allow the server to allocate additional space for SPX connections on a dynamic basis. The four connection entries in the SPX Statistics screen denote the maximum possible connections (for a workstation only), peak connections that occurred, aborted connections and watchdog aborted connections. The Aborted Connections entry indicates how many times an application aborted SPX connections, while the Watchdog Aborted Connections entry indicates the number of times a timer expired and SPX was aborted due to a lack of response from the distant end.

The remaining entries in Figure 6.12 indicate how many times programs operating on the node requested SPX to establish a connection to another node or to listen for a connection as well as the number of times each request failed. A value for Establish Connections Failed means that either the destination is not present on the network or cannot respond. Concerning the latter, a computer crash or reaching the limit on the maximum connections are reasons why no response may be received to an establish connection request. A value for Listen For Connections Failed indicates how many times programs on the node asked SPX to listen for a connection and failed because the node reached its limit of maximum possible connections.

6.2.6 Shell statistics

The workstation shell is the component of NetWare that interprets commands entered by the user, passes non-network commands to the operating system used by the workstation and processes and passes network commands to IPX and SPX for transmission onto the network. Thus, examining shell statistics provides the potential for denoting several types of network operating system related problems.

Figure 6.13 illustrates the Node Tracker Shell Statistics display for a selected workstation. The Shell Requests entry denotes the number of requests received by the shell to perform such

```
 The Frye Utilities - Node Tracker V2.00A        January 6, 1995 11:08:48am
                         Current Server: MDPC-1
 ┌══ Nodes ══┐    ┌═══════════ Shell Statistics ═══════════─View All┐
 │----00000100----↑│ 0000AAA1:0000F62E29AA <WS> GXHELD              │
 │0020AF3E1D64 WS  │                                                │
 │----0000AAA1---- │ Shell Requests                          51,797 │
 │0000F62E23D4 WS ▓│ Operator Aborts/Retries                    0/0 │
 │0000F62E2401 WS  │ Timeout Errors                               0 │
 │0000F62E24E0 WS  │ Write Errors                                 0 │
 │0000F62E24E6 WS  │ Invalid Reply Header Errors                  0 │
 │0000F62E2520 WS  │ Invalid Slot Errors                          0 │
 │0000F62E29AA*WS  │ Invalid Sequence Number Errors               0 │
 │0000F62E29BE WS  │ Packet Receiving Errors                      0 │
 │0000F62E29F1 WS  │ No Router Found Errors                       0 │
 │0000F62E2BDE WS  │ Being Processed Replies                      0 │
 │0000F62E2C49 WS  │ Invalid Server Slot Errors                   0 │
 │0000F62E2C64 WS  │ Cannot Find Route Errors                     0 │
 │0000F62E2CG5 WS  │ No Slots Available Errors                    0 │
 │0000F62E2CA4 WS  │ Network Gone Errors                          0 │
 │0000F62E2D8D WS  │ Server Down Errors                           0 │
 │0000F62E653A WS ↓│ Unknown Errors                               0 │
 └──────────────┘  └──────────────────────────────────────────────┘
     Config  Ipx  Spx  sheLl  sHelldriver  shellTable  Router  routerDriver
                        Press Ctrl fur main menu
     F1-Help F2-Server F3-Collect F4-Print F6-Freeze F8-Map F10-Cmds Esc-Menu
```

Figure 6.13   Using Node Tracker to examine the shell statistics for a network user

operations as reading and writing file data, opening and closing a
network file and similar network related operations. By itself this
entry simply denotes the activity of the shell. In attempting to
isolate the cause of network problems you would focus your
attention upon the error entries in the Shell Statistics display.

Timeout Errors

The Timeout Errors entry indicates the number of times the shell
initiated a request but did not receive a reply within the expected
time. Each timeout normally results in the shell transmitting a
subsequent request. A large number of timeout errors can indicate
a heavily utilized server, a heavily utilized network, or both.

Write Errors

The Write Errors entry indicates the number of times the shell
could not send a request to a file server. An entry indicates that

the request could not be sent after all permitted retries had occurred and results in a 'Network Error' message being displayed at the workstation. The crash of a file server or occurrence of a network problem after login to a server can result in a write error.

Invalid packets, receive and route errors

The three invalid errors denote a bad packet header, invalid connection number or a packet out of sequence. A Packet Receiving Errors entry normally indicates an IPX receiving error. This usually occurs when data is received faster that the workstation can process received information. The No Router Found Errors entry indicates the number of times the shell was unable to find a route for a packet. When a network error occurs the shell will attempt to reroute packets if the user selects a Retry option.

No Slots Available

Although most of the other error indicators in Figure 6.13 are self-explanatory, one deserves special mention. That error indicator is the No Slots Available Errors entry. This error entry indicates the number of times the workstation shell attempted to connect to a server but could not do so as the server had reached its connection limit. If this happens on a regular basis it indicates that you should consider upgrading to a version of NetWare that supports more users or adding an additional file server to your network.

Although NetWare utility programs, Frye Computer Systems' products and other third-party products can be used to display other network operating system parameters, the previously described parameters may be sufficient to diagnose the cause of the vast majority of NOS related problems. Of course, if these displays do not indicate the reason for a particular network operating system problem, you would then continue your use of one or more programs in an attempt to isolate its cause. In doing so the important thing to note is that the use of NetWare's built-in utility programs, Frye Computer's products or another vendor's product can provide you with an insight to the cause of one or more NOS problems, permitting you to initiate appropriate corrective actions.

FAULT AND PERFORMANCE MANAGEMENT WITH SNMP AND RMON

Testing and troubleshooting LANs as noted so far in previous chapters is a complex task, requiring a detailed methodology during which you examine the flow of data at various OSI Reference Model layers. From a network management viewpoint a LAN is no different than a WAN, requiring a series of efforts that fall into well-defined network management areas. Those areas include accounting, configuration, fault, performance and security management. If we consider the testing and troubleshooting aspects of a LAN or WAN, we are primarily concerned with fault and performance management areas. Fortunately, a set of standardized network management tools are available to assist us with those two network management areas. Those tools are the Simple Network Management Protocol (SNMP) and the Remote Monitoring (RMON) Management Information Base (MID). Through the use of those tools you may be able to detect and diagnose the cause of network problems as well as determine the reason behind a level of performance not commensurate with network user expectations. In addition, both SNMP and RMON are now included in many network management platforms which provide a standardized method for managing products produced by different vendors. Those network management platforms expand the use of SNMP and RMON to include accounting, configuration and security management, topics which I will briefly mention but which are beyond the scope of this book.

7.1 SNMP

The Simple Network Management Protocol (SNMP) represents a network management protocol which primarily uses the Transmission Control Protocol (TCP) transport mechanism to communicate, although it was designed to be transport protocol independent. This means it can be implemented on connection oriented protocols, such as HDLC, or on common LAN connectionless oriented protocols. The most common SNMP transport protocol is the TCP/IP User Datagram Protocol (UDP), with SNMP receiving on port 161 resulting in transmission on port 162 and vice versa. Originally intended as a mechanism to manage TCP/IP and Ethernet gateways connected to the Internet, this versatile network management application protocol has been considerably extended through an architecture which permits new products to be managed. Today, bridges, routers and individual workstations on local and geographically separated Token-Ring and Ethernet LANs as well as FDDI networks, CSUs and other devices can be managed from a central network management station. As I discuss the components of SNMP and their interrelationship the use of this application as a tool for fault and performance management applications will become apparent.

7.1.1 Architecture

SNMP consists of three basic components – an agent, a manager and a database queried by an agent.

The agent

The agent represents a program contained in either RAM or ROM in a managed network device. That managed network device can be a bridge, router, workstation network adapter card or minicomputer or host computer, or another device connected to a network. Each agent stores certain predefined management information and responds to the manager's request by transmitting the requested information.

The manager

The manager is a software program which operates on a network management platform. That platform includes other software applications which typically hide the complexities of SNMP and RMON from the user via a graphic user interface (GUI). The collection of hardware and software represents the network management station which monitors and controls agents.

The MIB

The third component of SNMP is the Management Information Base (MIB). The MIB conforms to a standard referred to as the Structure of Management Information (SMI) established for TCP/IP networks and can consist of statistical, status and configuration information. Unlike a conventional database stored on a computer file, a MIB can represent a combination of ROM and RAM memory locations, hardware DIP switch settings or files.

Component relationship

Figure 7.1 illustrates the relationship between the three SNMP components. Although I used an Ethernet bus based topology to illustrate the relationship between SNMP components, the devices being managed can be on a different type of LAN or on a local area network geographically separated from the network where the NMS resides.

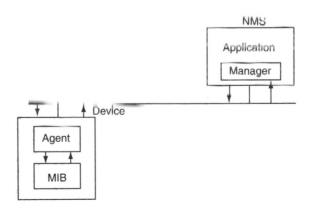

MIB = Management Information Base
NMS = Network Management System

Figure 7.1   SNMP component relationship

7.1.2 Operation

The ability to standardize network management was obtained by the standardization of the MIB and protocol commands. Concerning the MIB, in actuality a tree structure of objects is standardized to include the name, attributes and set of operations that can be performed on each object. Included within the MIB object structure is the ability to support undefined subtrees. The ability to add subtrees permits the MIB to be extended to vendor-specific product features that require management, such as the initialization of a bridge via the downloading of software or the transfer of communications to a backup circuit. Any enterprise, to include hardware and software vendors, colleges and universities and government agencies, can define its own management parameters and request their registration via the assignment of a subtree from the Internet Activities Board. Once registered, other vendors can then design their NMS to use SNMP commands to operate upon the objects in the registered subtree.

7.1.3 Commands

The first version of SNMP specified five types of commands or verbs, commonly referred to as Protocol Data Units (PDUs). Under SNMP Version 2 (SNMPv2) there were a few slight changes to the manner by which several previously defined commands operate as well as the addition of two new commands. Since an appreciation of SNMPv2 commands is best explained by first discussing the original SNMP commands I will first explain the operation of the original set of SNMP commands.

Table 7.1 lists SNMP commands and indicates their applicability to a particular version of the protocol. The Get-Request command is used to request the values of one or more MIB variables, while the Get-Next-Request is used to read values from the MIB. The latter command can be used to 'walk through' the entries in a MIB, one variable at a time. That is, a Get-Request command would be used to request the first variable in the MIB or a variable at a predefined location. Then, a series of Get-Next-Request commands could be issued to sequentially retrieve the remaining MIB variables.

A third command which is associated with the Get-Request and Get-Next-Request commands is the Get-Response command. That command is returned to answer the Get-Request and Get-Next-Request commands. In addition, the Get-Response command is returned to answer a Set-Request command described next.

Table 7.1 SNMP commands

Command	Applicability
Get-Request	SNMPv1 and SNMPv2[a]
Get-Next-Request	SNMPv1 and SNMPv2[a]
Set-Request	SNMPv1 and SNMPv2[a]
Get-Response	SNMPv1 and SNMPv2[a]
Trap	SNMPv1 and SNMPv2
Inform-Request	SNMPv2
Get-Bulk-Request	SNMPv2

[a] Enhanced under SNMPv2.

The Set-Request command is used by a manager to update one or more MIB values. Those values can represent the resetting of statistics or equipment configuration parameters. Owing to the original SNMP's lack of security, it became possible for unauthorized persons to change configuration parameters that could corrupt network operations. As a result, a number of equipment vendors elected not to support the Set-Request command within their SNMP agent implementation. Under SNMPv2 the addition of a mechanism to authenticate messages as well as protect the contents of messages alleviated the potentially improper use of the Set-Request command.

The fifth command supported by the original version of SNMP was an alert command formerly known as a Trap. The Trap is the only unsolicited command that an agent can send to a manager and is used to indicate a predefined significant event, such as a communications line failure or the cold or warm boot of hardware.

Under SNMPv2 several enhancements were incorporated into the 'get' commands and two new commands were added. One of the problems associated with SNMPv1 was the fact that if any variable in a list of variables to be retrieved could not be retrieved the entire get operation would fail and no data was returned. SNMPv2 permits an agent to process good variables in a request and return their values while filling the value field of 'bad' variables with a special problem reporting value. The two new commands added to SNMPv2 are Inform-Request and Get-Bulk-Request.

Inform-Request permits one manager to report information to another manager, permitting a hierarchy of network management stations to be established. The Get-Bulk-Request command permits a manager to retrieve a larger number of MIB variables than was possible under SNMPv1, thereby reducing the dataflow between manager and agent while increasing operating efficiency.

7.2 SNMP MANAGEMENT

Although the agent and manager are important components of SNMP, it is the MIB which governs your ability to obtain an insight into LAN operations. Thus, in this section I will discuss and describe two common LAN MIBs. First I will examine the

Table 7.2 Ethernet MIB statistics

Statistics counter	Description
Alignment Errors	A count of frames that are not an integral number of octets in length and do not pass the FCS check.
FCS Errors	A count of frames that are an integral number of octets in length but do not pass the FCS check.
Single Collision Frames	A count of successfully transmitted frames for which transmission was inhibited by exactly one collision.
Multiple Collision Frames	A count of successfully transmitted frames for which transmission was blocked by more than one collision.
SQE Test Errors	A count of the number of times an SQE test error message is generated.
Deferred Transmissions	A count of frames for which the first transmission attempt is delayed because the medium was busy.
Late Collisions	A count of the number of times a collision is detected later than 512 bit-times into the transmission of a frame.
Excessive Collisions	A count of the number of frames for which transmission fails due to excessive collisions.
Internal MAC Transmit Errors	A count of frames for which transmission fails due to an internal MAC sublayer transmit error.
Carrier Sense Errors	A count of the number of times the carrier sense condition was lost or never asserted when attempting to transmit a frame.
Frame Too Long	A count of frames received whose length exceed the maximum permitted frame size.
Internal MAC Receive Errors	A count of frames for which reception fails due to an internal MAC sublayer receive error.

Ethernet MIB to include statistics computed and optional chip set statistics. This will be followed by an examination of the Token-Ring MIB.

7.2.1 The Ethernet MIB

RFC 1650 dated August 1994 resulted in the definition of managed objects for Ethernet-like interfaces using SNMPv2. The MIB defined in the referenced RFC updates RFC 1398 as well as respecifies the RFC 1398 MIB so that it is compliant with SNMPv2 and SNMPv1. Under RFC 1650 twelve 32-bit counters are used to record statistics for a particular interface, while five optional statistics for an Ethernet chip set are defined. Table 7.2 lists the Ethernet MIB statistics as well as provides a brief description of each statistics counter. Table 7.3 provides similar information for the optional Ethernet chip set MIB statistics.

By examining the types of Ethernet statistics counted by SNMP you can obtain an appreciation for the ability of this network management tool to provide assistance with respect to isolating and resolving network problems. Although most of the entries in Tables 7.2 and 7.3 are appropriately described, the late collisions counter deserves a degree of elaboration. At a 10 Mbps operating rate 512 bit-times corresponds to 51.2 microseconds, which results in the detection of a collision beyond 64 octets into the transmission. When this situation occurs the late collision is also counted as a generic collision and is then included in other appropriate collision related statistics, such as excessive collisions.

Table 7.3 Optional Ethernet Chip Set Statistics

Collision Table	A collection of collision histograms for a particular set of interfaces.
Collision Entry	A cell in the histogram of per-frame collisions for a particular interface.
Collision Count	The number of per-frame media collisions for which a particular collision histogram cell represents the frequency on a particular interface.
Collision Frequencies	A count of individual MAC frames for which transmission occurs after the frame experienced exactly the number of collisions in the associated collision count object.

7.2.2 The Token-Ring MIB

Similar to Ethernet, SNMP defines a MIB for a Token-Ring interface. This MIB is defined in RFC 1231 and includes several mandatory tables and an optional table. Mandatory tables include Token-Ring configuration parameters and a table of statistics and error counters. The option table defined in RFC 1231 consists of timer values which govern network management on the ring by ring stations.

Table 7.4 provides an overview of the contents of the Token-Ring interface table. This table stores configuration and status information applicable to a Token-Ring interface to include the status of the ring, its operating speed, whether the interface is joining or leaving the ring and other information concerning what is occurring at the interface.

Table 7.5 lists the values associated with the object types listed in Table 7.4 as well as providing a brief description of the event associated with each object type value. The Commands object type values are integer values which reference the particular

Table 7.4 Token-Ring interface table

Object managed	Description
Index	Identifies the 802.5 interface for which the entry contains management information.
Commands	Used to set the state of the station.
Ring Status	The current interface status which can be used to diagnose problems after a station is added to a ring.
Ring State	The current interface state with respect to a station entering or leaving the ring.
Ring Open Status	Indicates the success or reason for failure of the station's most recent attempt to enter the ring.
Ring Speed	The operating rate of the ring.
Up Stream	The MAC address of the upstream neighbor station in the ring.
Active Monitor Participate	Returns information concerning whether or not the interface will participate in the active monitor selection process.
Functional	Controls the bit mask of all Token-Ring functional addresses for which the interface accepts frames.

Table 7.5   Token-Ring MIB status and parameters values

Object type and values	Description
Commands:	
1 (no-op)	No effect upon station
2 (open)	Station goes into open state and joins ring
3 (reset)	Station goes into a reset state
4 (close)	Station is removed from ring
Ring Status:	
0	No problems detected
32	Ring Recovery
64	Single Station
256	Remove Received
512	Reserved
1024	Auto-Removal Error
2048	Lobe Wire Fault
4096	Transmit Beacon
8192	Soft Error
16384	Hard Error
32768	Signal Loss
131072	No status, open not completed
Ring State:	
1	Opened
2	Closed
3	Opening
4	Closing
5	Open Failure
6	Ring Failure
Ring Open Status:	
1	No open attempt
2	Bad Parameter
3	Lobe Failed
4	Signal Loss
5	Insertion Timeout
6	Ring Failed
7	Beaconing
8	Duplicate MAC
9	Request Failed
10	Remove Received
11	Open
Ring Speed:	
1	Unknown
2	1 Mbps
3	4 Mbps
4	16 Mbps

Table 7.6   Token-Ring MIB statistics

Counter	Description
Line Errors	Counter incremented if there is a non-data bit (J or K symbol) between starting and ending delimiters of token or frame or an FCS error in the frame.
Burst Errors	Counter incremented when a station detects the absence of transitions for five half-bit timers.
AC Errors	Counter incremented when a station receives an Active Monitor Present (AMP) or Standby Monitor Present (SMP) frame in which A and C bits equal 0 and then receives another SMP frame with A and C bits equal to 0 without first receiving an AMP frame.
Abort Transmission Errors	Counter incremented when a station transmits an abort delimiter while transmitting.
Internal Errors	Counter incremented when a station recognizes an internal error.
Frame Errors	Counter incremented when a station is transmitting and its Return-to-Report (TRR) timer expires.
Receive Congestions	Counter incremented when a station recognizes a frame addressed to it but has no available buffer space, indicating the station is congested.
Frame Copied Errors	Counter incremented when a station recognizes a frame addressed to its address and detects the A bits set to 1, indicating a possible line hit or duplicate address.
Token Errors	Counter incremented when a station acting as an active monitor recognizes an error condition that requires the transmission of a token.
Soft Errors	Counter incremented when a Soft Error (those which are recoverable by the MAC layer protocols) occurs.
Hard Errors	Counter incremented when an immediately recoverable fatal error occurs. The Counter notes the number of times the interface is either transmitting or receiving beacon MAC frames.
Signal Loss	Counter incremented when the loss of signal condition is detected.
Transmit Beacons	Counter incremented when a beacon frame is transmitted.

Table 7.6 (*continued*)

Counter	Description
Recoveries	Counter incremented when a Claim Token MAC frame is transmitted or received after a Ring Purge MAC frame is received. This counter indicates the number of times the ring was purged and recovered back to a normal operating state.
Lobe Wires	Counter increments when an open or short circuit in the lobe data path is detected.
Removes	Counter incremented when a Remove Ring Station MAC frame request is received, resulting in a close state condition.
Singles	Counter incremented when the interface senses it is the only station on the ring.
Frequency Errors	Counter incremented when the interface detects that the frequency of the incoming signal differs from the expected frequency by more than the IEEE 802.5 standard.

command included in parentheses in Table 7.5. Access to the Command object is read–write, which enables a management station to control the state of a station.

The Ring Status object type is restricted to read-only access as this object defines the current interface status. By examining this object a NMS can determine a specific type of error. The Ring State object is also restricted to read-only access. This object type provides state information about opening (joining the ring) and closing (leaving the ring).

The Ring Open Status object type is also restricted to read-only access, providing information which indicates whether the last attempt to enter a ring was successful and, if not, why not. The Ring Speed object indicates the operating rate of the ring and has read–write access. This permits a management station to reset the speed if a station uses an adapter that was improperly configured.

I did not list the Up Stream, Active Monitor Participate and Functional object types from Table 7.4 in Table 7.5 as those object types, while included in the interface table, represent single table entries. The Up Stream object type is the MAC address of the upstream neighbor, while the Active Monitor Participate returns 1 for true and 2 for false depending on whether or not the station will participate in the Active Monitor selection process. The Functional object type is a bit mask for a

Table 7.7 Token-Ring Timer table objects

Object	Description
Return Repeat	The time-out value used to ensure the interface returns to its repeat state.
Timer Holding	The maximum period of time a station is permitted to transmit frames after capturing a token.
Timer Queue	The time-out value for queuing a Standby Monitor Present message for transmission after receiving an Active Monitor Present or Standby Monitor Present frame.
Valid Transmit	The time-out value used by the active monitor to detect the absence of valid transmissions.
Timer No Token	The time-out value used to detect a lost token.
Active Monitor	The time-out value used by the Active Monitor to generate Active Monitor Present frames.
Standby Monitor	The time-out value used by the standby monitors to ensure there is an active monitor on the ring.
Error Report	The time-out value which defines how often a station sends a Report Error frame to report the values in its error counters.
Beacon Transmit	The time-out value which defines how long a station continues beaconing prior to entering the bypass state.
Beacon Receive	The time-out value which determines how long a station will receive beacon frames from its downstream neighbor prior to entering the bypass state.

MAC address and is used to identify all functional addresses for the interface.

The Token-Ring statistics table provides a comprehensive count of error conditions that can be extremely useful in determining the cause of current problems or possibly evolving problems. Table 7.6 lists the Token-Ring statistics table counters as well as providing a brief description of the object tracked by the counter. In examining the entries in Table 7.6 it is important to review the contents of the Token-Ring frame's Ending Delimiter (ED) field whose contents govern several error conditions, such as Line Errors, AC Errors and Frame Copied Errors. Thus, you may wish to consider reviewing the Token-Ring frame operation information presented in Chapter 2 to obtain an appreciation for these error conditions.

The Token-Ring Timer table includes the values of many timers measured in units of 100-microsecond intervals. The timers are uniquely applicable to Token-Ring operations and as previously mentioned at the beginning of this section are an option to the Token-Ring MIB. Table 7.7 lists the Token-Ring Timer table entries as well as providing a brief description of each timer. Since the Token-Ring Timer table was designed to track the value of different timers required for Token-Ring operations, as you might expect access to each object is restricted to read-only.

7.3 RMON

Although SNMP can provide significant information about network attached devices, to do so it must poll public and private MIBs. While this action may not require a relatively broad section of bandwidth when occurring on a single LAN or LANs connected by local bridges, as soon as a network expands to encompass geographically separated networks connected by a WAN polling can represent a significant bandwidth problem. Recognizing this problem RMON was developed as a mechanism to support proactive monitoring of LAN traffic.

RMON was developed by the Internet Engineering Task Force (IETF) and became a standard in 1992 as RFC 1271 for Ethernet and later as RFC 1513 for Token-Ring. Under RFCs 1271 and 1513 RMON includes an 'Alarm Group' which enables thresholds to be set for critical network parameters. Then, when those thresholds are reached an alert will be automatically transmitted to the network management station.

An RMON agent can be either hardware or software based, operating on a computer connected to a LAN segment, a self-contained probe or built into another LAN device, such as a router. In addition to an Alarm Group RMON provides a standard set of MIBs which provide valuable network statistical information.

Through RMON you obtain a common platform from which you can monitor equipment from different vendors at the data link and physical layer. Hardware and software based RMON probes monitor all data packets transmitted and received, maintaining a historical record of events that can be used for fault diagnosis, performance tuning, and even network planning.

7.3.1 RMON groups

There are nine RMON groups considered to be generally common to both Ethernet and Token-Ring networks while a tenth group is only applicable to the latter network. Table 7.8 lists the ten RMON groups and includes a brief description or overview of the function of each group. While most of the MIB group objects in the first nine groups are applicable for the management of any type of network, some objects in different groups are only applicable to a particular type of LAN. For example, the Traffic Matrix Group provides statistics based upon pairs of nodes at the MAC layer, resulting in a count of packets and errors received and transmitted. Thus, the Traffic Matrix Group is very similar for both Ethernet and Token-Ring. In comparison, the Statistics Group varies considerably between Ethernet and Token-Ring

Table 7.8 Ethernet and Token-Ring RMON MIB groups

Common groups	Description
Statistics	Collects cumulative traffic and error statistics for the segment.
History	Collects and provides general traffic statistics based on user-defined sampling interval.
Host Table	Collects traffic statistics for each network node (device) in the table format.
Host Top N	Extends the host table by providing sorted host statistics based upon user-defined data selected, duration and number of devices (N).
Traffic Matrix	Collects amount of traffic and number of errors occurring between pairs of nodes at the MAC layer using a traffic matrix.
Alarms	Permits users to define thresholds and sampling intervals to generate alarms on any segment monitored by RMON agent.
Events	Creates entries in a log using packet matches and alarms. SNMP traps can be defined for any event for transmission to the NMS.
Filters	Permits capturing of packets that match a predefined criterion.
Packet Capture	Captures all packets or those meeting filtering criteria. Packets can be requested by the NMS and subsequently decoded.
Ring Station Statistics	Only applicable to Token-Ring LANs: captures ring station control, status information, order of stations on monitored rings, configuration and source routing data.

RMON MIB groups due to the key differences between the operation of each type of LAN which results in different access methods which require different methods of tracking.

In examining the groups listed in Table 7.8 I will defer a discussion of specific statistics maintained by Ethernet and Token-Ring RMON probes until later in this section. Doing so will facilitate a review of the use of the other groups common to Ethernet and Token-Ring RMON MIB groups.

History Group

The History Group provides historical views of the statistics collected by the Statistics Group. To do so, the History Group collects statistics based upon default or user-defined sampling intervals and bucket counters.

The RMON MIB has two defaults for trend analysis. The first provides 50 buckets or samples of 30-second sampling intervals over a period of 25 minutes. The second supports 50 buckets of 30-minute sampling intervals over a period of 25 hours. You can modify either default or add additional intervals to meet your specific requirement for historical analysis, varying the sample interval from one second to one hour.

Host Table Group

The Host Table Group maintains a series of traffic statistics in table form to include cumulative errors that represent a combination of all statistics error conditions. A host time table maintains the relative order by which each host was discovered by the agent. This feature assists in providing the management station with newly discovered addresses it is not yet aware of, reducing unnecessary SNMP polling traffic on the network.

Host Top N Group

This group extends the Host Table Group by providing sorted host statistics for N statistics. You can define data to be sorted and the duration of the study through the use of the network management station.

Host Top N counters maintain the statistics you select for study, while non-selected statistics over the same interval will not be available for later study. The actual number of studies you can invoke is limited by the resources of the RMON agent. The effect of the RMON agent maintaining the Host Top N counters is similar to the effect of the History and Host Table groups, reducing SNMP traffic as well as the processing load on the management station.

Traffic Matrix Group

The Traffic Matrix Group is used to store the amount of traffic and number of errors between pairs of nodes, with each node pair consisting of one source and one destination address. For each address pair the RMON MIB maintains counters for the number of packets, number of octets and error packets occurring between the node pair. Data generated by retrieving Traffic Matrix Group information can be extremely useful in attempting to determine if one or a few workstations are responsible for a majority of network traffic, if errors are primarily attributable to a specific workstation, and similar information that can significantly assist network managers and administrators in testing, troubleshooting and performance tuning operations.

Alarms Group

Through the use of the Alarms Group you can set thresholds which when reached generate an alarm. Both rising and falling thresholds can be set using either the absolute value of a statistic or its delta value. Here the latter can be used to provide notification of a rapid change in a monitored value which could indicate that a potential problem is about to occur. Since alarms are proactively generated without SNMP polling, once again SNMP traffic is reduced.

Events Group

The Events Group provides you with a mechanism to specify the number of events that can be stored in a probe and periodically transmitted to the network management station. Here the term event represents the occurrence of a trap condition. RFC 1157 specifies seven SNMP traps – link up, link down, warm start, cold start, authentication failure, Exterior Gateway Protocol (EGP) neighbor loss and enterprise specific. Three additional traps – rising threshold, falling threshold and packet match – are specified in the RMON MIB, resulting in up to ten distinct traps for which the Events Group can provide a notification of occurrence.

When a trap occurs the Events Group time stamps each event and adds a description of the event written by the manufacturer of the probe. This information is stored in a circular log in the probe, which can result in events becoming lost by overwriting unless they are periodically uploaded to the management station.

Filters Group

Through the use of the Filters Group you can define packets to be captured. RMON supports the use of AND and NOT operations and allows multiple filters to be combined through the use of the OR operator. By the use of one or more filters you can capture packets that meet a predefined address criterion, error condition, or another criterion that can assist your analysis of activity on a distant LAN segment.

Packet Capture Group

Through the Packet Capture Group you obtain the ability to create one or more capture buffers as well as to control recording of information into those buffers.

The actual placement of packets into a capture buffer is controlled by filters created through the use of the Filters Group. When a packet matches a filter it can be used to initiate a trigger to perform a trace, resulting in trace data filling a designated buffer. In comparison, the Packet Capture Group lets you assign matched filtered objects to one or more capture buffers and control whether trace buffers will wrap back to the beginning (circular buffer) and overwrite previously captured packets or stop when the buffer is full.

7.3.2 Ethernet statistics

The Ethernet Statistics Group contains statistics measured by a probe for each monitored Ethernet interface. Table 7.9 lists the Ethernet Statistics Group counters and provides a brief description of the contents of each counter.

Each of the RMON segment statistics listed in Table 7.9 is maintained in its own 32-bit cumulative counter. By examining certain error counter values you can obtain an insight into the

Table 7.9   Ethernet RMON segment stations

Counter	Description
Dropped Events	Number of events dropped due to a lack of resources.
Octets	The total number of octets of data received on the network to include FCS octets but not framing bits.
Packets	The total number of packets received.
Broadcast Packets	The total number of good broadcast packets received.
Multicast Packets	The total number of good multicast packets received.
CRC Alignment Errors	The total number of packets received with a length between 64 and 1518 bytes with either a bad FCS and either an integral or non-integral number of octets.
Undersized Packets	The total number of packets received that were less than 64 octets long.
Oversized Packets	The total number of packets received longer than 1518 octets not including framing bits but including the FCS.
Fragments	The total number of packets received that were less than 64 octets, excluding frame bits but including the FCS, and had a bad FCS.
Jabbers	The total number of packets received longer than 1518 bytes with a bad FCS.
Collisions	Total number of collisions detected.
Packets size distribution: 64 octets 65 to 127 octets 128 to 255 octets 256 to 511 octets 512 to 1023 octets 1024 to 1518 octets	Separate counters that provide the total number of packets in the indicated length ranges, excluding frame bits but including FCS octets.

potential cause of many network problems. For example, CRC alignment errors indicate a transmission problem which can result from improper cabling or electromagnetic interference. A series of undersized packets or oversized packets are typically caused by an improperly configured workstation, while a large number of collisions can indicate that the level of network traffic may require the LAN to be segmented.

Many network management systems will retrieve RMON statistics either on a user-defined polling schedule or on user demand to compute and present 'network health' statistics, in either a tabular or a graphic format. For example, a management station may use the packets counter and packets size distribution counters to provide a graph indicating the percentage distribution of packets by size. Since long packets primarily result from a file transfer or client–server response screen while packets of relatively short length are associated with interactive queries, this distribution provides you with an indication of the general activity occurring on the LAN. If, for example, the management station indicated that a relatively large percentage of packets were between 1024 and 1518 octets in length and users were complaining of poor LAN performance, the packet distribution would indicate that one or more network stations may be performing a significant amount of file transfer operations that are adversely affecting network performance.

7.3.3 Token-Ring extensions

As indicated in Chapter 2, a Token-Ring network includes many error detection facilities within its frame composition as well as the use of a series of MAC frames that control the configuration of a station and the propagation of station addresses from one neighbor to another, more formally referred to as neighbor notification. Recognizing the differences between Ethernet and Token-Ring, RFC 1513 which defined RMON for Token-Ring added media-specific objects applicable to Token-Ring networks that were referred to as Ring Station Statistics in Table 7.8. In actuality, the Ring Station Statistics Group represents an extension of RMON to encompass six areas, while Token-Ring statistics were subdivided into two groups – Token-Ring MAC Layer Statistics and Token-Ring Promiscuous Statistics. Table 7.10 lists the RFC 1513 RMON extensions as well as providing a brief overview of each extension.

In examining the entries in Table 7.10, I will defer a discussion of these two statistics groups to briefly provide additional information on a few other Token-Ring RMON extensions listed in that table. In doing so I will illustrate their applicability to a unique aspect associated with Token-Ring networks.

The Ring Station Configuration Control extension was developed as a result of the neighbor notification process associated with Token-Ring networks. As discussed in Chapter 2, that process permits a station to learn the nearest addressable upstream neighbor (NAUN) address. When a beacon occurs to report a

Table 7.10 Token-Ring RMON extensions

Extension	Description
Token-Ring MAC Layer Statistics Group	This extension tracks Token-Ring MAC statistics, diagnostics and event notifications on the local ring.
Token-Ring Promiscuous Statistics Group	This optional extension tracks non-MAC user data traffic on the local ring.
Ring Station Control	This extension tracks such status information as the ring state, active monitor, hard error beacon fault domain and number of active stations for each ring being monitored.
Ring Station Table	This extension provides diagnostic and status information to include station MAC address, status and isolating and non-isolating soft error diagnostics for each station on the ring.
Ring Station Configuration Control	This extension provides a description of the physical configuration of the network.
Ring Station Order	This extension returns a list of stations attached to the monitored ring in logical ring order.
Ring Station Configuration	This extension returns Token-Ring errors that may result from configuration problems.
Source Routing	This extension tracks source routing statistics which enable the efficiency of source routing to be monitored.

media fault the fault is reported as a 'fault domain' in which the addresses between two adjacent nodes where the problem occurred are reported. Thus, the exact location of the problem can be obtained by referring to a map which a management station can display from data kept by the Ring Station Configuration Control extension. To properly position each station on the network map the Ring Station Order extension tracks the order of each station relative to other stations on the ring. Thus, the Ring Station Configuration Control and Ring Station Order extensions provide a management system with the ability to correctly display a network map indicating the relative location of each station. Now that we have an appreciation for how a network management station can obtain data to indicate where

Figure 7.11 Token-Ring RMON Statistics Group

Object	Description
Dropped Events	The number of times the condition in which packets were dropped by the probe due to a lack of resources was observed.
Mac Octets	The total number of octets of data in good MAC packets received on the network.
Mac Packets	The total number of good MAC packets received.
Ring Purge Events	The total number of times the ring enters the ring purge state from the normal ring state.
Ring Purge Packets	The total number of ring purge MAC packets detected.
Beacon Events	The total number of times the ring enters a beaconing state.
Beacon Time	The total amount of time the ring was in the beaconing state.
Beacon Packets	The total number of beacon MAC packets detected.
Claim Token Events	The total number of times the ring enters the claim token state from the normal state or ring purge state. The claim token state provided in response to a beacon state is not counted.
Claim Token Packets	The total number of claim token MAC packets detected.
NAUN Changes	The total number of NAUN changes detected.
Line Errors	The total number of line errors reported in detected error reporting packets.
Internal Errors	The total number of adapter internal errors reported in detected error reporting packets.
Burst Errors	The total number of burst errors reported in detected error reporting packets.
AC Errors	The total number of Address Copied (AC) errors reported in detected error reporting packets.
Abort Errors	The total number of abort delimiters reported in detected error reporting packets.
Lost Frame Errors	The total number of lost frame errors reported in detected error reporting packets.
Congestion Errors	The total number of receive congestion errors reported in detected error reporting packets.
Frame Copied Errors	The total number of frame copied errors reported in detected error reporting packets.

Table 7.11 (*continued*)

Object	Description
Frequency Errors	The total number of frequency errors reported in detected error reporting packets.
Token Errors	The total number of token errors reported in detected error reporting packets.
Error Reports	The total number of soft error report frames detected.
Ring Poll Events	The total number of detected ring poll events.

Table 7.12 Token-Ring RMON Promiscuous Statistics Group

Object	Description
Dropped Events	Same as statistics group object.
Data Octets	The total number of octets of data in good frames received on the network in non-MAC packets.
Data Packets	The total number of good non-MAC packets received.
Data Broadcast Packets	The total number of good non-MAC frames received that were directed to an LLC broadcast address.
Data Multicast Packets	The total number of good non-MAC frames received that were directed to a local or global multicast or functional address.
Data Packets: 18–63 octets 64–127 octets 128–255 octets 256–511 octets 512–1023 octets 1024–2047 octets 2048–4095 octets 4096–8191 octets 8192–18000 octets 718000 octets	The total number of received good non-MAC frames within the indicated length ranges.

a fault lies on a network map, let's turn our attention to the statistics kept by a Token-Ring RMON MIB.

Table 7.11 lists the collection of MAC layer statistics accumulated by a Token-Ring RMON probe while Table 7.12 lists the optional promiscuous statistics a probe can accumulate. Not included in these tables but included in each group is a group Data Source object. That object functions in a similar manner to Ethernet Data Source objects, identifying the source of the data that the group is set up to analyze. The Data Source can represent the address of any Token-Ring interface on a probe connected ring.

As indicated in Table 7.11, the Token-Ring RMON Statistics Group provides a measurement of network activity as well as diagnostics and event notifications associated with MAC traffic. In comparison, the Token-Ring RMON Promiscuous Statistics Group tracks non-MAC traffic on the local ring being monitored.

7.3.4 RMON limitations

One of the problems associated with RMON is the fact that it is limited to tracking packets at layer 2 of the OSI Reference Model. This means that a pure RMON probe cannot provide information required to provide an application traffic monitoring capability. Recognizing this problem, several vendors have introduced RMON extensions which provide support for application traffic monitoring at layer 7 down through network traffic at layer 3. Through the use of such products as Frontier Software's NETscout Manager you can monitor Netscape, Notes, ccMail, WordPerfect Office and similar applications, viewing critical parameters that can be used to resolve network problems and alleviate potential network failures prior to their occurrence.

7.4 USING A MANAGEMENT PLATFORM

The ability to use SNMP and one or more RMON probes is dependent upon the use of a management platform. In concluding this chapter covering fault and performance management with SNMP and RMON, I will illustrate the use of the ProTools Foundation Manager with the firm's Cornerstone Probe. ProTools is a wholly owned subsidiary of Network General Corporation, a company primarily known for their LAN hardware decoding tools. Their ProTools subsidiary specializes in providing monitoring stations and remote probes that can be used to obtain a real-time network monitoring and analysis capability for a single local network or for the simultaneous monitoring and analysis of multiple remote networks.

7.4.1 Working with Foundation Manager

Figure 7.2 illustrates the Foundation Manager main menu. Under the conventional Windows menu bar is a ribbon bar which contains icons which when clicked upon provide quick access to such program options as starting or stopping agent monitoring, viewing outstanding alarms, configuring SNMP communications settings and performing similar actions. The middle of the ribbon bar which I set to 'Remote Token Ring Monitoring' is a pull-down menu you can use to invoke local or remote monitoring of Ethernet and Token-Ring networks, sort traffic, and other program features.

Directly under the ribbon bar is the solution bar which contains icons which when pressed enable you to quickly invoke different types of network monitoring. I will shortly provide an overview of the use of several solution bar icons to illustrate the typical view of information from an RMON probe via the use of a management station.

The vertical column pair of icons are referred to as the icon panel. Icons in the icon panel control the construction of paths

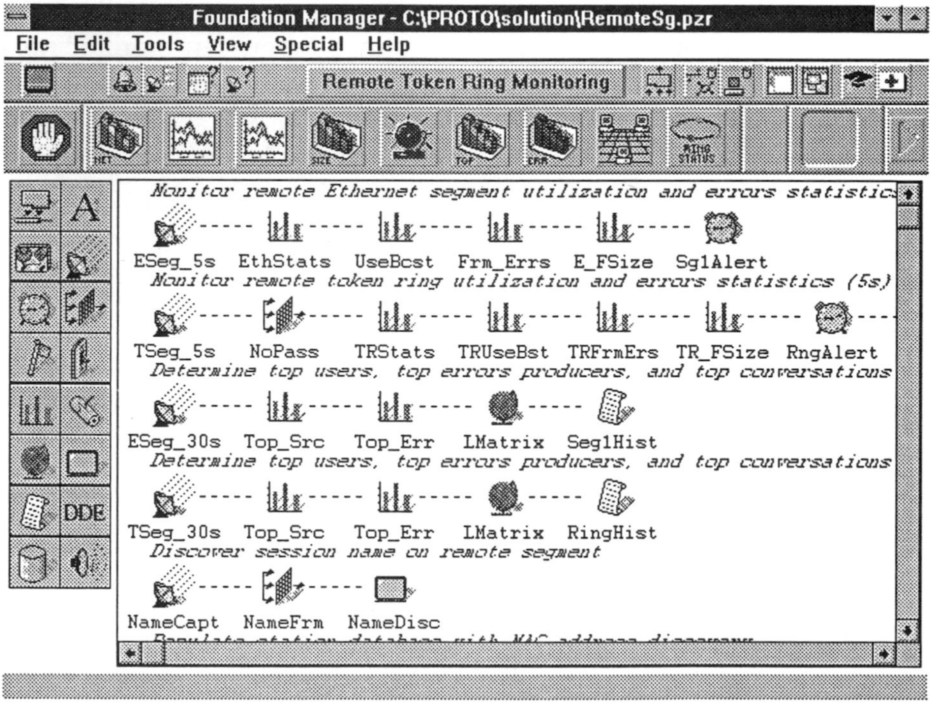

Figure 7.2 Foundation Manager main window

Foundation Manager uses to analyze a network to include the input of acquired frames into a file and their playback.

The center of the window, which is referred to as the path area, is where you load solutions or construct paths to perform a specific network analysis. To construct a path you drag an icon from the icon panel to the path area. For example, the top left icon in the icon panel is the Acquire icon. Moving it into the path area results in frames being acquired from the network. Once this occurs you can view and analyze data through the use of an optional protocol decoder module. In the remainder of this section I will focus my attention upon the use of several of the Foundation Manager's solution bar icons to display statistics captured by a remote Token-Ring probe.

7.4.2 Token-Ring statistics

Selecting the second icon in the solution bar which appears results in the display of Token-Ring statistics in a bar chart format. This is illustrated in Figure 7.3 by the contents of the window labeled 'Statistics – RMON Probe'. This window shows in

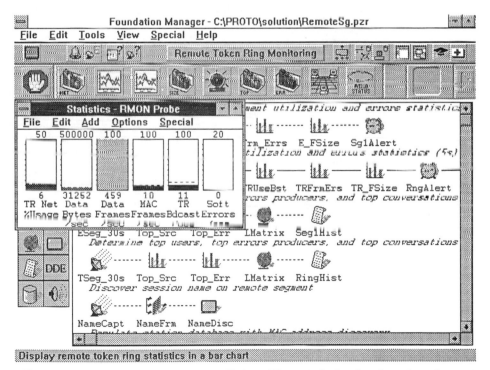

Figure 7.3 Displaying six remote Token-Ring statistics in a bar chart format

bar chart format six key Token-Ring statistics, ranging from the percentage of network usage (TR Net %Usage) to Soft Errors per second.

7.4.3 Displaying statistics by time

The third icon in the solution bar appears to resemble a line graph and is similar to the next icon to its right. Selecting either of those icons results in the tracking of different statistics over time via the use of line charts.

Figure 7.4 illustrates the display window obtained by selecting the first line chart icon which is the third icon from the left in the solution bar. The result of this action is the display of ring usage as a percentage and broadcasts/second in two colors on a common trend graph as illustrated at the bottom of Figure 7.4.

Selecting the second line chart in the solution bar produces a dual line graph display. This is illustrated in Figure 7.5. The top trend graph, which is new, displays data frames, line errors, data

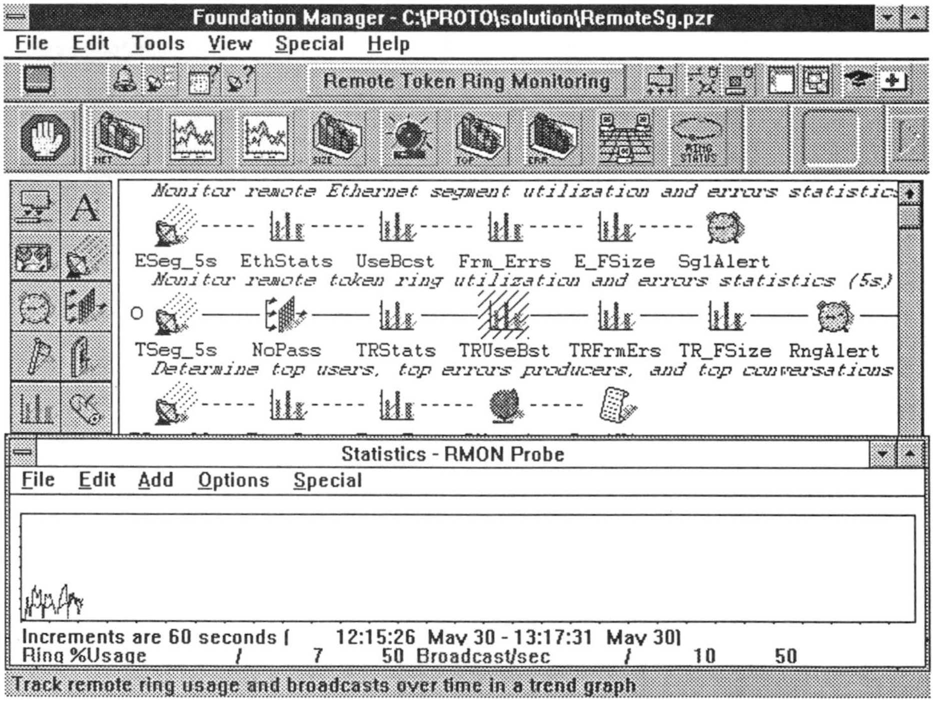

Figure 7.4 Selecting the first line graph icon in the solution bar results in the display of ring usage and broadcasts/second over time in a trend graph

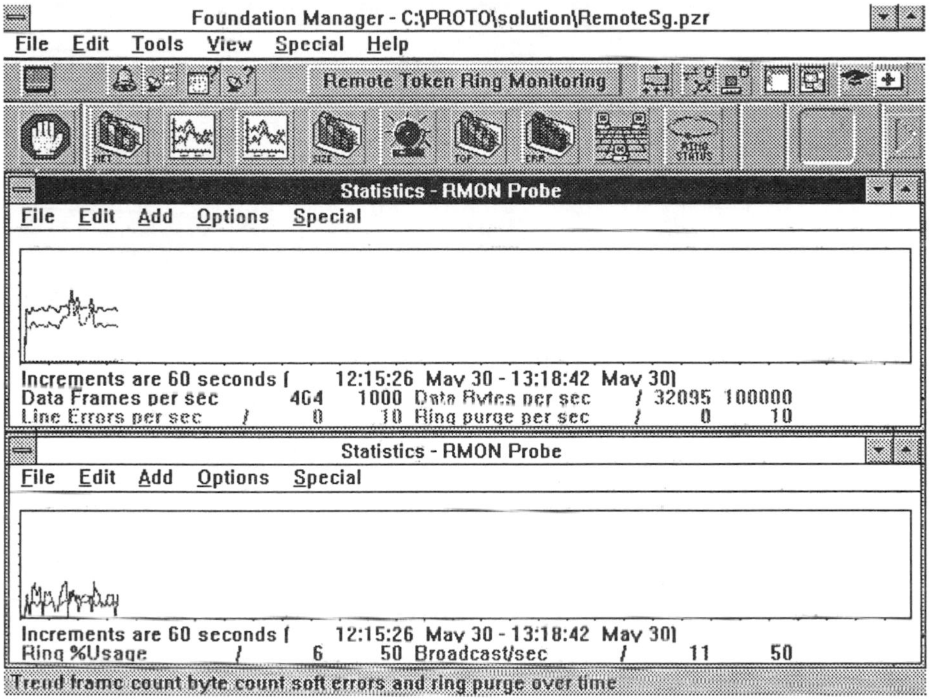

Figure 7.5 Selecting the second line graph from the solution bar results in a trend graph showing the value of four new variables over time

bytes and ring purges on a per second basis. The second graph which is shown at the bottom of Figure 7.5 represents the prior display. Thus, a total of six variables are plotted in two trend graphs.

7.4.4 Frame distribution

To obtain a visual display of the distribution of frames based upon their length you would select the fifth icon from the solution bar. That icon contains a bar graph and the label 'SIZE', which when selected results in a window which shows the frame size distribution on the remote ring. Figure 7.6 illustrates the result of the selection of the bar graph icon with the label 'SIZE'. By examining this display you can quickly obtain an indication of the type of operations occurring on the monitored LAN since long frames are primarily used for file transfer while short frames are normally associated with interactive operations.

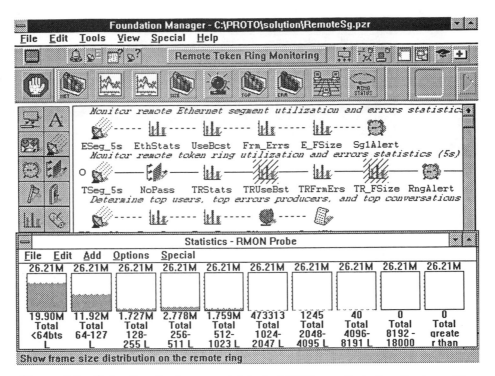

Figure 7.6 Selecting the bar graph labeled SIZE results in the display of the frame size distribution of frames of the monitored LAN

7.4.5 Other operations

The icon which appears to resemble a clock ringing is the alarm icon. Selecting that icon displays information about current alarm criteria as well as the alarm count and outstanding alarms. Currently Foundation Manager permits a user to set a value for approximately 40 variables for use as alarm criteria. For example, a ring usage exceeding 50 percent in 30 seconds could be used as the criterion to generate an alarm.

The bar graph icon labeled 'TOP' when selected will result in the display of information about the top five busiest users on the network. Similarly, the bar graph icon labeled 'ERR' results in the display of error information. While those displays can be valuable to many network users, I have found the selection of the last two icons in the solution bar to provide extremely valuable information.

The icon which appears to resemble PCs on a matrix results in the display of the latest 20 conversation pairs on the network. This information can be extremely useful in attempting to isolate certain types of query–response problems since direct monitoring

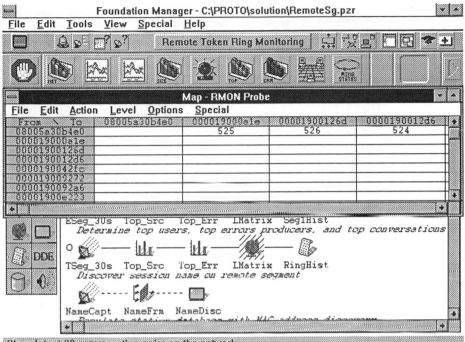

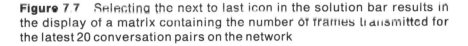

Figure 7.7 Selecting the next to last icon in the solution bar results in the display of a matrix containing the number of frames transmitted for the latest 20 conversation pairs on the network

by a conventional network analyzer would require a user to manually sort through addresses. As illustrated in Figure 7.7, the latest 20 conversation pairs are presented as a From\To matrix which facilitates viewing the activity between network nodes. Here the number in each cell represents the number of frames with the indicated source and destination; however, it also represents traffic in one direction. Traffic in the opposite direction would be listed in another cell.

The last icon in the solution bar is the ring status icon. Selecting that icon results in a display of MAC layer activity for the monitored ring. This is illustrated in Figure 7.8. Note that Foundation Manager provides a matrix of Token-Ring MAC layer activity based upon node address, making it relatively easy to isolate problems to specific LAN nodes.

Although the previously presented information provides an overview of the use of a management station controlling an RMON probe, it is not all-inclusive. Foundation Manager as well as other management platforms provide numerous types of statistical

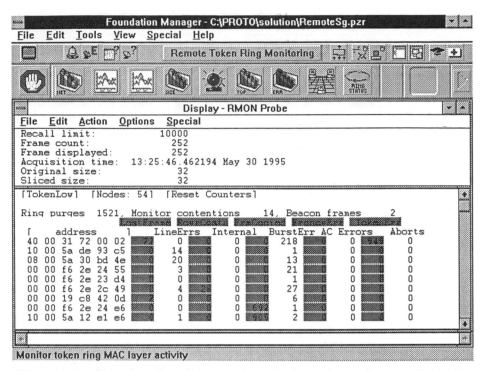

Figure 7.8 Selecting the rightmost icon in the solution bar results in the display of MAC activity in a matrix format by node address, facilitating the isolation LAN problems

charts and trend graphs that can be extremely important in obtaining a visual indication of the state of the current and future health of a network. By observing trend graphs you may be able to head off netware related performance problems prior to their observation by network users, a situation dear to the hearts of network managers and administrators.

PACKET DECODING

Preparing to write this chapter I deliberated between using 'packet' and 'protocol' in the title, selecting the former even though the primary focus of this chapter involves the decoding of two common LAN protocols. The reason for selecting the term 'packet' is the fact that packets are the mechanism used to transport data, while protocols govern the control of the flow of packets. Although many network related problems can be determined by protocol decoding, in actuality you are decoding packets. Thus, I felt it would be more appropriate to use the term 'packet' in the title of this chapter.

To effectively decode packets you must have a decoding tool as well as a basic understanding of protocols. Although there are a large number of LAN protocols, unfortunately space constraints preclude coverage of most protocols other than the two most commonly used ones. Since a majority of LANs primarily use either TCP/IP or NetWare IPX/SPX, in the first section of this chapter I will review those protocols. This review will include their relationship to the International Standards Organization (ISO) Open System's Interconnection (OSI) Reference Model, their packet format and field functions as well as key values associated with certain packet fields. Using this information as a base the second section in this chapter will illustrate packet decoding using a specific software LAN analysis program, although you can use any equivalent hardware or software decoding tool to obtain similar results. The rationale for packet decoding is to obtain an insight into the flow of data on a network. Many times you can locate network problems by observing the response or lack of response to certain packets or you may discover an ill-behaved application through packet decoding. Thus, packet decoding provides an additional insight into the state of the LAN that can be extremely useful for detecting network related problems. In addition, due to the manner by which certain devices transmit broadcast messages to make other devices aware of their presence, packet decoding can provide information useful for enhancing network performance.

8.1 NetWare IPX/SPX AND RELATED PROTOCOLS

NetWare primarily provides communications services using two protocols that are variations of the Xerox Network Systems (XNS) Internet Transport protocol – Internetwork Packet Exchange (IPX) and Sequence Packet Exchange (SPX). IPX is a best effort connectionless protocol, operating at the Network layer of the OSI Reference Model. In comparison, SPX is a connection oriented protocol which supports reliable peer-to-peer communications and operates at the Transport layer of the OSI Reference Model.

8.1.1 IPX and its header fields

Although IPX is a connectionless protocol it can be used in an implied verification mode. That is, file servers use IPX for request and reply packets. Thus, if a server responds to a request it is implied that it received the request. Conversely, if a station times out waiting for a response you can logically assume that the server never received the request. Figure 8.1 illustrates the format or structure of an IPX packet header.

Checksum field

The header contains a total of 30 bytes, of which the Checksum field was included for compatibility with the XNS packet header and is always set to hex FF-FF. Since adapter cards perform a hardware checksum on the entire IPX packet the Checksum field is not used.

Packet Length field

The Packet Length field is set by IPX and denotes the length of the complete IPX packet to include the header and data. The data field can vary from zero to a maximum of 576 bytes.

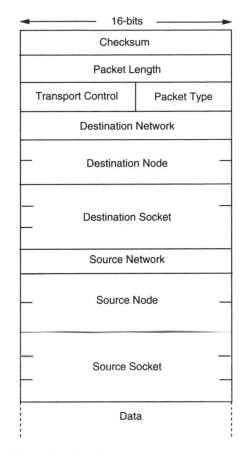

Figure 8.1   IPX packet header

Transport Control field

The Transport Control field is used by internetwork bridges and is initially set by IPX to zero prior to transmission. Thereafter, the Transport Control field contains the number of hops from source to destination.

Packet Type field

The Packet Type field denotes the type of service either offered or requested by the packet. Under XNS, Xerox defined eight packet types. Those types and their values are listed in Table 8.1. Under IPX the Packet Type field value is set to either 0 or 4, while SPX sets the value to 5.

Table 8.1 Packet Type field values

Value	Meaning
0	Unknown Packet Type
1	Routing Information Packet
2	Echo Packet
3	Error Packet
4	Packet Exchange Packet
5	Sequenced Packed Protocol Packet
16–31	Experimental Protocols
17	NetWare Core Protocol

Destination Network field

The Destination Network field contains the network number on which the station address in the Destination Node field resides. This is the administration assigned network number. NetWare uses four-byte network numbers as identifiers for servers on the same network segment. If the value of the Destination Network field is 0, it is assumed that the Destination Node is on the same physical network as the source node and that the packet is not transmitted through an internetwork bridge.

Destination Node field

The six-byte Destination Node field contains the physical address of the destination station. A destination address of hex FF-FF-FF-FF-FF-FF represents a broadcast packet which is sent to all nodes on the destination network.

Destination Socket field

The Destination Socket field contains the address of the packet's destination process, a term referred to as the destination socket address. Table 8.2 lists socket numbers used by Xerox under XNS as well as socket numbers Xerox assigned to Novell.

In examining the entries in Table 8.2 it's important to note that Novell also administers a list of sockets. Programmers can request Novell to register a socket number of their programs or can use the dynamic socket assignment of the NetWare shell. Dynamic socket numbers begin at hex 4000, while numbers assigned by Novell begin at hex 8000.

Table 8.2 Destination Socket addresses

Hex value	Meaning
Reserved by Xerox:	
1	Routing Information Packet
2	Echo Protocol Packet
3	Error Handler Packet
20–3F	Experimental
1–BB8	Registered with Xerox
BB9–	Dynamically assignable
Assigned to Novell:	
451	File Service Packet
452	Service Advertising Packet
455	Routing Information Packet
456	NetBIOS Packet
	Diagnostic Packet

Source Network field

The next field of the IPX header which follows the Destination Socket field is the Source Network field. This field contains the network number of the station transmitting the IPX packet. Similarly to the Destination Network field, the Source Network field uses the four-byte network number given to servers on the same network segment. If this field has a value of zero, this indicates that the physical network is unknown.

Source Node and Source Socket fields

The Source Node and Source Socket fields are set by IPX to indicate the physical address of the source node and the socket address of the process sending the packet, respectively. Similarly to the Destination Socket, the Source Socket can be static or dynamic and the same numbering convention as described for Destination Socket numbers is followed.

8.1.2 IPX Data field composition: SPX, SAP, RIP

As we will soon note, the structure of the IPX header provides a common foundation for the extension of information which converts an IPX header into a different transport mechanism. This extension occurs through the use of the Data field as its

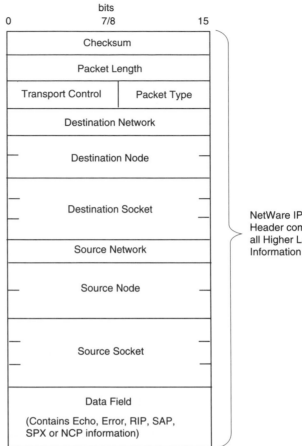

Figure 8.2 shows the NetWare packet composition.

NetWare IPX Packet Header common to all Higher Layer Information

bits		
0	7/8	15

Checksum

Packet Length

Transport Control	Packet Type

Destination Network

Destination Node

Destination Socket

Source Network

Source Node

Source Socket

Data Field

(Contains Echo, Error, RIP, SAP, SPX or NCP information)

RIP Information	SAP Information	SPX Information	NCP Information
Operation (2)	Operation (2)	Connection Control (1)	Request Type
Network Number (4)	Server Type (2)	Datastream Type (1)	Sequence Number
Number of Hops (2)	Server Name (48)	Source Connection ID (2)	Connection Number
Number of Ticks (2)	Network Address (4)	Destination Connection (2)	Task Number
• • •	Node Address (6)	Sequence Number (2)	Reserved
	Socket Address (2)	Acknowledge Number (2)	Function Code
	Hops to Server (2)	Allocation Number (2)	Data (variable length)
	• • •	0–534 octets of data	

Maximum 50 sets of network information

Maximum 7 sets of server information

( ) represents field length in octets

Figure 8.2 NetWare packet composition

composition results in the development of several types of transport mechanisms which Novell references as different types of NetWare protocols.

The Data field can contain Routing Information Protocol (RIP), Service Advertising Protocol (SAP), SPX, Echo, Error or NetWare Core Protocol (NCP) information. In fact, via the extension of the previously described IPX header the packet can be converted into a different type of packet, such as an SPX packet.

Figure 8.2 illustrates the composition of the NetWare packet Data field for RIP, SAP, SPX and NCP information. In the remainder of this section I will discuss the contents of the SPX packet header in terms of its 12-byte extension of an IPX header as well as the operation of SAP and RIP, since many problems as well as performance issues are attributable to those protocols.

SPX

In examining the composition of the data field which turns an IPX packet into an SPX packet you will note the addition of 12 bytes to the IPX header. Thus, I will focus my attention upon those bytes in discussing SPX.

Connection Control field

The first new field, Connection Control, contains four single-bit flags used by the protocol to control the bidirectional flow of data. Table 8.3 lists the Connection Control field single-bit flags and their meanings.

Table 8.3 Connection Control bit flags

Hex bit flag value	Meaning
10	(End-of-Message) A client sets this flag to signal its partner an end of connection. SPX passes it unaltered.
20	(Attention) A client sets this flag if a packet is an attention packet. SPX passes it unaltered.
40	(Acknowledgement Required) SPX sets this bit if an acknowledgment packet is required.
80	(System Packet) SPX sets this bit if the packet is a system packet.

Datastream Type field

The second field in the SPX extension is a one-byte flag which indicates the type of data contained in the packet. Known as the Datastream Type field, possible values include hex 0-FD for client defined, hex FE for End-of-Connection, and hex FF for End-of-Connection Acknowledgement. A Client Defined setting results from an application and is ignored by SPX. An End-of-Connection is generated by SPX when a client requests the termination of an active connection and represents the last message delivered on the connection. The third type of data, End-of-Connection Acknowledgement, is generated by SPX and is not delivered to connected clients.

Source and Destination Connection ID fields

Following the Datastream Type field is the Source Connection ID field. This field contains a number assigned by SPX at the packet's source. That field is followed by the Destination Connection field which contains a number assigned by SPX at the packet's destination. Since multiple connections active on a computer can use the same socket, the Destination Connection field provides a mechanism for demultiplexing incoming packets arriving on the same socket from different connections.

Sequence Number field

The Sequence Number field varies from hex 0 to FF-FF and is used to count packets exchanged in one direction on a connection. SPX wraps to 0 when the maximum value is reached.

Acknowledge Number field

The Acknowledge Number field contains the sequence number of the next packet SPX expects to receive.

Allocation Number field

The last field, Allocation Number, contains the number of listen buffers outstanding in one direction on the connection. SPX can only transmit packets until the sequence number equals the remote Allocation Number.

SAP and RIP

The Service Advertising Protocol (SAP) and Routing Information Protocol (RIP) govern the ability to have multiple servers on a common network or on geographically separated networks that can be recognized and then become accessible to client workstations. SAP and RIP are used to provide a request/reply sequence which provides a mechanism for workstations to be able to locate and access servers.

SAP operation and SAP fields

When a NetWare workstation loads NETX or VLM, the station transmits a SAP request onto the network. That request is a request for the nearest server unless altered by the use of the NetWare ATTACH command to request attachment to a specific server. Servers receiving the SAP request respond with SAP replies which include the server's network address. Since the first response is considered to represent the nearest server, the workstation responds to the first SAP reply it receives by broadcasting a RIP request. The RIP request and the RIP reply sent from a router to the workstation enable the workstation to construct a table which associates the hardware address of the router with a network address for the requested service. This enables the workstation to correctly address its packets to the service it seeks.

In addition to supporting the connection of clients to servers when NETX or VLM is loaded, SAPs support the ability of routers and certain network commands (SLIST) to know the presence of servers on a network. Every 60 seconds (default) servers broadcast a SAP to advertise their services as well as all known services. The SAP format which is shown in the second column in Figure 8.2 can contain up to seven sets of server descriptors whose contents specify information about the server.

The Server Type field specifies the type of server, such as file server or print server. The Server Name field contains the name of the server and explains how you can use the SLIST command to obtain a list of server names. The Network Address field is the internal network address.

In a NetWare environment there are two network addresses you must consider – the network address assigned by the administrator and the internal network address. The first network address is assigned by the administrator when a file server is configured. The internal address is used to support file service requests as such requests are routed from a workstation's network address to a NetWare server's internal network address where the file service processes reside. The Node Address field is a six-byte address which represents the data link address of the server, normally the Ethernet or Token-Ring adapter address. The two-byte Socket Address field is similar to that for other IPX sockets, representing the internal address of a service, such as a Print Server.

The information carried in SAPs is used by servers and routers to construct Server Information Tables (SITs). SITs contain the information required to associate network services with network locations; however, they do not provide information required to send packets to a destination network. The information necessary to transmit packets to a destination network is contained in the Routing Information Table (RIT) which is constructed via RIP broadcasts which also occur every 60 seconds.

RIP operation

The RIP packet shown in column 1 of Figure 8.2 is used by routers to construct Routing Information Tables. RIP packets received on one port are updated via the incrementation of the Hops and Ticks fields and transmitted to all other attached networks. In examining the IPX extension to construct a RIP packet the Hops field contains the distance in routers that must be traversed to reach the destination network. In comparison, the Ticks field contains the time in one-eighteenth second increments required to reach the destination network.

Under RIP a network is considered to be unreachable if it is 16 hops away. This enables routers to gracefully exit a network and allow other routers to reconfigure themselves to provide a better route. Here the router exiting a route simply broadcasts that it is 16 hops away from the networks it no longer supports.

8.1.3 Performance issues

Because SAP and RIP broadcasts occur every 60 seconds or whenever a change occurs in a network they can cause performance problems due to the bandwidth they consume. This is especially true when an internetwork consists of LANs connected by relatively slow 56 Kbps WAN links.

The first types of packets you should check when WAN performance becomes an issue are SAP and RIP. In fact, when constructing a WAN interconnection it is extremely important to consider restricting the flow of SAP and RIP packets via filtering. In doing so you may cause a slight delay for some users performing an SLIST or similar internetwork related command dependent upon SAP updates while improving internetwork communications capability for transferring files or performing client–server interactive communications across WAN links.

8.2 TCP/IP

TCP/IP represents a collection of network protocols that provide services at the Network and Transport layers of the ISO's OSI Reference Model. Originally developed based upon work performed by the US Department of Defense Advanced Research Projects Agency Network (ARPANET), TCP/IP is also commonly referred to as the DOD protocols or the Internet protocol suite.

Figure 8.3 illustrates the relationship of TCP/IP protocol suite and the services they provide with respect to the OSI Reference

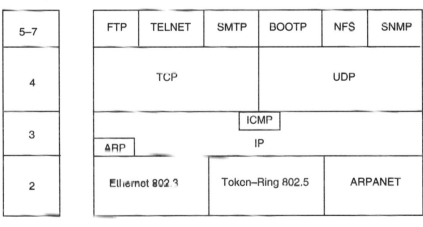

Legend:
ARP   Address Resolution Protocol
BOOTP   Bootstrap Protocol
FTP   File Transfer Protocol
ICMP   Internet Control Message Protocol
NFS   Network File System
SMTP   Simple Mail Transfer Protocol
SNMP   Simple Network Management Protocol
UDP   User Datagram Protocol

Figure 8.3   TCP/IP protocols and services

Model. In the remainder of this section I will review IP and TCP packet headers as well as discuss the use of several related network and transport layer protocols and higher level protocols implemented over TCP and its related protocol suite.

8.2.1 Datagrams versus virtual circuits

In examining Figure 8.3 you will note that the Internet Protocol (IP) provides a common Layer 3 transport for TCP and UDP. TCP is a connection oriented protocol, which requires the acknowledgement of the existence of the connection and for packets transmitted once the connection is established. In comparison, UDP, a mnemonic for User Datagram Protocol, is a connectionless mode service that provides a parallel service to TCP. Here 'datagram' is a term used to identify the basic limit of information transported across a TCP/IP network. A datagram can be transported either via an acknowledged connection oriented service or via an unacknowledged, connectionless service, where each information element is addressed to its destination and its transmission is at the mercy of network nodes. Datagrams are routed via the best path available to the destination as the datagram is placed onto the network. An alternative to datagram transmission is the use of a virtual circuit, where network nodes establish a fixed path when a connection is initiated and subsequent data exchanges occur on that path.

Two additional network layer protocols in the TCP/IP suite are ICMP and ARP. TCP implements transmission via the use of a virtual circuit, while IP provides a datagram oriented gateway transmission service between networks.

8.2.2 ICMP and ARP

The Internet Control Message Protocol (ICMP) provides a mechanism for communicating control message and error reports. Both gateways and hosts use ICMP to transmit problem reports about datagrams back to the datagram originator. In addition, ICMP includes an echo request/reply that can be used to determine if a destination is reachable and, if so, is responding. The Address Resolution Protocol (ARP) maps the high level IP address configured via software to a low level physical hardware address, typically the ROM address of the network interface card (NIC).

8.2.3 TCP

In examining Figure 8.3 you will note that TCP provides services at the transport layer for more commonly used application suite protocols, such as FTP, TELNET and SMTP. Figure 8.4 illustrates the TCP header format, while Table 8.4 identifies the functions of the fields within the header.

In examining the entries in Table 8.4 it is important to note that TCP has a rich set of features and a full discussion of the operation of TCP, IP and their application protocols is included in several well-known book series. Thus, instead of describing at length TCP and IP operations I will examine the contents of certain protocol header fields which serve as a basis for testing and troubleshooting operations.

Source Port and Destination Port fields

The Source Port and Destination Port fields can contain many additional values besides those listed in Table 8.4. Quite often, the application filtering of a router is used to bar one or more types of packets based upon the value of the source or destination port field. For example, consider FTP which sends control information on port 21 while the actual data transfer occurs on port 20. By filtering TCP packets with source port addresses of 20 and 21 the router would prohibit inbound FTP from external networks. Conversely, filtering those addresses in the destination

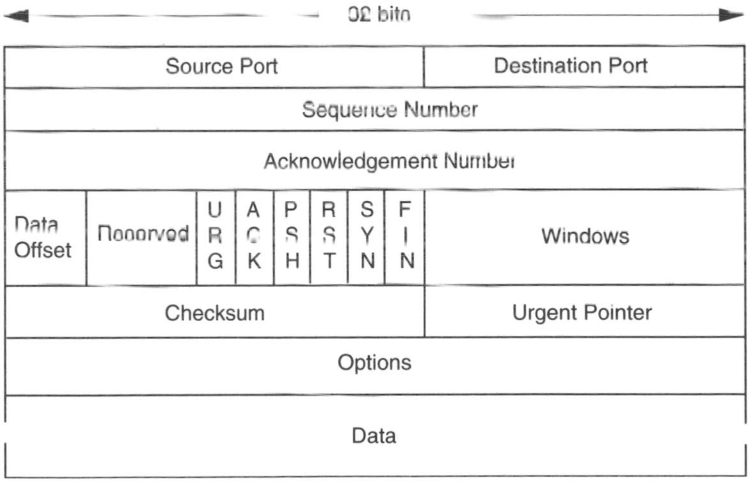

32 bits		
Source Port		Destination Port
Sequence Number		
Acknowledgement Number		
Data Offset / Reserved / URG ACK PSH RST SYN FIN		Windows
Checksum		Urgent Pointer
Options		
Data		

Figure 8.4   TCP header format

Table 8.4 TCP header fields

Field	Description
Source Port	The address that identifies a process or service in the sender's host. Examples of well-known application ports include: FTP 20, 21 Finger 79 SMTP 25 SNMP 161, 162 TELNET 23 Whois 43
Destination Port	The address that identifies a process or service in the receiver's host.
Sequence Number	This field usually represents the sequence number of the first data byte of a segment. If a SYN or a control flag is present the sequence number is the Initial Sequence Number (ISN) of the connection and the first data byte is numbered $ISN + 1$.
Acknowledgement Number	When the ACK bit is set, this field contains the next sequence number that the sender expects to receive.
Data Offset	This field indicates the number of 32-bit words contained in the TCP header.
Control Bits	Control bit flags can be set to perform the following functions: URG – urgent pointer used to indicate there is urgent data coming SYN – used to indicate a connection request ACK – used to indicate the acknowledgement field is relevant RST – reset causes the connection to be reset PSH – push tells the receiver to immediately deliver the data.
Window	The value in this field indicates the number of data bytes, commencing with the one indicated in the acknowledgement field that the sender can accept.
Checksum	This field protects the TCP header and data.
Urgent Pointer	When the URG flag bit is set the value in this field represents the last byte of urgent data.

port field would preclude outbound FTP from your network. Upon occasion, filtering templates can become quite complex and good intentions can easily result in certain applications going into the proverbial bit bucket. Through the packet decoding process you can easily identify filtering mistakes by observing the fact that packets transmitted on one network do not pass through a router.

In addition to examining the values in the source and destination port, packet decoding can be used to check the operation of the protocol as well as ascertain if the implementation of the protocol is working as intended. Included in TCP are end-to-end flow control, error control, connection setup and the exchange of status information. Thus, TCP provides a mechanism for the orderly exchange of information to include data integrity which you can examine via packet decoding.

8.2.4 IP

As previously mentioned, IP provides a datagram oriented gateway service for transmission between subnetworks. This provides a mechanism for hosts to access other hosts on a best effort basis but does not enhance reliability as it relies on upper layer protocols for error detection and correction. As a Layer 3 protocol IP is responsible for the routing and delivery of datagrams. To accomplish this task IP performs a number of communications functions to include addressing, status information, management and the fragmentation and reassembly of datagrams when necessary.

8.2.5 IP header format

Figure 8.5 illustrates the IP header format while Table 8.5 provides a brief description of the fields in the IP header. In examining the IP header a common network problem relates to the IP address carried in the source and destination address fields. Thus, a description of IP addressing is warranted as from experience it contributes to a large number of network related problems that are easily recognized from packet decoding.

8.2.6 IP addressing

The IP addressing scheme uses a 32-bit address which is divided into an assigned network number and a host number. The latter

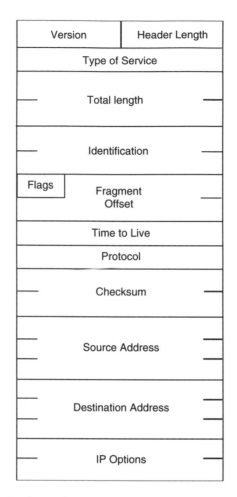

Figure 8.5   IP header format

can be further segmented into a subnet number and a host number. Through subnetting you can construct multiple networks while localizing the traffic of hosts to specific subnets, a technique I will shortly illustrate.

IP addressing numbers are assigned by the InterNIC network information center and can fall into one of five unique network classes, referenced as Class A through Class E. Figure 8.6 illustrates the IP address formats for Class A, B and C networks. Class D addresses are reserved for multicast groups, while Class E addresses are reserved for future use.

In examining Figure 8.6 note that by examining the first bit in the IP address you can distinguish a Class A address from Class B

Table 8.5 IP header fields

Field	Description
Version	The version of the IP protocol used to create the datagram.
Header Length	Header length in 32-bit words.
Type of Service	Specifies how the datagram should be handled.

```
0     1    2    3  4  5   6  7
┌──────────────┬──┬──┬──┬────────┐
│  PRECEDENCE  │D │T │R │ UNUSED │
└──────────────┴──┴──┴──┴────────┘
```

PRECEDENCE indicates importance of the datagram
D when set requests low delay
T when set requests high throughput
R when set requests high reliability

Field	Description
Total Length	Specifies the total length to include header and data.
Identification	Used with source address to identify fragments belonging to specific datagrams.
Flags	Middle bit when set disables possible fragmentation. Low order bit specifies whether the fragment contains data from the middle of the original datagram or the end.
Fragment Offset	Specifies the offset in the original datagram of data being carried in a fragment.
Time to Live	Specifies the time in seconds a datagram is allowed to remain in the Internet.
Protocol	Specifies the higher level protocol used to create the message carried in the data field.
Header	Checksum Protects the integrity of the header.
Source IP Address	The 32-bit IP address of the datagram's sender.
Destination IP Address	The 32-bit IP address of the datagram's intended recipient.
IP Options	Primarily used for network testing or debugging.

```
0       1     2     3  4    5     6  7
┌──────┬──────────────┬──────────────┐
│ COPY │ OPTION CLASS │ OPTION NUMBER │
└──────┴──────────────┴──────────────┘
```

When copy bit set it tells gateways that the option should be copied into all fragments. When set to 0 the option is copied into the first fragment.

Option class	Meaning
0	Datagram or network control
1	Reserved for future use
2	Debugging
3	Reserved for future use

The option number defines a specific option within a class.

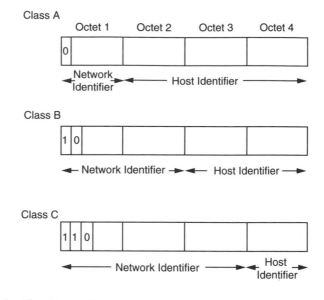

Figure 8.6 IP address formats

and C addresses. Thereafter, examining the composition of the second bit position enables a Class B address to be distinguished from a Class C address.

An IP 32-bit address is expressed as four decimal numbers, with each number ranging in value from 0 to 255 and separated from another number by a dot (decimal point). This explains why an IP address is commonly referred to as a dotted decimal address.

In examining Figure 8.6 note that a Class A address has three octets available for identifying hosts on one network or on subnets which provides support for more hosts than other address classes. Thus, Class A addresses are only assigned to large organizations or countries. Since the first bit in a Class A address must be zero, the first octet ranges in value from 1 to 127 instead of to 255.

A Class B address uses two octets for the network identifier and two for the host or subnet identifier. This permits up to 65 536 hosts and/or subnets to be assigned. In a Class C address three octets are used to identify the network, leaving one octet to identify hosts and/or subnets. Since one octet only permits 256 hosts or subnets to be identified, many small organizations with a requirement to provide more than 256 hosts with access to the Internet must obtain multiple Class C addresses.

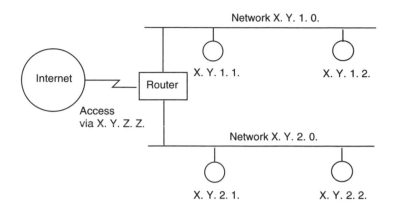

IP datagrams with the destination address X. Y. Z. Z. where Z can be
any decimal value represent a Class B network address that can
consist of 256 subnets, with 256 hosts on each subnet.

Figure 8.7   Class B subnetting

Subnetting

Through the use of subnetting you can use a single IP address as
a mechanism for connecting multiple physical networks. To
accomplish subnetting you logically divide the host portion of an
IP address into a network address and a host address.

Figure 8.7 illustrates an example of the IP subnet addressing
format for a Class B address. In this example all traffic routed to
the address XY, where X and Y represent the values of the first
two Class B address octets, flows to a common location connected
to the Internet, typically a router. The router in turn connects two

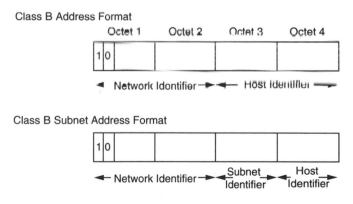

Figure 8.8   Class B network address location with two physical networks
using subnet addressing

or more Class B subnets, each with a distinct address formed by the third decimal digit which represents the subnet identifier. Figure 8.8 illustrates a Class B network address location with two physical networks using subnet addressing.

Subnet masks

The implementation of a subnet addressing scheme is accomplished by the partitioning of the host identifier portion of an IP address. To accomplish this a 32-bit subnet mask must be created for each network, with bits set to 1 in the subnet mask to indicate the network portion of the IP address, while bits are set to 0 to indicate the host identifier portion. Thus, the Class B subnet address format illustrated in the lower portion of Figure 8.7 would require the following 32-bit subnet mask:

11111111   11111111   00000000   00000000

The prior mask would then be entered as 255.255.0.0 in dotted decimal representation into a router configuration screen as well as in software configuration screens on TCP/IP program stacks operating on each subnet. Concerning the latter, you must then configure each station to indicate its subnet and host identifier so that each station obtains a full four-digit dotted decimal address.

Although the above example used octet boundaries for creating the subnet mask this is not an addressing requirement. For example, you could assign the following mask to a network:

11111111   11111111   00001110   00001100

The only submask restriction is to assign 1's to at least all the network identifier positions, resulting in the ability to extend masking into the host identifier field if you desire to arrange the specific assignment of addresses to computers. However, doing so can make it more difficult to verify the correct assignment of addresses in routers and workstations. Therefore it is highly recommended that you should implement subnet masking on integral octet boundaries.

8.2.7 Using Ping

In concluding my short examination of TCP/IP I would be remiss if I did not mention the use of one application that can be of considerable assistance when performing testing and troubleshooting operations. That application is Ping, which results in a packet being transmitted to a predefined IP address. If the network is functioning correctly and the destination host is operational the host will echo the packet back. Thus, the receipt of a Pinged packet will indicate that a destination host is both operational and accessible via network communications facilities and equipment. Thus, an inability to access the desired location is probably attributable to an application or the improper configuration of an application instead of a network problem or a distant host being offline.

8.3 USING LANSleuth

To illustrate the application of packet decoding requires the use of a protocol analyzer. In this section I will illustrate packet decoding through the use of LANSleuth, a software based analyzer developed by Systems and Synchronous, Inc. of Naperville, Illinois. This program operates under Microsoft Corporation's Windows environment and turns a personal computer into a LAN analyzer.

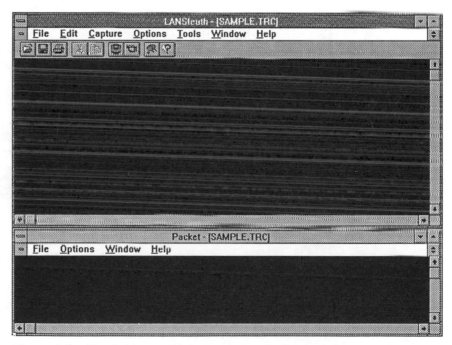

Figure 8.9 The initial LANSleuth screen display subdivides the screen into an upper Trace window and a lower Packet window

8.3.1 Trace and packet windows

Figure 8.9 illustrates the initial LANSleuth display screen which is subdivided into two horizontal windows. The trace window is the upper window. This window will display summary information of packets that satisfy any predefined criteria, such as protocol, packet type, station address and similar matching constraints developed through the use of the program's filter capability. The packet window in the lower portion of Figure 8.9 is where detailed information concerning a packet highlighted in the Trace window is displayed.

8.3.2 Use of filtering

The operating rate of a LAN can result in a packet flow rate of 1000 or more per second. At that rate it's easy to reach the situation where it becomes difficult, if not impossible, to separate packets of interest when attempting to solve a network problem from other packets. In addition, at a high packet flow rate you can rapidly run out of memory and disk space to store packets. As a

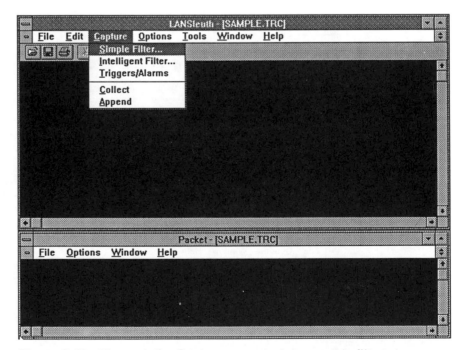

Figure 8.10 Through the Capture menu you can create filters to govern the type of packets captured as well as invoke the collection of packets

result, it is important to have a filtering capability included in a LAN analyzer, regardless of whether it's a hardware or software based analyzer. LANSleuth is no exception, as this program includes two types of filters that can be initiated from the program's Capture menu.

Figure 8.10 illustrates the options of the LANSleuth program's Capture menu. The simple filter option allows you to specify the collection of packets based upon an address matching criterion. Then, those packets flowing on the network that meet the predefined address matching criterion will be collected and displayed in the Trace window. In comparison, the intelligent filter option provides you with a much more sophisticated filtering capability.

In addition to supporting address matching, an intelligent filter supports filtering based upon specific protocol fields. Figure 8.11 illustrates a portion of LANSleuth's intelligent filter capability. In this example clicking on the initial filter button, which is obscured from view, results in the display of the program's protocol choices – FRAME, SNA, AppleTalk, TCP/IP and Novell. Selecting Novell results in the display of a second field of Novell packets. In Figure 8.11 the Service Advertising Protocol (SAP)

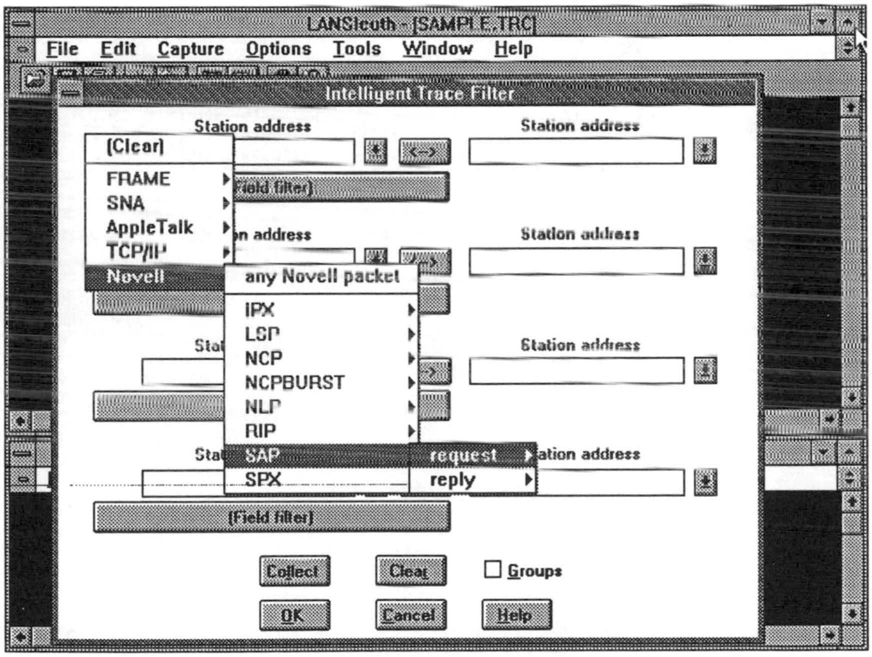

Figure 8.11 Through the use of intelligent filters you can restrict the capture of packets based upon station address and protocol

packet was selected, resulting in another menu in which the entry
'request' was selected. Thus the intelligent filter being constructed in Figure 8.11 is designed to result in Novell SAP request
packets being captured. Since SAPs are the means by which
servers advertise their services on a Novell network, the absence
of periodic SAP packets generated by a server can be used as an
indication of a communication failure or a server failure. Thus,
initiating a trace based upon capturing SAP packets can provide
you with information that can be useful for diagnosing server
problems.

8.3.3 Initiating IPX packet capturing

After you set your intelligent filters you can use either the collect
or the append Capture menu option to initiate packet capturing.
Figure 8.12 illustrates the program's Trace and Packet windows
after I initiated a packet capture operation. Note that moving the
highlight bar over an entry in the Trace window results in a
portion of detailed information about the packet being displayed
in the Packet window. In examining the highlighted packet,

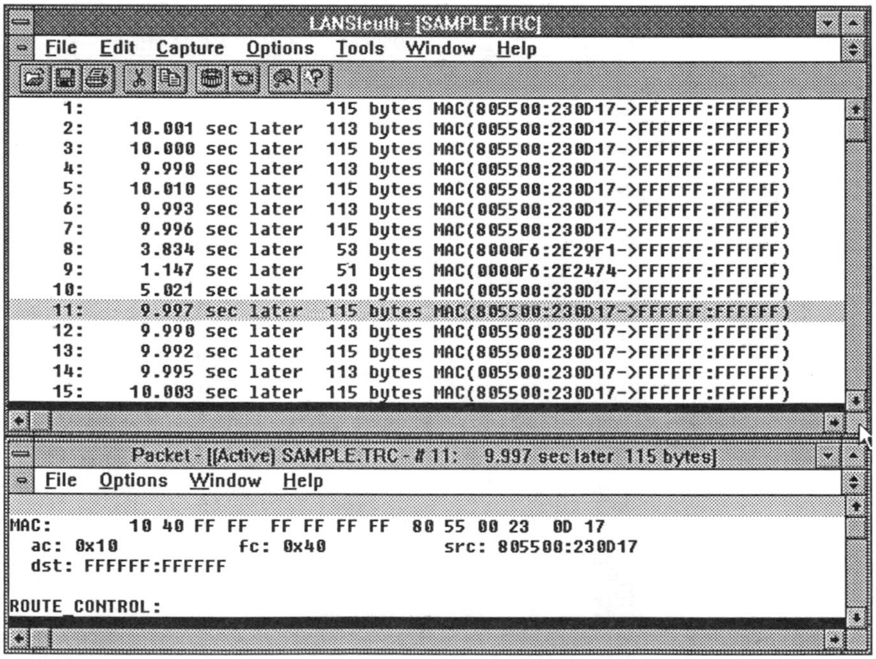

Figure 8.12 The LANSleuth Trace and Packet windows after capturing
SAP packets

number 11, the Trace window shows a packet number generated by the program strictly as a reference. That reference number is followed by the time the packet arrived with respect to the prior packet, its size, MAC address and destination address. Since a SAP packet is a broadcast packet, its destination is correctly indicated as all hex F's.

The Packet window is the key to the analysis of information flowing on the network. Although initially this window is relatively small to enable you to see more packets in the Trace window, once you select a packet you can either print the full contents of the packet window or enlarge it to view additional packet details prior to having to scroll through the window. Figure 8.13 illustrates the expanded packet window while Figure 8.14 shows the information obtained by using the program's print facility. The latter is exactly the same as the former but permits you to have a hard copy which eliminates scrolling. If you examine the contents of Figures 8.13 and 8.14 you will note that neither display provides information concerning the type of LAN frame used to transport the SAP packet. Through the use of the program's Options menu, you would select the Full Packet Detail option which will provide informational text detailing the contents of the protocol fields. This is illustrated in Figures 8.15

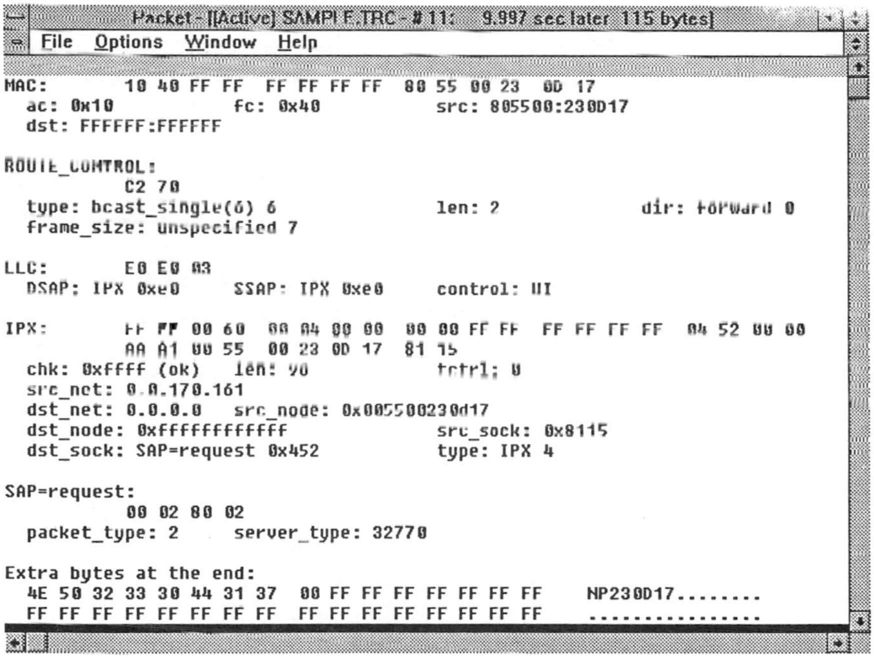

```
Packet - [[Active] SAMPLE.TRC - #11:    9.997 sec later  115 bytes]
  File   Options   Window   Help

MAC:       10 40 FF FF  FF FF FF FF  80 55 00 23  0D 17
  ac: 0x10           fc: 0x40           src: 805500:230D17
  dst: FFFFFF:FFFFFF

ROUTE_CONTROL:
          C2 70
  type: bcast_single(6) 6              len: 2              dir: forward 0
  frame_size: unspecified 7

LLC:      E0 E0 03
  DSAP: IPX 0xe0     SSAP: IPX 0xe0     control: UI

IPX:       FF FF 00 60  00 04 00 00  00 00 FF FF  FF FF FF FF  04 52 00 00
           00 A1 00 55  00 23 0D 17  81 15
  chk: 0xFFFF (ok)    len: 90                    trtrl: 0
  src_net: 0.0.170.161
  dst_net: 0.0.0.0     src_node: 0x005500230d17
  dst_node: 0xFFFFFFFFFFFF            src_sock: 0x8115
  dst_sock: SAP=request 0x452         type: IPX 4

SAP=request:
          00 02 80 02
  packet_type: 2     server_type: 32770

Extra bytes at the end:
  4E 50 32 33 30 44 31 37  00 FF FF FF FF FF FF FF   NP230D17........
  FF FF FF FF FF FF FF FF  FF FF FF FF FF FF FF FF   ................
```

Figure 8.13   LANSleuth expanded packet window

```
(Active) SAMPLE.TRC - # 11:      9.997 sec later  115 bytes


MAC:      10 40 FF FF  FF FF FF FF  80 55 00 23  0D 17
   ac: 0x10            fc: 0x40            src: 805500:230D17
   dst: FFFFFF:FFFFFF

ROUTE_CONTROL:
          C2 70
   type: bcast_single(6) 6                len: 2              dir: forward 0
   frame_size: unspecified 7

LLC:      E0 E0 03
   DSAP: IPX 0xe0      SSAP: IPX 0xe0      control: UI

IPX:      FF FF 00 60  00 04 00 00  00 00 FF FF  FF FF FF FF  04 52 00 00
          AA A1 00 55  00 23 0D 17  81 15
   chk: 0xffff (ok)   len: 96           tctrl: 0
   src_net: 0.0.170.161
   dst_net: 0.0.0.0    src_node: 0x005500230d17
   dst_node: 0xffffffffffff            src_sock: 0x8115
   dst_sock: SAP=request 0x452         type: IPX 4

SAP=request:
          00 02 80 02
   packet_type: 2     server_type: 32770

Extra bytes at the end:
   4E 50 32 33 30 44 31 37  00 FF FF FF FF FF FF FF    NP230D17........
   FF FF FF FF FF FF FF FF  FF FF FF FF FF FF FF FF    ................
   FF FF FF FF FF FF FF FF  FF FF FF FF FF FF FF FF    ................
   00 00 AA A1 00 55 00 23  0D 17 81 15 00 01          .....U.#......
```

Figure 8.14 Printed contents of the LANSleuth expanded packet window (Figure 8.13) in its default mode

and 8.16. Figure 8.15 illustrates the contents of the Packet window after the Full Packet Detail was selected. Figure 8.16 shows the full contents of the window obtained by printing the contents of the window.

Both the scrollable window shown in Figure 8.15 and its printed contents shown in Figure 8.16 represent the full packet details to include information about the LAN frame used to transport the SAP. Since a Token-Ring LAN was the transport mechanism used to transmit SAP packets, the selection of the Full Packet Detail option results in the display of LAN frame information to include the content of the token's Access Control (AC) field and Logical Link Control (LLC) information carried in the Information field within the Token-Ring frame. Most hardware and software analyzers include this capability which allows you to focus your decoding effort on a specific layer or to perform a full decoding to examine other layers in the protocol stack. Although LANSleuth is limited to decoding at one specific layer or all layers, some hardware and software products provide an additional capability by enabling decoding to occur at any specified layer. Yet another option you may wish to consider if

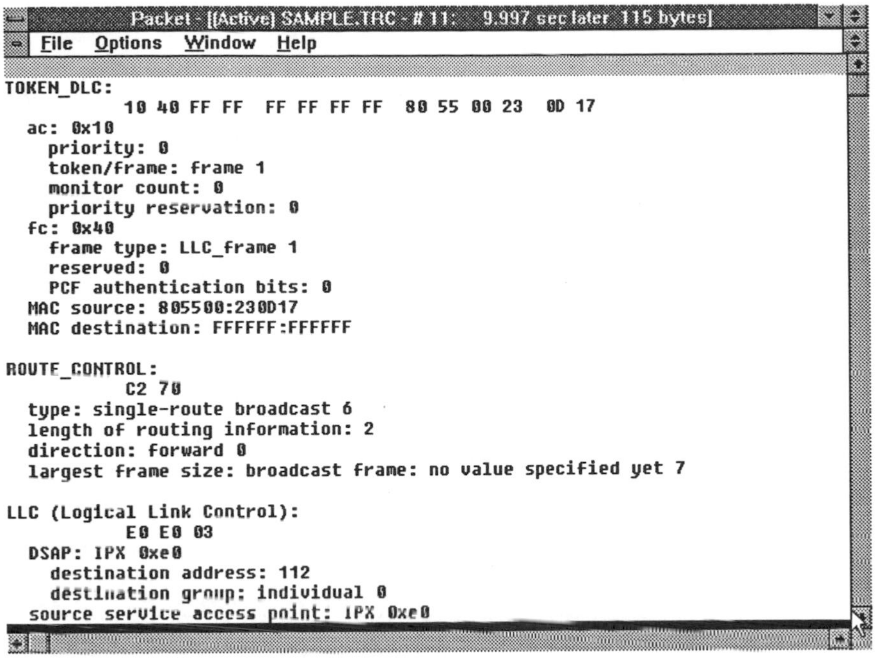

```
┌────────────────────────────────────────────────────────────┐
│   Packet - [(Active) SAMPLE.TRC - # 11:   9.997 sec later 115 bytes]│
│  File  Options  Window  Help                                 │
├────────────────────────────────────────────────────────────┤
│ TOKEN_DLC:                                                   │
│           10 40 FF FF  FF FF FF FF   80 55 00 23   0D 17      │
│   ac: 0x10                                                    │
│     priority: 0                                               │
│     token/frame: frame 1                                      │
│     monitor count: 0                                          │
│     priority reservation: 0                                   │
│   fc: 0x40                                                    │
│     frame type: LLC_frame 1                                   │
│     reserved: 0                                               │
│     PCF authentication bits: 0                                │
│   MAC source: 805500:230D17                                   │
│   MAC destination: FFFFFF:FFFFFF                              │
│                                                               │
│ ROUTE_CONTROL:                                                │
│           C2 70                                               │
│   type: single-route broadcast 6                              │
│   length of routing information: 2                            │
│   direction: forward 0                                        │
│   largest frame size: broadcast frame: no value specified yet 7│
│                                                               │
│ LLC (Logical Link Control):                                   │
│           E0 E0 03                                            │
│   DSAP: IPX 0xe0                                              │
│     destination address: 112                                  │
│     destination group: individual 0                           │
│   source service access point: IPX 0xe0                      │
└────────────────────────────────────────────────────────────┘
```

Figure 8.15 Using the Full Packet Detail option for the Packet window

your organizational budget permits is an expert decoding system. This type of decoder not only decodes packets at any or all layers in the protocol stack but in addition includes a degree of built-in intelligence. That built-in intelligence examines the contents of packets and uses a database to report possible causes of noted abnormalities. Although many users of expert systems are quite pleased with the results obtained from their use, other persons question the problem recognition ability of some systems beyond recognizing commonly encountered problems. Thus, the ability to visually work with the display or printed copy of a packet decode may be required regardless of the type of decoder used. To do so requires knowledge about the composition of packets as well as the values associated with packet fields. While you do not have to memorize packet field values, you should have access to appropriate vendor manuals to determine if the value of a specific field is causing a problem or is the result of the occurrence of a problem.

To illustrate the investigation of the contents of a decoded packet I will focus my attention upon SAP packet number 11 which was decoded in Figures 8.13 and 8.14 and for which I obtained a full decode by selecting the LANSleuth Full Packet Detail option which resulted in the additional packet details being

```
(Active) SAMPLE.TRC - # 11:        9.997 sec later   115 bytes


TOKEN_DLC:
            10 40 FF FF  FF FF FF FF  80 55 00 23   0D 17
  ac: 0x10
    priority: 0
    token/frame: frame 1
    monitor count: 0
    priority reservation: 0
  fc: 0x40
    frame type: LLC_frame 1
    reserved: 0
    PCF authentication bits: 0
  MAC source: 805500:230D17
  MAC destination: FFFFFF:FFFFFF

ROUTE_CONTROL:
            C2 70
  type: single-route broadcast 6
  length of routing information: 2
  direction: forward 0
  largest frame size: broadcast frame: no value specified yet 7

LLC (Logical Link Control):
            E0 E0 03
  DSAP: IPX 0xe0
    destination address: 112
    destination group: individual 0
  source service access point: IPX 0xe0
    destination address: 112
    destination group: individual 0
  control: UI

IPX (Novell Netware IPX/SPX):
            FF FF 00 60  00 04 00 00  00 00 FF FF  FF FF FF FF  04 52 00 00
            AA A1 00 55  00 23 0D 17  81 15
  IPX checksum: 0xffff (ok)
  packet length: 96
  transport control: 0
  source network: 0.0.170.161
  destination network: 0.0.0.0
  source node: 0x005500230d17
  destination node: 0xffffffffffff
  source socket: 0x8115
  destination socket: SAP=request 0x452
  IPX packet type: IPX 4

SAP=request (Service Advertising Packet):
            00 02 80 02
  packet_type: 2
  server_type: 32770

Extra bytes at the end:
  4E 50 32 33 30 44 31 37  00 FF FF FF FF FF FF FF    NP230D17........
  FF FF FF FF FF FF FF FF  FF FF FF FF FF FF FF FF    ................
  FF FF FF FF FF FF FF FF  FF FF FF FF FF FF FF FF    ................
  00 00 AA A1 00 55 00 23  0D 17 81 15 00 01         .....U.#......
```

Figure 8.16 Printed contents of the LANSleuth packet window once the Full Packet Detail was selected

displayed in Figures 8.15 and 8.16. Although Figures 8.15 and 8.16 contain the same packet decoding information, I will use the printout contained in Figure 8.16 as it displays the full decode while Figure 8.15 only displays a portion of the decode in the scrollable window.

In examining Figure 8.16 note the section labeled 'IPX (Novell Netware IPX/SPX)' which contains the contents of the 30-byte IPX header. LANSleuth displays both the hex value of the 30 bytes in the IPX header as well as the names of the ten fields in the header and their values. In examining the IPX header note that the destination node value is set to hex all F's, while the destination socket is set to hex 452. A server broadcasts its identity on socket hex 452 upon initialization and every 60 seconds thereafter. Thus, the destination node correctly has a value of hex FF-FF-FF-FF-FF-FF which represents a broadcast packet. The source socket number of hex 8115 is above hex 8000. This indicates that the server is transmitting the SAP on a static socket assigned by Novell. In comparison, if the socket value was between hex 4000 and hex 7FFF it would indicate a dynamically assigned socket.

Although LANSleuth provides a well-defined decode for the IPX header, to investigate the SAP requires additional effort. For example, the entry under the 'SAP=request' heading only lists four bytes and provides the decoding for two fields, with the remainder of the SAP listed under the heading 'Extra bytes at the end' in Figure 8.16. You can easily verify that those extra bytes are the SAP since the packet length in the IPX header has a value of 96 and there are 30 bytes in the IPX header. Thus, 66 bytes must be in the data field which contains the SAP. Since the values for only four bytes are listed under the 'SAP=request' heading, the extra bytes at the end must equal 62 which they do. Thus, you could use the NetWare SAP packet composition previously illustrated in Column 2 of Figure 8.2 to manually decode additional SAP field values.

9

NETWORK TUNING
TECHNIQUES

The tuning of a network can be considered to represent the adjustment of one or more configuration parameters or settings or the use of specific types of hardware or software. Settings can be performed via software or involve the adjustment of dip switches or jumpers on hardware. As such, tuning can involve changes to adapter cards, workstation files, a network operating system and bridges, routers and gateways or the installation of a variety of different hardware or software products. Thus, network tuning encompasses a wide variety of hardware and software products.

Although any tuning effort is worthwhile if the end result improves network performance, the tuning effort requires personnel resources. Many times, the resources of knowledgeable personnel are scarce and you must prioritize your tuning effort. In doing so you should primarily focus your attention upon enhancing the performance of internetworking equipment and communication circuits used to connect geographically separated networks. The rationale for doing so is the fact that the operating rate of wide area network transmission facilities is normally a fraction of the operating rate of local area networks. Thus, most network bottlenecks first occur on or at the LAN to WAN interface. By first focusing your tuning effort upon the LAN to WAN interface you can usually maximize the benefit you can obtain from the use of your key personnel.

Following the above rationale I will focus my attention primarily upon tuning techniques to enhance the flow of data between local area networks. However, owing to the ability to obtain a relatively high improvement in LAN performance through the implementation of certain relatively easy to implement tuning techniques, I

Table 9.1 Tuning techniques to consider

- Reduce the Ethernet collision window
- Use Ethernet frame truncation performing equipment
- Use device filtering capability
- Use precedence and express queuing
- Employ compression performing devices
- Use the switched network to overcome leased line congestion
- Consider NIC performance

will also cover a few techniques appropriate to individual types of local area networks.

Table 9.1 lists server tuning techniques I will cover in this chapter. The first two, as their names imply, are only applicable to Ethernet networks. The following five techniques are applicable to any type of local area network.

9.1 REDUCE THE ETHERNET COLLISION WINDOW

One of the more effective methods to increase the performance of an Ethernet LAN is obtained by taking advantage of the collision window. First, however, I will provide a review of Ethernet CSMA/CD operations to illustrate the concept behind the window.

9.1.1 The CSMA/CD access protocol

Ethernet uses a CSMA/CD access protocol in which stations first 'listen' to the wire prior to transmitting. If a station does not hear that the wire is in use it will then proceed to transmit data. Unfortunately, this access protocol can result in an increase in the probability of the occurrence of a collision as the distance between workstations increases. To illustrate this consider Figure 9.1 which shows the collision detection process.

At time t_0 both Stations A and B are listening to the wire and do not hear any activity. At time t_1 Station A begins transmitting and Station B still hears no activity as it requires time for the signal generated by Station A to propagate down the wire.

Assuming Station B now has data to transmit, it begins transmission at time t_2. At time t_3 the signal transmitted by Station A collides with the signal generated by Station B,

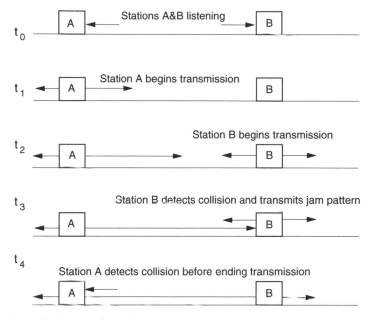

Figure 9.1   Collision detection process

resulting in an increase in the voltage level that is first detected by Station B as it is closer to the location where the collision occurred. Upon detecting the collision Station B transmits a jam pattern which Station A then detects. Both stations then use a random exponential backoff algorithm as a timer which governs when each station can attempt to repeat the previously discussed process. As already indicated, decreasing the distance between the two stations reduces the probability that one station will have initiated transmission which another station fails to hear, then assuming it can transmit, resulting in a collision.

9.1.2 Enhancing CSMA/CD performance

While you obviously cannot move all workstations in a network very close to one another, you can enhance CSMA/CD perfor-mance by locating workstations that have a high level of communications near one another. Three good candidates for consideration in addition to highly active user workstations are file servers, print servers and gateways. Each of those devices receives a lot of traffic and generates responses to that traffic.

9.1.3 Locating high activity stations

In Chapter 2 I reviewed the format of the Ethernet frame, while in Chapter 5 I examined the use of a program called TokenVision developed by Triticom. That company also markets a product called EtherVision that can be used to monitor the transmission on an Ethernet/IEEE 802.3 network.

Through the use of EtherVision or a similar product you can monitor the flow of frames by source or destination address. Figure 9.2 illustrates the EtherVision Source Address monitoring screen. Although I only monitored the network for approximately three minutes when the screen was captured, the ability of the program to count frames transmitted by different stations provides you with the information necessary to identify high activity network devices. Then you can use that information in conjunction with a network map to determine if it is practical to reduce the collision window between highly active network devices.

9.2 USE ETHERNET FRAME TRUNCATION PERFORMING EQUIPMENT

In Chapter 2 I noted that the minimum Ethernet frame length is 72 bytes when six-byte addressing is used. This means that if the data field only contains one character, 45 pad characters are added to that field to obtain a 72-byte frame length.

Although the addition of pad characters is a necessity due to the structure of the CSMA/CD access protocol, when frames are transported over a wide area network transmission facility they can represent a significant overhead which reduces inter-LAN communication performance.

9.2.1 Frame truncation

Frame truncation represents the removal of pad characters prior to the transmission of a frame over a WAN link and the reinsertion of pad characters at the opposite end of the link. You can consider Ethernet frame truncation to represent a type of compression; however, more technically it represents a pattern replacement technique. In addition, unlike some compression techniques that are standardized, Ethernet frame truncation represents a proprietary method of WAN data reduction implemented by a few remote bridge and router vendors. Regardless of

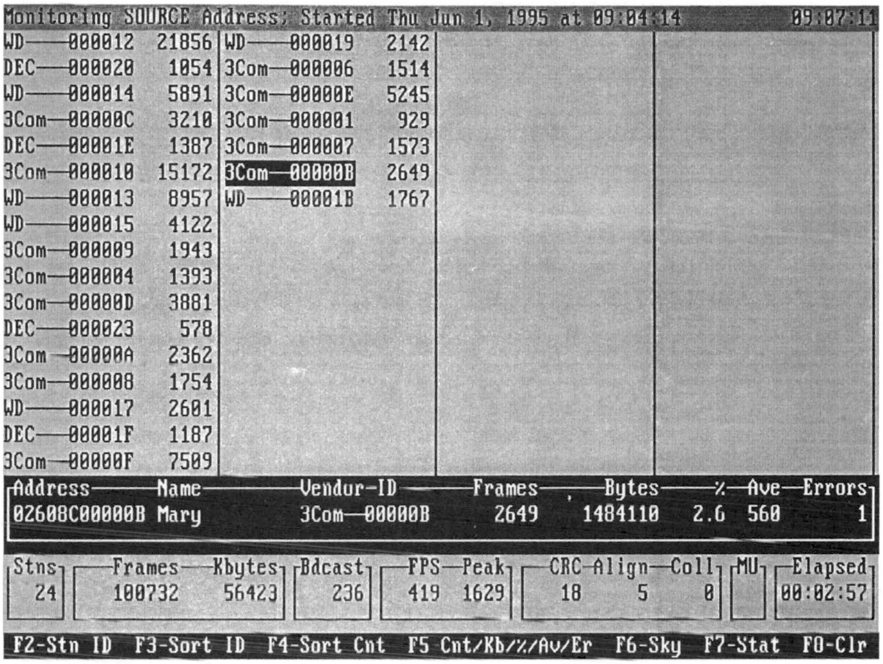

```
Monitoring SOURCE Address; Started Thu Jun 1, 1995 at 09:04:14        09:07:11
WD-----000012  21856 WD-----000019  2142
DEC----000020   1054 3Com---000006  1514
WD-----000014   5891 3Com---00000E  5245
3Com---00000C   3210 3Com---000001   929
DEC----00001E   1387 3Com---000007  1573
3Com---000010  15172 3Com---00000B  2649
WD-----000013   8957 WD-----00001B  1767
WD-----000015   4122
3Com---000009   1943
3Com---000004   1393
3Com---00000D   3881
DEC----000023    578
3Com --00000A   2362
3Com---000008   1754
WD-----000017   2601
DEC----00001F   1187
3Com---00000F   7509
┌Address------Name-----------Vendor-ID -----Frames-----Bytes------%--Ave--Errors┐
 02608C00000B Mary            3Com---00000B    2649    1484110   2.6  560       1

┌Stns┐ ┌Frames---Kbytes┐ ┌Bdcast┐ ┌FPS--Peak┐ ┌CRC-Align--Coll┐ ┌MU┐ ┌Elapsed┐
  24    100732   56423     236      419  1629     18     5     0        00:02:57

 F2-Stn ID  F3-Sort ID  F4-Sort Cnt  F5 Cnt/Kb/%/Av/Er  F6-Sky  F7-Stat  F0-Clr
```

Figure 9.2 Using EtherVision to monitor network activity by station address

the name of the technology, its implementation provides you with the ability to reduce the adverse effect of transporting pad characters across relatively low speed WAN links.

9.3 USE DEVICE FILTERING CAPABILITY

Due to the significant difference between the operating rates of LANs and WANs any unnecessary traffic you can remove from flowing over a wide area network can significantly boost the performance of your internetwork operation. The key to removing unnecessary traffic is the use of the device filtering capability of bridges, routers and other types of communications products to include LAN switches.

9.3.1 Types of filtering

There are several types of filtering you can consider, each of which may provide you with the ability to better utilize your wide area network transmission facility. Examples of different types of filtering commonly supported by remote bridges and routers include address filtering and frame type and upper protocol filtering. Some devices provide you with the ability to specify an offset from the beginning of a frame to establish a filtering capability. This feature provides you with the ability to establish one or more filters based upon different frame fields.

9.3.2 Filtering operation

To illustrate the potential effect obtained from filtering consider the internetwork illustrated in Figure 9.3. Here three geographically separated LANs are connected by the use of two 56 Kbps digital leased lines. The three LANs have a total of five file servers, each indicated by a square box containing a letter.

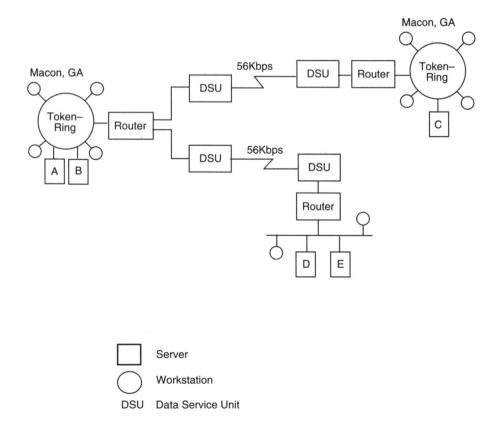

Figure 9.3 By filtering unnecessary NetWare Service Advertising Protocol packets you can enhance the performance of relatively low speed WAN transmission facilities

Assume the network with file servers A and B uses both TCP/IP and IPX protocols, while the other networks are TCP/IP based networks. Let's further assume that server A is the only NetWare server. Under NetWare the server transmits a Service Advertising Protocol (SAP) message every 60 seconds. That message consists of a minimum of 66 bytes. Thus, unless filtered, every hour $66 \times 60 \times 8$ bits are unnecessarily transmitted over the two WAN links to the distant networks. In the remainder of this section I will illustrate the construction of a few filters through the use of the CrossComm Corporation Integrated Management System (IMS), a network management system which operates under the Hewlett-Packard Open View network management platform.

9.3.3 CrossComm router filtering

The CrossComm IMS provides access to one of the more sophisticated filtering capabilities incorporated into the vendor's routers. Through the use of CrossComm filters you can define one or more filter patterns that can be applied to one or more router ports. Since patterns are defined based upon fields within a frame you can define what CrossComm refers to as a SmartFilter to filter particular types of packets, protocols and address and combinations of packet types, protocols and addresses. In fact, you can define up to four SmartFilters that can be applied to a router port which can provide a very sophisticated filtering capability.

The CrossComm IMS supports several types of filters to include address, protocol and SmartFilter patterns. By moving the mouse pointer over the system module of a displayed physical router the CrossComm management system generates a menu which provides access to each of three filters. Figure 9.4 illustrates the selection of the configuration option when the pointer was placed on the system module of a related router, resulting in a menu of selectable options to include the three filter options being displayed.

By selecting the SmartFilter Patterns entry from the menu displayed in Figure 9.4 you obtain the ability to list currently defined filter patterns or define new patterns. Figure 9.5 illustrates the display of the CrossComm SmartFilter Pattern specification dialog box. You can select one of eleven predefined patterns via the use of the lower scrollable box in Figure 9.5, with SNA shown selected. You can enter a name in the upper box which will activate the 'Zoom/Add' button, enabling you to define a filter pattern that will be associated with the filter name you enter into the Defined Patterns box.

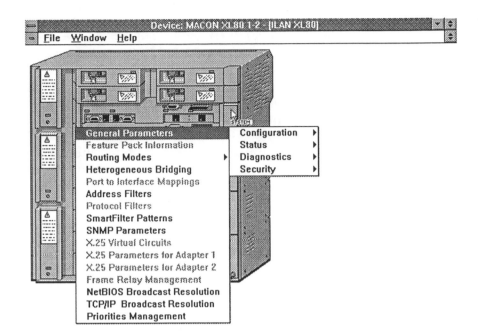

Figure 9.4 By positioning the pointer over the system module of a router the CrossComm network management system generates drop-down menus which provide the ability to define, delete and revise filters

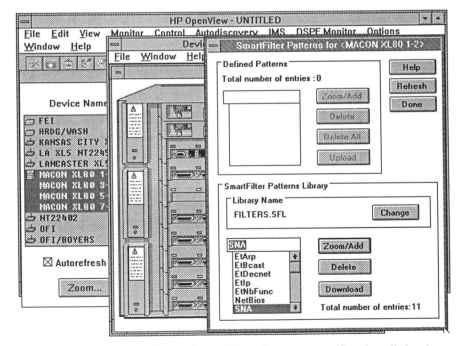

Figure 9.5 The CrossComm SmartFilter Pattern specification dialog box

To illustrate a simple example of the use of a SmartFilter let's assume I want to filter NetBIOS packets flowing onto ports 2 and 3 of a router. First, I would enter a relevant name for the filter I wish to construct into the Defined Patterns box at the top of Figure 9.5. Doing so would permit me to press a selectable upper 'Zoom/Add' button. This action would result in the display of a SmartFilter Pattern Definition dialog box, similar to the one illustrated in Figure 9.6.

In the SmartFilter Pattern Definition dialog box illustrated in Figure 9.6 the start of range hex value of F0 was entered as NetBIOS frames are identified by a hex F0 at offset 0 in the data portion of a Token-Ring frame. CrossComm permits you to specify an offset value based on either frame origin or data origin as well as define up to 16 bytes or octets for a pattern to be matched from the specified offset. Although I could add up to three additional patterns in the definition dialog box, let's assume I just want to filter NetBIOS packets.

Once a SmartFilter pattern or group of patterns are defined they must be applied. To do so you must associate a pattern with a source or input port and one or more destination or output ports.

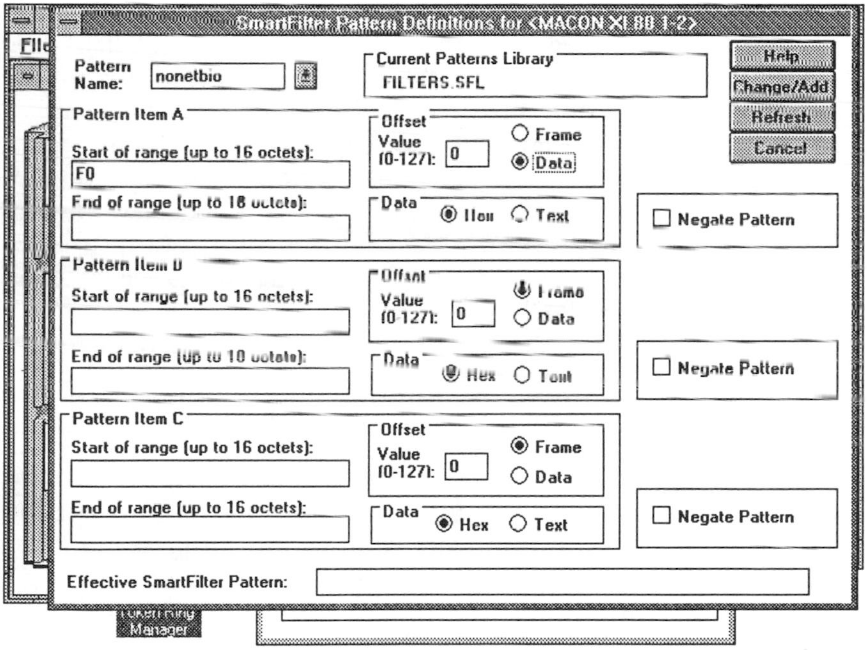

Figure 9.6 The CrossComm SmartFilter Pattern Definition dialog box

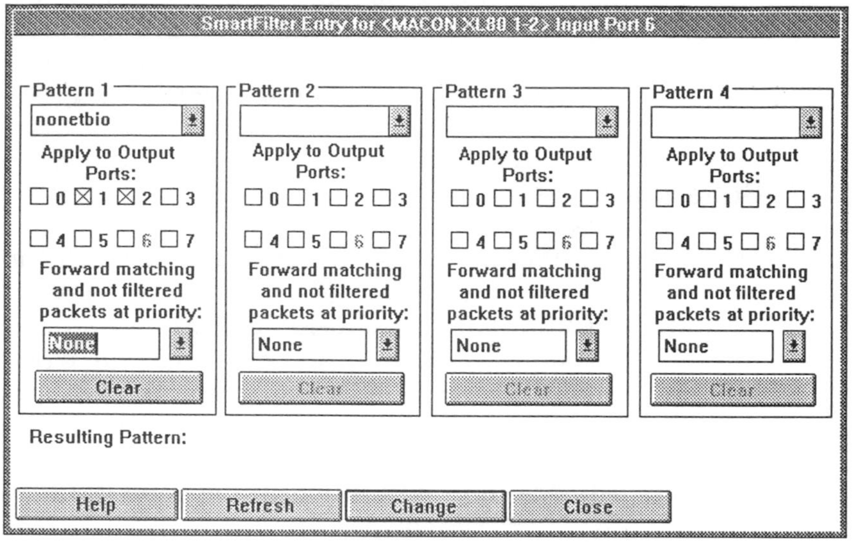

Figure 9.7 The CrossComm SmartFilter Entry dialog box

To apply a filter you would move a pointer over the port module on the router display you wish to filter. Then you would select the Apply SmartFilters option from the port menu, resulting in the display of the SmartFilter Entry dialog box which is shown in Figure 9.7. In this example the previously constructed filter was applied to ports 1 and 2, inhibiting NetBIOS packets from flowing from one LAN to the other LANs via the applied ports.

While the preceding filtering examples were relatively elementary, they illustrate the ease by which some remote bridge and router management systems permit filter construction. By carefully examining the necessity of different types of frames and filtering out unnecessary ones, you may be able to significantly enhance the performance of your WAN transmission facilities.

9.4 USE PRECEDENCE AND EXPRESS QUEUING

The connection of a remote bridge or router to a local area network results in a speed mismatch between the device's LAN and WAN connections. Data flowing from one local area network to another arrives at the remote bridge or router at the LAN operating rate but must be transmitted to the distant LAN at the operating rate of the wide area network transmission facility. To accomplish speed or data rate conversion the bridge or router must have a minimum amount of buffer memory. However, what happens when several frames follow one another on the LAN, each addressed to a distant LAN?

9.4.1 Buffering

To minimize the potential loss of frames both remote bridges and routers typically include an expanded buffer area beyond that required just for speed or data rate conversion. By obtaining the ability to store frames arriving from the LAN the remote bridge or router minimizes the probability of frames becoming lost and stations then retransmitting those frames, in effect minimizing LAN performance degradation.

The buffering used by most routers is based upon a simple first-in, first-out (FIFO) queuing scheme which is illustrated in Figure 9.8. As the name of the queuing scheme implies, the frames received from the LAN are transmitted onto the WAN in the order in which they are received by the bridge or router.

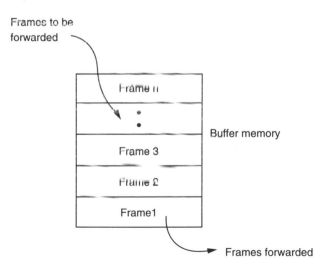

In a first–in, first–out queuing system the first frame that arrives at a device is the first frame forwarded.

Figure 9.8   First-in, first-out queuing

9.4.2 FIFO queue problems

Although frames normally arrive at the bridge or router
randomly, this is not always the case. In fact, a FIFO queuing
mechanism can have a significantly adverse effect upon interactive query response operations. To illustrate this I will use
Figure 9.9 in which geographically separated Token-Ring and
Ethernet LANs are shown connected to one another via a pair of
remote bridges.

In examining Figure 9.9 let's focus our attention upon
transmission from the Ethernet LAN to the Token-Ring LAN.
Assume station E first initiated a file transfer to station C and
transmitted for precisely one second, with a data field of 1500
bytes per frame which is the maximum capacity of an Ethernet
frame. Assuming the station has an Industry Standard Architecture (ISA) adapter card capable of transferring 300 000 bytes/
second, then in one second 300 000 bytes at 1500 bytes/frame
would result in 200 frames being transmitted.

If you examine Figure 9.9 and focus your attention upon the
timing chart under the remote bridge that connects the Ethernet
LAN to the WAN, the line labeled $E_1 \rightarrow C_1$ denotes the first frame
which flows from station E_1 to station C_1. At a 56 Kbps operating
rate the remote bridge can forward $56\,000/(8 \times 1500)$ or
approximately five frames per second without considering the
protocol overhead of each frame. Thus, at the end of one second

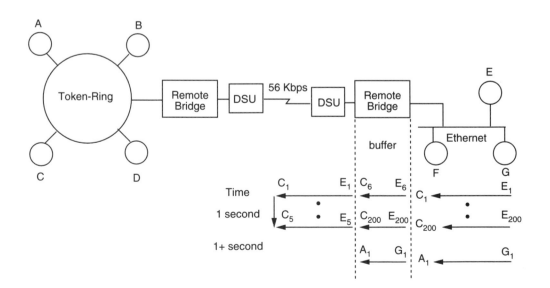

Figure 9.9 Queuing delay problems

five of the 200 frames arriving at the remote bridge would be serviced, while 195 frames would occupy the bridge's buffer, assuming buffer memory could hold that amount of traffic. Thus, at a time of one second into the transmission the chart to the lower left of the bridge shows the lines $E_1 \rightarrow C_1$ through $E_5 \rightarrow C_5$ indicating that frames 1 through 5 passed through the bridge. Directly under the buffer, the lines labeled $E_6 \rightarrow C_6$ through $E_{200} \rightarrow C_{200}$ indicate the remaining 195 frames in the remote bridge's buffer. Now, at precisely one second after station E initiated the file transfer let's assume station G initiates a response to a server query originated on the Token-Ring network. This is indicated by the line $G_1 \rightarrow A_1$ in Figure 9.9. Since there are 195 frames queued in the remote bridge the arrival of station G's frame requires

$$\frac{195 \text{ frames} \times 1500 \text{ bytes/frame} \times 8 \text{ bits/byte}}{56\,000 \text{ bits/second}}$$

or approximately 42 seconds until the bridge begins to place the frame on the WAN. Obviously, this is an unacceptable delay and most remote bridges and routers minimize the potential delay of a file transfer inhibiting interactive query–responses by limiting the amount of buffer memory in the device. Even so, it is not uncommon for relatively short delays of 3 to 5 seconds to result in session time-outs, especially when time dependent protocols such as SNA are transported. Thus, a method is required to prioritize traffic through bridges and routers.

9.4.3 Traffic prioritization

One method used to prioritize traffic is precedence queuing. Under precedence queuing the size of frames is used to subdivide the buffer area of remote bridges or routers into separate queues. Then, by varying the extraction rate from each queue to favor the queues containing relatively short frames the scheme ensures interactive transmission does not get stuck in a queue behind a file transfer.

Figure 9.10 illustrates an example of precedence queuing in which data is sorted into three queues based upon frame length. In this example relatively short frames are extracted at a rate three times that of the longest frames. Although Figure 9.10 illustrates precedence queuing based upon frame length some equipment vendors also offer this technique based upon protocol transmitted or another selectable criteria.

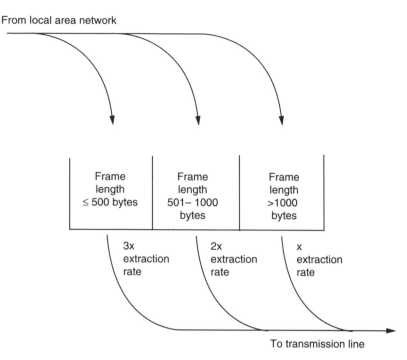

Figure 9.10 Procedure queuing operations

9.4.4 Benefits

In examining the use of remote bridges and routers it is important to note that you can significantly reduce retransmissions and session time-outs via precedence queuing. In doing so you also reduce the level of LAN utilization, which can be of considerable assistance if your LAN has a high level of utilization. In fact, reducing the utilization of an Ethernet LAN by only a few percent if it is above a 50 percent utilization level can significantly improve throughput. This is because the probability of occurrence of collisions increases with an increase in network traffic, and eliminating retransmissions indirectly reduces the collision rate on the LAN. Thus, the use of precedence queuing by remote bridges and routers can enhance both local and wide area network operations.

9.5 EMPLOY COMPRESSION PERFORMING DEVICES

Through the use of data compression you can reduce the quantity of information transported across a wide area network. This in turn can result in several performance gains since compression enables more data to be transported in a set amount of time. First, a compression performing remote bridge or router can service frames faster than a device that does not perform compression. Thus, time delays associated with queued frames will be reduced, enhancing network performance. Secondly, since queues are reduced, this means the probability of a buffer being filled when a frame arrives is reduced thereby reducing the probability of a lost frame and the retransmission of the frame on the local area network. Thus, although data compression is limited to such hardware products as remote bridges, routers, modems and DSUs, the use of this technology can improve both local and wide area network performance.

9.5.1 Methods

Most compression performing internetworking hardware and software products are based upon the use of the well known Lempel–Ziv string compression algorithm. Where vendor products can be differentiated from one another is in the use of a second compression method. Some products use a two-level compression method, with the output of the Lempel–Ziv algorithm recompressed using either arithmetic or Huffman coding, further increasing the compression ratio. Whereas Lempel–Ziv string compression may result in an average compression ratio of $3:1$, through the use of a two-level compression technique the compression ratio may be increased to $3.5:1$ to $4:1$.

9.6 USE THE SWITCHED NETWORK TO OVERCOME LEASED LINE CONGESTION

Internetwork traffic tends to have capacity utilization peaks similar to local area network use. Thus, you can normally expect the period shortly before lunch and following the afternoon break to represent peak periods of internetwork transmission.

9.6.1 Network traffic characteristics

Although no two networks exhibit identical nor even near-identical traffic patterns, the traffic peaks internetworks experience do have some common characteristics. Those characteristics enable the use of the switched telephone network to provide an economical solution to network congestion. Two of those common characteristics include a relatively low number of periods of relatively short duration per day where the utilization of a leased line linking two geographically separated local area networks degrades internetwork performance.

Often the upgrade of an existing leased line or the installation of a second leased line represents an expensive solution to short duration congestion problems. One economical technique you can consider to overcome leased line congestion is obtained through the use of a pair of bandwidth-on-demand inverse multiplexers.

9.6.2 Bandwidth-on-demand multiplexer operation

Figure 9.11 illustrates the use of a pair of bandwidth-on-demand inverse multiplexers to connect a Token-Ring network to an Ethernet LAN. In its monitoring mode of operation the inverse multiplexer connects the two LANs by the transparent transmission of remote bridge traffic via a 64 Kbps digital circuit. During the monitoring mode one inverse multiplexer functions as a master device while the other operates as a slave. The master device measures the utilization level of the WAN leased line. If the utilization level reaches some predefined level and maintains or exceeds that level for a predefined period of time, one or more 56 or 64 Kbps switched calls are made to the slave unit to establish one or more secondary circuits. Once this occurs the inverse multiplexer will attempt to load balance the traffic while monitoring the composite utilization of the group of transmission lines. After their utilization falls below a predefined threshold the inverse multiplexer will gracefully disconnect the switched digital calls after all traffic is routed back onto the leased circuit.

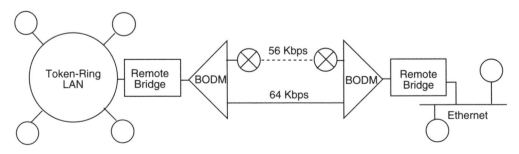

Figure 9.11   Bandwidth-on-demand

9.6.3 Economics

Since the cost of a switched 56 Kbps call varies between 5 and 10 cents per minute it provides a most economical method to relieve minor periods of leased line congestion. Thus, the use of a bandwidth-on-demand inverse multiplexer provides an economical method for automating the use of the switched digital network to overcome leased line congestion.

9.7 CONSIDER ADAPTER CARD PERFORMANCE

Until recently there were essentially three methods by which network adapter cards transferred data onto a LAN – via a Direct Memory Access (DMA) transfer, through the use of an I/O port, or via shared memory with a computer.

A DMA transfer permits the transfer of information between the adapter card and computer memory to occur simultaneously with other operations. Although a DMA transfer can be viewed as a form of multitasking, it requires a contiguous memory area and setup time. Here the setup time involves the placement of a starting and ending address into the DMA chip and those operations slightly decrease throughput.

The shared I/O transfer method involves the use of an I/O port between the adapter card and the computer. This method is normally the slowest method of data transfer.

The third method used by adapter cards is shared memory. In this technique the adapter memory becomes part of the computer's memory This avoids the transfer of frames from the adapter to the computer and until recently provided the highest level of wire transfer capability.

9.7.1 Parallel tasking

The three previously discussed techniques until recently had one common constraint in that operations were performed sequentially. Recently several vendors have introduced shared memory network adapter cards that use parallel tasking.

Through the use of parallel tasking an adapter can begin processing one frame as it comes off the wire while another frame is being prepared for placement onto the wire. Through the use of parallel tasking the delays between transmission and reception of data are reduced, resulting in a station achieving a higher transmission capability.

9.7.2 Full-duplex operation

In addition to parallel tasking new Ethernet and Token-Ring adapters can now be obtained to support full-duplex transmission. Although the use of a full-duplex adapter requires the connection of a workstation to a switching hub, it permits a theoretical doubling of transmission.

From a practical viewpoint most workstations rarely require a simultaneous transmission and reception capability and the use of a full-duplex adapter might at best increase your wire transfer capability by a few percent. Where a full-duplex adapter card can make a significant improvement to LAN performance is when used in a server. This would enable the server to transmit information in response to a prior query while receiving a new query. Thus, the use of a full-duplex network adapter card in a file server can actually result in a doubling of server throughput when the server is required to simultaneously transmit and receive data.

The seven tuning techniques presented in this chapter represent methods that can provide a relatively large payback in terms of enhancing network performance. Some techniques may be easy to implement, requiring either the movement of a cable or the use of a built-in remote bridge or router feature. Other techniques, such as changing server network adapter cards, may also require the installation of a LAN switch whose cost must be considered. Regardless of the effort and cost of implementing any tuning technique it is important to realize that the end result may alleviate a more costly upgrade or network segmentation. Thus, it is important to compare the cost and time required to implement any tuning technique against the cost and effort required to alleviate a utilization problem that may be compounded by inaction.

INDEX

Index compiled by Geoffrey Jones